TALK
ON THE
WILD
SIDE

Why Language Can't Be Tamed

LANE GREENE

PUBLICAFFAIRS
New York

PublicAffairs
Hachette Book Group
1290 Avenue of the Americas, New York, NY 10104
www.publicaffairsbooks.com
@PublicAffairs

The Economist in Association with Profile Books Ltd. and PublicAffairs

Printed in the United States of America

Originally published in 2018 by Profile Books Ltd. in Great Britain.
First US Edition: November 2018

Published by PublicAffairs, an imprint of Perseus Books, LLC, a subsidiary of Hachette Book Group, Inc. The PublicAffairs name and logo is a trademark of the Hachette Book Group.

Print book interior Typeset in Milo by MacGuru Ltd

Library of Congress Control Number: 2018956609

ISBNs: 978-1-61039-833-6 (hardcover); 978-1-61039-834-3 (ebook)

LSC-C

10   9   8   7   6   5   4   3   2   1

For my mother, Sharon Lane Greene

Contents

Introduction: The Case of the Missing Whom

SHERLOCK DEPICTS THE WORLD'S most famous fictional detective as – to be blunt – a bit of a prig. On the BBC show, Benedict Cumberbatch's Sherlock Holmes is curt with those not as smart as he is, which is everyone. Cumberbatch is talented and charming, but I still find his Sherlock tiring.

The third episode opens in a jail in Minsk. Holmes is interviewing a man accused of murdering his wife, and he is begging Holmes to take his case. The man speaks British English with a working-class accent and grammar. As he pleads with Sherlock to help him, Sherlock gets as fed up with him as I do with Sherlock.

Guy: She's always getting at me, saying I weren't a real man.

Sherlock: Wasn't a real man.

At this point, I rewound the video to see if I had heard rightly. Did Sherlock really just correct his grammar? Yes, on second viewing, he had. The sequence goes on:

Guy: Me old man was a butcher, and he learned us how to cut up a beast...

Sherlock: Taught...

Now the poor guy is losing his nerve.

Guy: Then I done it...

Sherlock: Did it...

Undone by Sherlock's hectoring, he breaks down, and confesses: he has repeatedly stabbed his wife. Sherlock wants no part of representing a murderer. He saunters out. As he does, the man makes one last plea:

Guy: Without you, I'll get hung for this.

Sherlock: No, not at all.

At this point, there's a long pause, and a tight shot on Sherlock's smirk: "*Hanged*, yes."

... and cue the title music, giving the audience another minute to think on the fact that Sherlock's grammatical precision is part of his uncompromising brilliance.

When the title sequence is over, the very next scene takes place in the apartment Sherlock shares with John Watson, played by a hangdog Martin Freeman. Watson is chiding Sherlock for his lack of practical knowledge about the world. Sherlock, lying on the couch and bored by the conversation, says, "It doesn't matter to me who's prime minister, or who's sleeping with who."

Once again I grabbed my remote and rewound, to my wife's annoyance. Had Sherlock really said "who's sleeping with who"?

My wife has what we call "HBO brain". In those long multi-season shows with dozens of characters, she can remember who's in love with whom, who's betrayed whom, who has an alliance with whom and so on. I can't, and I'm constantly asking her to tell me what's going on. Her ability to keep all the characters' motivations in her head helps her make sensible predictions about what's going to happen. I am just carried along by the stream, vaguely confused the whole time.

So when I spotted Sherlock's "who's sleeping with who" I thought, aha! I've noticed a clue, and my wife has missed it. The pre-title-sequence scene had shown Sherlock to be an uncompromising grammatical pedant. And just a minute later, he's saying "who's sleeping with who" rather than the standard formal English "who's sleeping with whom". I just knew that this lack of *whom* was going to come up later in the plot.

And... it just never did. It was an oversight. The writers had spent two solid screen minutes setting Sherlock up as a man so unbending in his grammar that he will taunt a man fearing a date with the hangman. But those same writers didn't even notice the Case of the Missing Whom.

Who murdered *whom*? For some readers, the answer will be simple:

it was the middlebrow intellectuals in the writer's room, and the murder weapon was the drop in grammatical standards in schools since the 1960s. For the many educated, intelligent and thoughtful people who worry about the state of the English language, the omission of *whom* in an expensively produced, high-end BBC show is not just a minor oversight on a television show. It is serious business. Well-educated writers at a prestigious institution, even a national crown jewel like the BBC, are abusing a core feature of English grammar. And other people – foreigners, the young (the children!) – are watching. They learn the prestige form of English from the BBC; indeed "BBC English" used to be synonymous with a high standard. If the writers of *Sherlock* are allowed to get away with murdering *whom*, something valuable – clarity, precision, logic in the next generation – will be lost.

For the worriers, the story of *whom* goes like this: once upon a time, schoolchildren learned not just English but Latin grammar. They knew that words have a feature called "case". "Case" distinguishes the subject of a sentence from the objects. In Latin, all nouns have an ending that shows their case. In English, only the pronouns do. *He* is in the nominative case, for a subject. *Him* is in the objective, for a direct or indirect object.

Who is also a pronoun, and like *he*, it is in the nominative case. Its objective form is *whom*: *You saw **whom**? She's sleeping with **whom**?* For a certain kind of English-speaker, saying (as Sherlock did) "who's sleeping with *who*", neglecting that case ending, betrays a drop in care and attention to the crucial relationships in a statement. It's critical to know which word is the subject of a sentence, and which is the object.

But how does Watson react to Sherlock? Is he confused by "who's sleeping with who?" Of course not. Watson, like the writers and the vast majority of the viewers, simply didn't notice. That is not because he has low standards, too. Watson (like the viewer) understood perfectly well what Holmes meant. So here we come to the real mystery: if *whom* is so important, why is there no difficulty whatsoever understanding a sentence that omits it?

This is because there are two overlapping ways to communicate what's a subject and what's an object in English. One is case: the difference between *he* and *him* or *who* and *whom*. But the other is word order. *He saw him* has *he* in the subject position and *him* in the object slot. But in *Steve saw John*, Steve is just as obviously the subject and John is just as obviously the object, despite the lack of case marking on *Steve* and *John*. You can't say *Steve saw John* when John did the seeing and Steve was the seen. Flipping the word order while keeping the same meaning is possible in some languages, like Latin, because the case endings on all nouns, including names, convey who is seeing and who is seen. But this isn't possible in English.

About a thousand years ago, English was, in fact, Latin-like, with case endings on all nouns, and flexible word order. But today's language has these endings left on just a few pronouns, and a relatively fixed word order. Why exactly this happened is a matter of debate. One theory has it that languages naturally cycle between "synthetic" (Latin) and "analytic" (English) states. Synthetic languages gradually lose all those word endings, and other elements like word order and little helping words step in to do the work that the old endings did. Then some of those little extra helping words get fused back together with the bigger, content-filled words, and they gradually become endings again, with the process of that fusion lost to history. Think of a solid-looking metamorphic rock: it began as a more loosely composed sedimentary one, but pressure and time fuse those elements together. But then other forces – glaciers, erosion – break them apart again. The resulting sediment gloms together again into a sedimentary rock, which fuses again into metamorphic rock, and so on.

By this theory – that languages cycle between different types, like our rocks here – English has perhaps simply lost all of its case endings temporarily. It is in an analytical, not synthetic, period in its long history. This makes the current status of English interesting to linguists, but hardly signals a catastrophic collapse in its structure. (We'll look at this theory in detail in Chapter 4.)

Another theory, this one more specific to English, is that English's case endings are a victim not of sloppy education, whether in the 1060s or the 1960s, but of conquest. First, Germanic-speaking Anglo-Saxons conquered England from the continent, and brought their case-rich variety of old German. Then Vikings conquered them, and many settled in England; over the years and centuries, the Vikings learned that heavily inflected Old English imperfectly, and dispensed with some unnecessary endings. Then came another conquest, in 1066, by the Norman French, and once again – so goes the theory – imperfect learning, this time by the Normans, simplified the inflection system further still, meaning that all of those grammatical endings gradually became lost.

One big statistical study looked beyond English at thousands of languages, and found some support for this second theory. Languages with a big geographic spread, lots of speakers, and lots of neighbours had simpler inflection systems (including not only case endings on nouns but tense and other kinds of endings on other words like verbs and adjectives). It seems that when a language is in contact with lots of second-language learners, those endings become sanded away over time, as water and sand smooth the jagged edges off a stone. The result is no less a stone, but it is a different kind: a change, but a natural one that is nothing to worry about.

*

This book is about different ways of looking at questions like the Case of the Missing Whom in language. There are broadly two schools of thought. One goes by the ugly label "descriptivism". This is the approach of scientific scholars of language. People in linguistics departments look at the facts of language – like the gradual loss of case endings in English – and try to come up with generalisations about why these changes happen. Those generalisations are things like our theory that highly inflected languages naturally become less so before becoming more inflected again, or the idea that having lots of neighbours tends to simplify languages.

This book is mostly about – and to a certain extent written for – the other camp. People in this second camp are sometimes called "prescriptivists": rather than seeking to describe language from a distance, they are actively involved in trying to dictate what the language does. They resist changes in the language, like the gentle decline of *whom*. They assume that changes result not from natural, unstoppable, forces, but from human laziness or fuzzy thinking.

A dislike of change over time also overlaps with a dislike of other kinds of disorder in the language. Prescriptivists don't like multiple forms of a language hanging around. The idea of using "who's sleeping with who" in casual chitchat while writing "who's sleeping with whom" in a formal paper seems to invite confusion. For such prescriptivists, the rules should be the rules all the time. And they are as picky with word meanings as they are with grammar, often insisting on making distinctions that most people can't be bothered with. If you've ever been told that *healthy* can only refer to a living thing (a healthy child, a healthy plant), and that things that contribute to health are *healthful* (healthful food, for example), you've met a prescriptivist.

In this book I focus on the nature of language itself. In so doing, I will argue why the sticklers are wrong to worry about the health of the language. English and other languages do not need – and often even suffer from – the efforts to engineer, perfect or preserve language that are likely to prove frustrating for the engineers, protectors and preservers.

In other words, I am more optimistic than the grouches, seeing language as a robust, organic and evolving phenomenon that needs relatively little intervention. Prescriptivists tend to hold a competing view: that language is elegant but delicate, an easily threatened logical system for conveying meaning without loss or confusion, which could crumble if we don't mind it carefully.

Language is a wild animal like a wolf, well adapted for its conditions and its needs. But there are those who want to tame language, to teach it to behave. Their ideal language would be a show dog, one that will come, sit, fetch, shake hands and roll over on command.

In what ways is language "wild"? It is unstable over time. It is vague, where speaker and listener do not always understand the same thing by the same sentence. Sometimes it is inefficient, offering many more words than are needed to convey meaning. It is ambiguous, with surprisingly many sentences lending themselves to radically different interpretations. It varies quite a bit by situation: people observe some grammar rules on some occasions, and other rules on others. Finally, language borders are fuzzy – it is often surprisingly hard for even experts to tell where one language and its dialects end, and a neighbouring related language begins.

Language tamers treat these qualities of language as something like the wild behaviours that must be bred out of a domestic dog to make it behave properly. But language can never fully shed its wild nature.

It evolved not to be perfect, but to be useful. And some people go even further, making sweeping claims about language, logical thought and the state of the human mind itself. They worry that if we can't use proper grammar anymore, then we can't think straight, with dire consequences for the human race. We'll meet one particularly zealous language reactionary who makes this case explicitly in Chapter 2. Many people, though in less radical terms, share his view.

This book will argue that by misunderstanding the deep nature of language, the language tamers set themselves up for failure and disappointment. By its nature, language is ambiguous, changing, incomplete, redundant and illogical; not all the time, but a lot of the time. Those who think that language should ideally always be unambiguous, stable, complete, efficient and logical will make themselves miserable by observing the real, natural, messy thing every day. The language tamers have an expensive show dog that nonetheless insists on barking at invisible cats and marking its territory on the living-room rug.

Like all metaphors, this shouldn't be taken too far: language doesn't literally have paws or canine teeth, and it doesn't literally pee on the rug. It's not even an animate thing with wishes or an inherent personality. Language is a human behaviour. But in some way I do mean the metaphor to be taken seriously. Language is a product of the continuing evolution of an animal called *homo sapiens*. Like other animal behaviours, it's fantastically useful – and inherently flawed. Humans walk upright, giving them use of their hands, but also bad backs. Evolved traits will be useful almost by definition (they usually wouldn't survive among the population otherwise). But they will also show weaknesses. Evolved traits don't progress towards perfection as if guided by a creator. They inch forward blindly, being shaped sometimes by natural selection (maladaptive features don't tend to survive) and sometimes by accident (random changes happen over time, and some of them stick).

Many other metaphors lend themselves to describing the way language really is versus how the sticklers wish it would be. Language, as a product of human ingenuity, can be seen a bit like another human product: our children. Parents want their kids to be perfect: to sit still in class, take notes, get A grades, respect adults, eat their vegetables and go to bed without a fuss. But real kids sometimes fidget, skip their homework, hate their teacher, struggle with a subject, throw a tantrum, demand ice cream for dinner, and act as though they need never go to bed. They can be partly tamed out of these behaviours, but never fully.

Yet most kids, though not perfect, are *resourceful*: they're on a developmental plan that calls for them to master physical and cognitive skills, self-control and good social behaviour on a timeline that makes sense for their growing brains. Watch a three-year-old manipulate her father into a third story at bedtime, or a 13-year-old argue like a master lawyer for some extra allowance, and it is hard not to be amazed at children's robustness and inventiveness in a world full of people much more powerful than they are. Language is a bit like that: it is hardly perfect, but its adaptability and resourcefulness are to be marvelled at.

When you begin seeing language this way, you start to see more and more such analogies. Language is not like computer code, which crashes on even small mistakes, and needs to be constantly debugged. It's a bit more like a recipe, which can be modified by individual users according to taste, where different conditions (the quality of your cookware, the altitude, the hardness of the local water) will call for a few changes, and where mistakes can easily be survived with a little creativity and will on the part of the chef.

Written language is a bit like classical composition, with well-established conventions of harmony and melody. A wrong note really will sound wrong. Spoken language (which is – as we will see later – the original form of language of which writing is an offshoot) is more like jazz. Jazz has its own conventions, but on-the-fly improvisation and constantly changing styles mean that a blue note in a blistering run may be what gives it its verve. In jazz, like speech, even clear mistakes can be forgiven: "wrong" is all in the ear of the beholder.

To sum up: language is not so much logical as it is useful. It is not composed; it is improvised. It is not well behaved; it is resourceful. It is not delicate; it is hardy. It is not always efficient, but its redundancy makes it robust. It is not threatened; it is self-renewing. It is not perfect. But it is amazing.

*

But the most visible, powerful and influential language commentators hardly ever show this kind of optimism and faith in the languages they love. Pessimists think the language was once in good shape, but now is in danger of falling apart. Too many parents and teachers lament "kids today" as the reason nobody can use the language properly anymore. Other writers, editors and writers on usage act as self-appointed guardians of language against the corrupting tendencies of its users: in this view, language has always been a hair's breadth from chaos, and needs constant vigilance in order to stop it from going wild. And this kind of thinking is of a piece with a broader fear of decline: decline in language, decline in manners, decline in politics, decline in morals. If the pessimistic language tamers can convince you that the language is a short step away from chaos, they can convince you the same is true of the world in general.

Other language tamers are not quite so exasperated or afraid. You can – and I think that you really should – have strong opinions about language, and take pride in using it well. But this is not the same thing as being an authoritarian scold or a garment-rending prophet of doom. The best language tamers are like consistent and patient parents who constantly nudge their children this way and that, but understand that imperfection is all part of the process. They understand the value of order and clarity but don't expect 100% compliance. They are pragmatists not perfectionists, craftsmen and not theoreticians. We will look at some of the best of them – scholars, lexicographers and grammar gurus – in this book.

They are, though, in a minority. The public conversation about language is dominated by a kind of middlebrow irascibility, rather than by patient examination of language facts and their consequences. My aim here is to get those who really love language into the habit of stopping and looking into the facts before instantly reaching for the kids-these-days complaints of decline. Who, exactly, am I talking about here? Those I have called grammar grouches can be teachers: they grade awkward young writers' work daily, and so can get the impression that the use of language by today's young people is worse than ever. Or they can be letter-to-the-editor-type readers of magazines and newspapers. These readers wonder, understandably enough, how typos slip through layers of proofreaders and editors, and assume that standards are no longer as high as they once were. Or they can be journalists and editors themselves, their whole life being using words well. When they see words misused by the powerful people they cover, they take the lesson that language requires eternal watchfulness.

Some language tamers are truly radical. They realise that normal human languages are messy and inaccurate, and propose sweeping changes to existing languages – or even new languages – to correct the deficiencies of natural language. The Big Brother regime of Orwell's *Nineteen Eighty-Four* was a kind of language tamer, the kind that worried that the wrong ideas could spread if you let people use words like "freedom". Newspeak was their stripped-down, re-jiggered language meant to make such subversive thoughts literally unthinkable.

In real life, radical language tamers usually have more benign motivations. Esperanto was invented not just to promote international harmony, but was made "tame" from the start. It is completely orderly, with none of the maddening irregularities that bedevil ordinary languages. An even more extreme example – Lojban, to which we turn in Chapter 1 – eliminates not just irregularity but ambiguity and illogic from language. What's so radical about that? We'll see that natural human languages are, in fact, hugely ambiguous and illogical much of the time, and how different from a real language a truly tamed language would be.

*

When prescriptivists and descriptivists, sticklers and scholars, conservatives and liberals argue about language, they're often talking about two different things. Language, after all, has two major instantiations in the world: speech and writing. (Sign languages are a third, but they behave a lot like spoken languages.)

When linguists talk about language, they are almost always focusing on speech. That's because linguistics as a discipline focuses on language as a universal human faculty. All cognitively normal people speak. Deaf people "speak" with sign languages that are as richly developed as the spoken kind. Children learn the language of their community without any overt instruction, almost as if by magic. By the age of two they are using basic phrases, and by four they can construct a huge variety of sophisticated sentences.

Linguistics as a discipline is focused on this universal ability. Its specialists are often to be found, when not in the Linguistics department of the local university, in Psychology or Cognitive Science, around other people studying human thinking and human nature. Or they might be in Anthropology or the departments of foreign languages, looking at a broad variety of different languages and specialising in a few. While linguists can often be emotionally animated by their subject, they don't find languages they don't like, or don't respect; they don't divide the world into good and bad language. If we go back to our animal analogy, they are zoologists. If they find a new language or a new fact about a language that overturns what they thought they knew, it is a discovery worth popping open the champagne for. They are, most of all, curious.

Writing is very different from speech, and demands a different kind of analysis. We don't know how long humans have been speaking something that could be called human language – most estimates run from 50,000 years ago to 200,000 years ago – but it's certainly a very long time. The reason we don't have much more idea than that is because we can only reason from non-linguistic evidence to try to figure out how long people have been talking. Does the existence of grave sites mean people had religion, and therefore language? What about art or tools?

The only direct evidence of ancient language itself is, of course, writing – and that is only a few thousand years old. So writing is only a small fraction as old as speech. Moreover, writing is only done by a subset of the world's people: about 15% of the world's adult population still cannot read or write after decades of a push for literacy in the poorest parts of the world[1]. Humans learn to read and write only after a lot of explicit instruction, and many of them struggle mightily to get it right.

Finally, only a fraction of the world's languages – a few hundred out of 7,000 or so – are written on a regular basis. Many have writing systems but are almost never written, and many more have never been written at all. But it is scientifically illiterate to say that speakers of these unwritten languages are "without language". In fact, when linguists set out to describe them, they often find incredible complexities that seem to put the well-known written Western languages to shame. (Remember the theory that "big" languages get simpler over time. Small isolated languages without much contact with the outside world can afford amazing complexities that wouldn't survive if outsiders had to learn them on a regular basis.)

So there's a good scientific case to be made that when we talk about "language" with no further qualification, we should be talking about speech, not writing. Speech is older by far, and it is universal. It is learned with such speed and so little explicit teaching that some scholars call it an "instinct". Some other linguists, admittedly, disagree. But all concur that the combination of the various pieces of the language faculty, and their incredible expressive flexibility, are uniquely human. Writing is uniquely – but not universally – human.

So another way of stating the theme of this book is that the language authoritarians often mistake formal writing and speech that aims to ape formal writing for the only "real" and acceptable language. Yes, the norms of edited, high-quality published writing – composed, error-free, stable, unambiguous, efficient, and so on – truly are important in writing. They represent language at its most precise and controlled. But the vast majority of human language use is oral. What's more, in today's world of e-mail, text, Twitter, Facebook, chat and who-knows-what to come next, more writing than ever before in history is quick and informal – like speech, meant to convey a message at speed to someone the writer knows. A new kind of writing is emerging, a variety that John McWhorter of Columbia University calls "fingered speech".[2]

The kind of writing an excellent writer does for a public audience – trying to make a complicated case or an intricate story both clear and compelling to a lot of strangers – is one of civilisation's most important vehicles of culture. Mastering it is a goal that serious writers (and public speakers) should aim for. But they should always aim for it knowing that they are using an imperfect, evolved animal behaviour. Language today is partly tame and partly wild, and the two will always be in tension. There are real goals worth pursuing: clarity, simplicity, stability, and the like are good things, language behaving as it should. But these are destinations that are never quite reached, just as a domesticated animal never quite loses its wild nature. Losing your cool when language is messy is a little like expecting a dog never to bark, or to mark its territory.

What's more, elegant formal written language isn't the only form of language that matters. Language is a many-faceted thing. Slang and dialect, jocular play with non-standard forms, teen-speak, text-speak, corporate jargon, political waffle and all the other kinds of language typically loathed by the letter-to-the-editor type have their places. These forms are not a threat to language's health. Their persistence shows that they fill a need. Not all language is well behaved, nor does it need to be.

*

Nobody really murdered *whom*. It is alive and well, being used millions of times every day. But in plenty of other cases, it is being replaced by *who*, and it is being perfectly understood. *Whom* might be completely on its way out, or it might have a long life as an alternative to *who*, one formal, one informal. But its disappearance is not the disappearance of grammar, or of high standards, or of care and respect for language. All of these will survive even when everyone alive today is gone. Did you notice *whom* missing in that "Who, exactly, am I talking about here?" from four pages ago? If you did, you might be the kind of reader I still have some work to do on to convince that it's going to be all right. And if you didn't, well, you're in the good company of Benedict Cumberbatch, Martin Freeman, the writers of *Sherlock*, and many other highly literate people, some of whom we'll meet in this book. While professional writers, editors and teachers still prize knowing how *whom* is traditionally used, those who don't should not hang their heads if they haven't mastered it yet. It's tricky because it's rare, and so it's increasingly confusing.

A wolf is not just evolved: it keeps evolving, because it has to. And though language will continue to change, the whole system never loses its strength and resilience. The loss of almost all of English's case system didn't result in a net loss of expressiveness, with English-speakers grunting "Me Tarzan" at each other. It resulted in a different language, one that went from "Ic beo Tarzan" to "I'm Tarzan". Today's English is a wonderful language for that and so much more.

Those who love language may mourn – or try to stop – an individual change in its early stages, if they feel it would be a loss to clarity or eloquence. But they needn't worry about the language as a whole.

Languages don't decline; not when Beowulf was losing his cases, not in the 1960s, not in the text-message era, not today and not tomorrow.

None of this optimism – that language is robust and will survive any change that comes – should be taken to mean that I preach a slovenly, let-it-all-hang-out approach. Using language well matters hugely, even if keeping *whom* around doesn't. I'm passionate about good writing, and not only as a reader and a writer. I'm also an editor at *The Economist*, where I have edited hundreds of thousands of words. When I see grammar errors, I fix them. When I see the same ones again and again, my own inner grouch comes out. I have my own peeves – I like to see *literally* used literally. You probably have your own strong opinions on language too, and you wouldn't be human if you didn't.

It's perfectly possible to reconcile strong opinions on individual points of grammar and usage – including dislike of a particular usage, or fear that a change to the language might introduce confusion – with a belief that the language on the whole is built to adapt, to minimise confusion. And that case is provable; today's "error" becomes tomorrow's grammar, and today's uneducated mistake becomes tomorrow's prestige standard, as we'll see in Chapter 4, focused on language change.

This book is a love-letter to language: to its elegance, expressiveness and power, but also to its endurance, adaptability and sturdiness. Scientists have never found a language that has fallen to pieces. It's not in language's nature. Humans need it to do too many important things. And language doesn't exist out there on its own (though I've described it as a living thing, it's really just a behaviour of another living thing – human beings). So in paying tribute to language's true nature, we also pay tribute to its speakers. In trusting the people over the pessimists, we extend the same respect to our fellow *homo sapiens* that we do when we choose democracy over benevolent dictatorship, or market economics over central planning. The collective wisdom of humans in their billions – the "spontaneous order" they generate without even trying – is greater than anything even the most brilliant language tamer could ever dream up.

1

Bringing the universe to order

THE 17TH CENTURY SAW an explosion of science. It was the century of Newton and Leibniz, Galileo and Kepler, Bacon and Descartes. All in their different ways helped advance the notion that the world was more systematic and predictable than it had theretofore seemed. They weren't the first or last to think this way, but for so many of them to do so at the same time meant that there was something distinctly in the air: a belief that the world was orderly, or at least through the application of human reason could be made more orderly.

That went for language, too. Language invention – the creation of languages more logical and rule-governed than the ones you heard on the street – was a common hobby in the 17th century. John Wilkins was a bit more diligent than most. Like many scholars of the age, he was a polymath, since few scientific fields were big enough to occupy a first-class "natural philosopher" full-time for long. He was able, but not brilliant: unlike many of his famous contemporaries and collaborators, he is not known for any enduring intellectual breakthrough. Instead he wrote works whose titles give a sense of his restless range: *The Discovery of a World in the Moone*; *Mercury, Or the Secret and Swift Messenger*; *Mathematical Magick* and *A Discourse Concerning the Beauty of Providence*, among others. Like most scientific men of the age, he was a devout Christian, something he would have regarded as his most important identity. He died a bishop (of Chester).

His most enduring contribution to scholarship – though it hardly endured – was in language. Natural languages were a mess, he thought. Even Latin was not good enough for science and serious work. So Wilkins devised what he called "a Philosophical Language", and in 1668, introduced it to the Royal Academy, which he had helped found, in London.

Wilkins's language had a remarkable structure. In it, each word would hold a sort of perfect schema encoding its own meaning. Like the "kingdom-phylum-class-order-family-genus-species" taxonomy of biology, the successive syllables and letters of each word would single out its membership in gradually more specific categories. *Zi-* is for beasts, adding a *-t-* singles out doglike beasts (including wolves), and a final *-α* specifies an ordinary dog itself. *Zita*.

What could make more sense? The great scientists of the age – Robert Hooke (who named "cells" in biology) and Robert Boyle (who worked out the relationship between temperature, pressure and volume of a gas) among them – promised to study and even write in the language. King Charles II said he wanted to learn it as well. The Royal Society promised to take on the task of perfecting the language.

Had his language succeeded, Wilkins might well have entered the pantheon of great minds of the age. It didn't. And so while he was one of the few people to head colleges at both Oxford and Cambridge, and invented a precursor to the metric system, he is mainly remembered as a quixotic, even sad figure, dying in the agony of kidney stones, the treatment for which may have killed him.

He might hardly be remembered at all but for an essay that Jorge Luis Borges wrote about his language. The Argentine short-story writer and essayist noted that Wilkins[1] had been dropped from the 14th edition of the *Encyclopaedia Britannica*, which was hardly a shame given that the 13th edition had had a bland 20-line list of biographical details on Wilkins's various positions and publications. But Borges had more respect for him.

Borges noted that it's common and popular to assume that the forms of words are more closely connected to their meaning than they really are.

> All of us have once experienced those neverending discussions in which a dame, using lots of interjections and incoherences, swears to you that the word "luna" is more (or less) expressive than the word "moon".

But he didn't buy it himself.

Apart from the evident observation that the monosyllable "moon" perhaps is a more suitable representation of such a very simple object than the bisyllable "luna", there is nothing to add to such a discussion.

Borges understood, as Ferdinand de Saussure had done around the turn of the century, the idea of the "arbitrariness of the sign". "Luna" doesn't really sound more or less like the thing in the night sky than "moon" does.

Plato, in his dialogue *Cratylus*, had once put a host of folk-etymologies into the mouth of Socrates, in which the form of a word revealed something deeper about its meaning.

Hermogenes: What is the meaning of the word "hero"? [Greek: *heros*]...

Socrates: All of them sprang either from the love of a God for a mortal woman, or of a mortal man for a Goddess; think of the word in the old Attic, and you will see better that the name *heros* is only a slight alteration of Eros, from whom the heroes sprang: either this is the meaning, or, if not this, then they must have been skilful as rhetoricians and dialecticians, and able to put the question (*erotan*), for *eirein* [to speak] is equivalent to *legein* [to say].

Many scholars don't think Plato even believed these fanciful etymologies. Today, all serious language scholars accept the arbitrariness of the sign, except in the case of a very few words, like onomatopoetic ones.

Wilkins's language was different. Far from mere onomatopoeia, the entire definition of the word was present in the word's form itself – as non-arbitrary as you can get. But Borges saw the problem underlying the project: to build a language based on a categorisation of the universe you had to have a proper categorisation of the universe to start with. But unfortunately, as Borges wrote, "it is clear that there is no classification of the Universe not being arbitrary and full of conjectures. The reason for this is very simple: we do not know what thing the universe is."

Take Wilkins's word for "flame": *deba*, from *de*, an element, plus

-b- denoting the first element, fire, and then *-a*, a part of that element: flame. What could be more obvious? Except that modern readers will trip over the idea of fire as an element. Those with a decent science education today know more than the eminent Wilkins did about what the universe is made of: the "earth, air, fire, water" system of "elements" seems to us childish, replaced by one in which a hundred-odd elements are defined by their number of protons and electrons. Imagine if Wilkins's language had taken off in his time, and was still spoken widely today: we would still be in a world of 17th-century ontology in which fire was an element but uranium was not.

One alternative to living in the science of 400 years ago would be to constantly rejig the system as new information poured in: once it was discovered that fire was not matter at all, and that the elements were things like tin, lead and nitrogen, fire's name would have to change in Wilkins's language. But this would undercut much of the logic of the language itself: if we don't know what the universe is, nor even what fire truly is, why build a language on the taxonomy of the universe in the first place? Learning it would be like buying a buggy beta version of a piece of software; you could only hope it would get better in future. Only learning a language is a lot harder than buying a bit of software.

A final alternative – if Wilkins's language could be made to work – would be to accept that the taxonomy underlying the language was always going to be a bit arbitrary and a bit wrong. The linguist Arika Okrent, in her lovely book *In the Land of Invented Languages*, describes trying to find "shit" in Wilkins's classification scheme. (Classy people, linguists.) She couldn't find it under "Corporeal Action", and only finally unearthed it under the category of "Motion" (sub-category "purgation"). This was hardly obvious. In other words, you had to memorise plenty of arbitrary things about Wilkins's own mental ideas – that to "shit" was a kind of motion rather than a corporeal action – in order to learn and use the word.

Why not just learn an arbitrary sign in the first place, no matter whether *shit, merde* or *Scheisse*? That brings us back to the arbitrariness of the sign that underlies almost every word in every natural language. Wilkins's system was hardly truly universal, in the sense of being based on a transparent and correct understanding of the world that everyone had access to. You had to know the contents of Wilkins's mind – or spend forever paging through his taxonomy, as Okrent did with "shit" – to make it work.

Of all the works that Wilkins wrote, few seemed to presage his late interest in language. With one exception: *Ecclesiastes*, a plea for the plain style, and against scholasticism, in preaching. Like many writers of the Reformation and its aftermath, he seemed to believe that transparent language was critical to Christian learning and devotion. Taken together with his philosophical language, it seems to indicate a worldview in which transparent language would practically force a kind of transparent thought.

Wilkins hoped that his language would further science, in the classically 17th-century belief that an international group of scholars, reading each other's work, would make slow but steady progress. It didn't work out that way, for his language at least. Wilkins died in the hopes that his fellows at the Royal Academy and his illustrious scientist friends would be as good as their word and keep developing his language. But they didn't, because they couldn't. Writing it was laborious, as Wilkins learned in his few pained efforts. Nobody, including him, could speak it. The messy real world resists being brought to order.

*

When people think of invented languages today, they hardly think of Wilkins and his doomed quest for the advancement of science. There are plenty of more popular reasons for inventing languages. One is fun: language invention as a joy in its own right. If you know where to look, the internet bursts with people inventing languages, and sharing ideas mainly with each other – they have no hope of getting anyone to actually speak them.

People also create languages for fictitious worlds. The first *Star Wars* movies made no real effort. (Somehow, *yotó yotó*, in *Return of the Jedi*, was supposed to mean "Fifty thousand, no less"). But the Klingon of *Star Trek* has a full grammar and a big vocabulary, and even a translation of *Hamlet*. Klingon's eager learners take achievement in the language seriously, offering lapel badges for those who move up the ranks in mastery. Klingon follows in the footsteps of Elvish, created by J. R. R. Tolkien (a linguist himself) for his fictional world, and is a predecessor of sci-fi and fantasy languages like Navi'i (from the film *Avatar*) and Dothraki and Valyrian (created for HBO's *Game of Thrones*).

But many language inventors fall into a third category: the language inventor as an extreme kind of language tamer. Not content with merely making natural languages more orderly, they insist on starting from scratch: they believe that the originals are fatally messy, and they must invent better languages in order to fix real-world problems that arise from the faulty ones handed down from our ancestors.

Esperanto is the world's most famous invented language: it has a big international community of enthusiastic learners, a flag, an anthem, and something like its own culture. It was invented by Ludwig Zamenhof as an idealistic project to create the world's foremost second language: an auxiliary language, one that people who did not share a first language would speak when they met each other. Zamenhof was born in one of the quintessential central European zones where nationalisms overlap on nationalisms, a Jew in Bialystok, then in the Russian Empire, today in Poland, the child of Russian and Yiddish-speaking parents, where Belarusian was also heard on the streets. (He is best known by the German version of his first name, but is also variously Ludwik, Ludoviko, and Leyzer; the Latinised version familiar to English-speakers is "Lazarus".)

Zamenhof's upbringing in this world convinced him that people didn't like each other because they didn't understand each other, and his language was a reflection of that. After a flirtation with Zionism, he spent the rest of his life as an opponent of nationalisms of all kinds. Trained as an ophthalmologist, he eventually found his calling as "Dr Esperanto", which means, in the language he created, "one who hopes".

Esperanto is not meant to replace natural languages, but to make sure that when foreigners meet and speak a *lingua franca* they have a neutral one, one without cultural baggage. Using French or English as a *lingua franca* unfairly privileges native speakers of those languages, Esperantists feel. Esperanto, by contrast, belongs to no one, and so to everyone.

More to the point, it is utterly regular. Spelling is completely regular. Nouns end in -o. Adjectives end in -a. Adverbs end in -e. Present-tense verbs end in -as. Many opposites are formed by adding the prefix mal-: *bona* is good, *malbona* is bad, *varma* is warm, *malvarma* is cool.

With these few rules you've learned as much as you would get in weeks of instruction in Spanish or French. Esperanto really is as easy as its fans say. All you need to do is learn vocabulary, and if you know a bit of a Romance language or of German (Zamenhof borrowed words from the big European languages, including English), you'll be picking words up in a snap.

Esperanto was "tame" from the start, but only as a by-product of its founder's intention. Zamenhof wanted as many people as possible to learn it frictionlessly as a second language. The real goal was peace and understanding between nations, a truly idealistic aim given the age of nationalism into which it was born in 1887. The multi-ethnic Russian, Austro-Hungarian and Ottoman empires were full of restive small peoples who wanted the same things the French, Spanish and Italians had: a state. Most of these nations, in their self-perception, were largely based on language; Czechs were those who spoke Czech, and Bulgarians those who spoke Bulgarian. Nationalists wanted to break Europe up into ethnically pure states, one for each nation and language. Zamenhof argued that while the nationalisms of the strong were unjust, the nationalisms of the weak were unwise; as long as people divided themselves up and fought for bits of the map, the strong would oppress the weak. He wanted to unite them with his new language.

Esperanto's simplicity didn't make it perfect. It uses a few letters with odd unfamiliar diacritical marks like ĥ and ŭ. It has a grammatical marked accusative (*kato*, "cat", becomes *katon* when the cat is the direct object of a sentence, as in *mi amas la katon*, "I love the cat.") Yes-no questions are marked by the presence of an odd little word, *ĉu*, probably because Zamenhof's Russian has a similar word, *li*. Since the creation of Esperanto, other language inventors have sought to create an even more simple and elegantly learnable language. But none of those languages have equalled Esperanto's success.

*

Success, that is, by name recognition and number of learners. But there are other ways to measure success. While Esperantists want speakers, others prioritise the elegance of a language itself. Perhaps the most radical experiment in conceptual minimalism comes in the form of a language with no verbs, nouns or adjectives. Zamenhof merely boiled down the big European languages, stripping irregularity as he went. But if you could build a language up rather than boil it down, with no need to respect any of the rules of the world's existing natural languages, what would it look like? What are the engineering limits of a language? James Cooke Brown, a sociologist at the University of Florida in the mid-1950s, wanted to find out, with no less an ambition than resolving a raging debate about the relationship between language and the mind.

In the early 20th century, Edward Sapir, a linguist, and Benjamin Lee Whorf, who had studied with him, developed "linguistic relativity": the idea that the world looks different depending on the native language of the speaker. Sapir formulated a cautious version of this idea; Whorf went further, declaring that the messy phenomena of the world were ordered in the mind by a speaker's native language. Far from seeing an objective reality, people saw only what their language conditioned them to see.

Brown, a sociologist of modest academic success who also dabbled in science-fiction and sailing, and made a supporting income by inventing a board-game, "Careers", was one of those restless and multi-talented people whose attention eventually turned to language. He wanted to test a version of this hypothesis, formulating the strongest possible paraphrase of Whorf's theory:

> The structure of the language spoken by a people determines their world view; that is it sets limits beyond which that world view cannot go. Thus the native speaker of any language is fated to see reality, and thus to think about it, exclusively on the terms and by the rules laid down for him by that language – unless he learns a new one.

"Determines". "Cannot go". "Exclusively". "Fated". If this full-strength statement of Whorf's hypothesis were true, building a better language – repairing the defects inherent in natural language itself – would be something like a key to unlocking the full logical powers of the mind. Brown's idea was indeed a radical experiment. Why not invent a language totally different in structure from any living language, and see what that does to its speakers' thinking?

It was an idea of its time, the dawn of the Space Age, a moment of rapid technological progress and economic growth, but also of the Cold War. Scientific and military competition with the Soviet bloc – and the threat of nuclear war – made it seem quite urgent that the country's minds were put to their best use. It was also around the intellectual peak of behaviourism, the psychological school that taught that all animal behaviour – including human language – was little more than conditioned responses to stimuli. If the mind was really so malleable, so suitable for conditioning, who knew what it might be conditioned to do?

Brown's creation, begun in 1955, was Loglan, a *log*ical *lan*guage based on predicate logic. In Loglan, it is impossible to be ambiguous: sentences take the form of a predicate – the core words of the language – and several arguments. A predicate-word like "to give" (*donsu* in Loglan) has three potential arguments – giver, the thing given and the recipient – and those arguments always appear in a fixed order. Part of knowing Loglan is to know what arguments each predicate takes, and their order.

What kind of word is *donsu*? Loglan's predicates combine the features of noun, verb and adjective. This was, Brown said, to avoid "making the metaphysical distinction between 'processes' and 'things' and between 'substances' and 'attributes' that have long troubled Western thought... We wish to impose as little metaphysics as possible on the speakers of Loglan." So *donsu* might mean "he gives", or preceded by *le* it becomes "the giver", or in other contexts, "giving" itself.

Predicates can be used with other predicates, like *vedma*, "selling", with little words called "operators" clearing up any ambiguity. *Le* means "the", or roughly "the one who", so *le donsu vedma* would mean "the giver sells" and *le vedma donsu* would mean "the seller gives" – with no need to change the form of *vedma* or *donsu*. In yet other contexts, *donsu* might be neither noun nor verb but adjective, meaning "generous".

The vocabulary was built up in its own ingenious way. Brown wanted Loglan to be independent from any culture. But he also wanted it to be learnable to as many people as possible. So he took the world's eight biggest languages by number of speakers (Mandarin Chinese,

English, Hindi, Russian, Spanish, Japanese, French and German) and found the words he wanted to coin in all of them. He then translated those words into a simplified spelling system created for Loglan. (That is, English's "blue" comes out *blu*.) Then he found which sounds were shared between the eight languages, and came up with different candidate Loglan words. The word that was chosen would be the one that had the most sounds in common with the words in the eight natural languages, with extra points for having the sounds in the same order. So *blanu*, "blue", has all of the sounds of English *blue*, Chinese *lan* and German *blau*, most of French *bleu*, half of Spanish *azul*, none of Japanese *ao* or *kon*, and so on. After these similarities were weighted by the language's size (so similarity to Chinese counted for more than similarity to German), Brown calculated a "learnability score". The highest-scoring word became the Loglan word. Brown put a lot of stock in the fact that he "discovered" words by this method, rather than coining them himself.

Finally, Loglan had another unique design feature: what Brown called "audiovisual isomorphism", or the quality that the audio and written stream carried exactly the same information. In English, it can be hard to tell "an ice-cream man" from "a nice cream man" spoken at full natural speed – just ask all the users who have posted on the website KissThisGuy.com, about misheard song lyrics. "Excuse me while I kiss the sky/kiss this guy", the eponymous example from Jimi Hendrix, shows how easy it is to hear a string of syllables and chop them up into nonsense rather than their intended meaning. These are called "mondegreens", for the song in which "laid him on the green" was misheard as "Lady Mondegreen". "Gladly, the cross-eyed bear" is perfectly homophonous with "Gladly the Cross I'd Bear".

Lojban makes this kind of thing impossible. Basic predicates have five sounds, always alternating consonants (C) and vowels (V) in either CCVCV or CVCCV order. They can be combined in equally predictable eight- or eleven-letter forms. Similarly, the "operators" and "attitudinals" have predictable sequences of consonants and vowels. Loglan was so designed that it's impossible for something like "kiss the sky" to be heard as "kiss this guy": the misheard version would violate Loglan's sound structure.

Why go to all this trouble to invent a language to test the Whorfian hypothesis? Brown reckoned that to discover whether language really does strongly influence thought, or even control it, scientists couldn't merely examine Japanese-speakers next to French-speakers and see if they thought differently. It would be impossible to know whether a host of other cultural factors were responsible for any differences researchers might find. So he had the idea to teach Loglan to people of different nationalities. Then they would be compared to a control group of their countrymen who hadn't studied Loglan.

Brown introduced Loglan to the world in *Scientific American* in 1960. He began boldly: "It would be surprising if ... Loglan were not superior to any of the natural languages in its ability to facilitate thought, if indeed thought is liable to such facilitation." In other words, if Whorfianism is even a little bit true, Loglan might be the world's best language.

But after going on to outline the grammar, the word-building rules and the pronunciation of Loglan, he seems to have realised that what he was putting forth was not exactly easy. The *Scientific American* article concludes more cautiously:

> We are by no means certain that Loglan is a thinkable language, let alone a thought-facilitating one. But there is some prospect that this instrument will facilitate experimental investigation into the distinguishing human faculty of symbolic communication.

In other words, as nearly every scientific article says, "more research is needed." Brown himself was trying to raise interest (and money) for his idea of what that research should be. His idea was to expose speakers of his eight languages to an intensive eight-month training in Loglan. Then he could test them against a control group of speakers of those same languages who had not learned Loglan, and see if there was any difference in logical thinking.

The "language governs thought" idea has always been an intellectually attractive one. Brown's article was a minor sensation. He initially got hundreds of letters, and donors supported his development of Loglan. A group of followers agreed to learn and propagate the language.[2] But he never got his improbable plan – to expose experimental subjects to eight months of intensive Loglan – off the ground. Funding for his project began drying up.

A group of Loglan enthusiasts, led by Bob Le Chevalier, who thought they had his tacit blessing, had continued adding words and ideas to Loglan. When he found out, Brown was furious: Loglan was his. Like many language inventors, he was prone to proprietary thinking about his creation, and to feuding over exactly what it needed and what it didn't. He called Le Chevalier an "unpaid employee" and sued for copyright infringement, asking a court to agree that Loglan was, in effect, his own intellectual and creative product, like a book or a song. Most of the supporters realised that Brown's singlemindedness was becoming more of a liability than an asset, and followed Bob Le Chevalier into the rival Logical Language Group, which reformulated the language. Brown lost his lawsuit anyway, but from now on, Loglan would be sidelined, with a new language – Lojban – taking its place. (Lojban, unlike Loglan, was named with "native" roots on its own principles: *logji* means "logic", and *bangu*, "language".) Lojban has most of the structure of Loglan, with most of the differences being in vocabulary.

But in the six decades since Loglan was first proposed, neither it nor Lojban has ever gone beyond a small hard core of learners, probably numbering today in the low hundreds. To put that into perspective, a big language like Spanish has about 1,000 times as many speakers as Esperanto, history's most successful invented language.[3] Esperanto in turn has about 1,000 times as many speakers as Lojban.

Languages spread because they are useful: most people learn a second language because there are a lot of people who speak it that they want to talk to. This makes it hard for any constructed language to take off. Why learn a language that nobody yet speaks? No matter how awesome its properties, would you learn the greatest language in the world if it would allow you to talk only to its creator?

But the hypothesis behind Brown's creation of Loglan was not really about communication, and regardless, its learners have always had a special kind of motivation. It was about seeing whether learning a logical language makes you a more logical thinker. It can be seen as the idea of language taming taken to the extreme: that all natural languages are deficient, compromised by culture, and that an entirely new, unambiguous language based on logic would make for better thinkers.

But Brown did not really show any ambition to *replace* lesser languages with Lojban; he seemed to be primarily interested in testing the Sapir–Whorf hypothesis by teaching it as a second language. Some Esperantists still believe in the *fina venko*, or "final victory", when everyone on earth learns Esperanto. Not even the most enthusiastic Lojbanist expects that of Lojban. Wilkins thought his language would revolutionise science in 1668. Zamenhof thought that Esperanto would further world peace in 1887. Loglan/Lojban was conceived as a way to test the properties of the human mind – but by the 21st century it was little more than a hobby for a few hundred people.

*

John Cowan is male, works with computers, and describes his interest in language as that of someone "inclined to be interested in complicated domains that have lots of little moving parts". He's a prolific commentator on language websites, hugely knowledgeable and entirely self-taught in linguistics, having never finished a degree in communication and mass media at City College of New York. He fits the profile of an enthusiastic Lojbanist. Twenty years ago, he wrote a grammar and description of the language filling 795 single-spaced pages.

But Cowan has never been fluent in Lojban, saying that he's no good at memorising vocabulary. (Most good Lojbanists, he says, are also good at learning natural languages.) While the early generation of Loglanists around James Cooke Brown were interested in the Sapir–Whorf hypothesis, very few would accept Brown's strong formulation of it today.

Is that because it's too hard to speak at a conversational pace? Lojbanists insist that some speakers really can speak Lojban fluently. But even Bob Le Chevalier, who led the breakaway group that made Loglan into Lojban beginning in 1987, describes himself as just "moderately skilled" today.[4] In any case, unlike Esperanto, nobody speaks Lojban with anything like native comfort. Listening to conversations of some of the current avid learners on the lojban.org website shows conversations proceeding in fits and starts, filled with agonisingly long pauses as the speakers work out what they want to say next.

Cowan says his fellow Lojbanists are divided as to whether Lojban is harder or easier to learn than a natural language. Those who think it's harder point to the many different ways in which the same statement can be expressed. Since there isn't a native-speaking Lojban community to set norms, none is any more natural than any other (and none really looks like what speakers are used to in their own native languages). What's more, making a mistake in a natural language usually results in a garbled but mostly comprehensible statement, like "the rat eat the cheese." In Lojban, Cowan says, a mistake will usually mean saying something grammatical but nonsensical, like "the rat cheeses the eater." But Cowan doesn't think that the logical properties of Lojban make it any harder to learn than natural languages.

Geoffrey Sampson, a linguist who reviewed Cowan's *Complete Lojban Language* for an academic journal in 1999,[5] cautioned against dismissing Lojban as a hobbyist's fancy. If a group of people came into existence that used Lojban regularly, he concluded,

> the question will arise why natural languages are not more like Lojban (if people can speak logically transparent languages, why don't they?). If not then one will ask what differences between Lojban and natural languages make the latter but not the former usable. The creators of Lojban have put into their language everything which we know to matter for human communication; if the language fails, natural languages may have other crucial properties that we have not yet noticed.

"If people can speak logically transparent languages, why don't they?" It's a good question, and Lojban hasn't answered it yet, with its small user numbers and their difficulty speaking the language fluently. If the strong Whorfian proposition were true, and speaking Lojban made you think more logically, it should have spread considerably since 1960. Who wouldn't want to think more logically?

On the other hand, if Lojban is harder than, say, Spanish as a second language, why? Is it because people are too illogical to grasp the underlying logic of Lojban? This looks unlikely: Lojban came after mathematicians and philosophers developed the formal symbolic apparatus of modern logic. Intelligent people with a certain bent seem to have no trouble thinking logically, when they set their minds to it.

But speaking in real time is a different matter. While experienced Lojbanists write without too much trouble, they seem to struggle in speech. What's going on? One possibility is that Lojban does not fit the template of the kind of languages humans are supposed to learn. This is the "language instinct" hypothesis, whose most famous proponents are Noam Chomsky and Steven Pinker. They claim that all human languages share underlying features that the brain is primed to learn. This could be one reason why children speak so fluently by age five despite little instruction, and while highly intelligent adults seem to struggle mightily with Lojban: the brain doesn't want inflexible predicates and arguments. It wants nouns and verbs, or something like them.[6] Perhaps Lojban can be acquired as a second language, but not as a first one, because it doesn't fit the brain's template of a language.

The only way to test this hypothesis would be the ultimate Whorfian experiment: to raise a child in Lojban. At least one couple – Bob Le Chevalier, the first president of the Logical Language Group, and his wife Nora Tansky – have exchanged their wedding vows in Lojban. (As relentlessly unambiguous as Lojban is, those vows should be at least as binding as most, if not more so.) But there are no known plans in the works for a Lojban-native child.

While writing this, I heard a reporter for the BBC talking about the prospects for Snapchat, the messaging app popular with teens and young adults, and stating that "158 million people use the app every day." There are two very different ways to hear that same short set of words. One is that Snapchat has a hugely loyal base: there is a distinct group of 158 million people who use the app every single day. But there's another perfectly possible understanding of those same words: that on any given day, 158 million people use Snapchat, but tomorrow's 158 million will be a different subset of the global population. The grammar of the BBC reporter's statement looks more like the former. I read three other news reports with similarly ambiguous statements, before reading Snapchat's original wording: "on average, 158 million people use Snapchat daily." The "on average" closes the case for the second reading: not a dedicated must-use-daily base of 158 million people, but daily figures of all users that average to 158 million.

The ambiguity would never have sent me to Google – would

never have been possible – in Lojban. Cowan dutifully translates the possibilities for me. The first is:

pa mu bi ki'o ki'o prenu cu pilno la .snaptcat. ca'o ro djedi

one five eight thousand thousand person (cu) use (la) Snapchat during each day

Or, roughly, "each of the same set of 158 million persons use Snapshot each day."

The second is:

ca'o ro djedi pa mu bi ki'o ki'o prenu cu pilno la .snaptcat.

during each day one five eight thousand thousand person (cu) use (la) Snapchat.

during each day, 158MM [million] persons (not necessarily the same ones) use Snapchat.

Should the BBC switch to Lojban? Unlike English, it is exactly the kind of language that sticklers (including many journalists) think people should speak. It makes you communicate information precisely, after working out exactly what you want to say in your own mind. Many sticklers assume a lay version of the Sapir–Whorf hypothesis themselves: that thought itself depends on language. They worry that lack of careful attention to grammar threatens the entire enterprise of clear communication and even clear thinking.

So before going on with more typical language tamers, those who think English is (or should be) perfectly logical, it's worth listening to speakers of the world's most logical language, which does not allow ambiguity and which requires careful assembly. They don't hold the kind of folk-Whorfian beliefs that many sticklers of English grammar do. Few Lojbanists still believe that thought depends on language and that logical thinking proceeds necessarily and inevitably from logical language. In Cowan's words, most people learn Lojban for the same reason he does: it's fun, "cool", even a "toy".

Asked whether, even anecdotally, Lojban speakers report becoming more logical over the years, Cowan says that it looks more likely to be the other way around: people interested in logic come to Lojban. A user called "solpahi" on a Lojban chat forum ventures a bit of support for Cooke's old hypothesis, saying that learning Lojban makes him more aware of the constant ambiguity of natural languages. But he does not endorse the view that Lojban makes you logical.

*

Lojban marks the high point of an arc of logical-language invention that began with people like John Wilkins and his analytical language, taxonomising the world's knowledge. Not quite on that arc is Esperanto, a language that was logical only to the extent that it stripped the irregularity from natural languages' grammar, but which still behaves like an easy European language. Wilkins's language is a historical curio. Esperanto never proposed to be a vehicle of pure thought, but merely put itself forward as a humble alternative to the world's existing *lingua francas*.[7]

Lojban is the closest thing to a logical language going. If the world's most extreme would-be language tamers have mostly given up on the idea of better thinking through better language, this has consequences for the many others out there banging the drum for their version of grammar, claiming it as the equivalent of logic itself.

2

Is language logic?

IF YOU HAD TO INVENT an extreme grammar-stickler for a stereotype, what would he look like? He needn't be a he, of course. But if he were, you might imagine him British, expensively educated, silver-haired, imperious to the point of arrogance, convinced of his rightness to the point of unreason. In other words, you would probably picture someone a lot like Nevile Martin Gwynne.

Gwynne didn't start life as a professional grammarian. The son of a family whose vast fortune dwindled to a modest one, he went to Eton before becoming a chartered accountant and then a businessman. His conversion to Catholicism cost him his marriage and convinced him to quit business: giving his reasons, he has said "you are always telling lies of a small kind." He retired in the 1980s, moved to Ireland and, when he needed some extra income, began teaching online. When Toby Young, a right-leaning British journalist, began praising Gwynne's teaching of Latin and grammar to Young's children, Gwynne's reputation grew. It is never too late to make a mark on the world, it seems: after turning 70, he published his first book, an impish yet somehow also imperious work, *Gwynne's Grammar*.[1]

Since its publication in 2012, Gwynne's book has gained him sudden renown: not long before a humble tutor, he was suddenly being introduced as an expert in television interviews. Prince Charles thanked him for producing "something so extraordinarily useful" in the *Grammar*. The *Daily Telegraph*, a conservative British newspaper, *First Things*, a religious-themed American magazine, and the master of Eton College have heaped praise on its no-nonsense, traditional methods.

So what are these methods? To begin, Gwynne lays out an extravagant, pseudo-logical "proof".

Step one. For genuine thinking we need words. By 'genuine thinking' I mean: as opposed to merely being – as animals are capable of being – conscious of feeling hungry, tired, angry, and so on, and wanting to do something about it. Thinking cannot be done without words.

Step two. If we do not use words rightly, we shall not think rightly.

Step three. If we do not think rightly, we cannot reliably decide rightly, because good decisions depend on accurate thinking.

Step four. If we do not decide rightly, we shall make a mess of our lives, and also of other people's lives to the extent that we have an influence on other people.

Step five. If we make a mess of our lives, we shall make ourselves and other people unhappy.

If it can be shown that Gwynne's grasp on grammar is shoddy, then (step two) he can't think rightly. At this point you could dispense with the rest of the proof, but you can follow it to the end to see that he should also be unhappy, and making other people unhappy, too.

But he seems quite pleased with himself. He went on to produce two more books, *Gwynne's Latin* (2013) and *Gwynne's Kings and Queens* (2018), a history of England. He gives frequent televised interviews and takes part in public debates with a kind of cheeky charm. Meanwhile a lot of people say nice things about his grammar teaching, including Gwynne's own future king. But according to his proof, he should be miserable, because his grammar is a mess. Something is wrong in the proof somewhere.

A few good tests can tell you quickly whether you should take a self-appointed authority on grammar seriously. One of them crops up as early as his preface, before he has even begun laying out grammar rules properly:

[T]he use of "he" to embrace either "he" or "she" now being held by some people to be offensive to women. The result of this has been unfortunate, to say the least. Because saying "he or she", "him or her" and "his or hers", when speaking about people generally, is often disagreeably clumsy, a way of avoiding doing so has arisen which is offensive to logic and common sense and shockingly illiterate when in writing. In place of "he or she", and the rest, the words "they", "them" and "their" are now often used, even when referring to only one person, as in "Anyone who considers this modern practice acceptable has lost their mind."

This is where a habitué of the grammar wars can put *Gwynne's Grammar* down with a pretty good idea of what the rest will be like. "Offensive to logic", "illiterate", even something that only people who have "lost their mind" would say? The hyperbole is common to Gwynne's writing, and that of his stablemates in grammatical sticklerism. It is also ahistorical and ungrammatical.

Think quickly: a group of friends at dinner has just left the room and you discover an umbrella on the table. You call out after them to let them know: "Someone left [possessive pronoun] umbrella!" If you are like the vast majority of English-speakers, you'll naturally say "someone left *their* umbrella." Don't worry. You are not illiterate, nor out of your mind, and you haven't offended logic.

Modern English doesn't have a good "epicene" pronoun, meaning one common to both genders, when you want to refer to "someone", or a generic "student" or "doctor". Instead, English has only several awkward options. Gwynne insists that only one – perhaps the most awkward one – is acceptable. He would have you say "someone has left *his* umbrella," in the dogged insistence that "he" logically includes "she" where necessary.

There are plenty of other places where *his* is awful if it's truly meant to be generic: "of Steve, Julie, Emily, Laura and Danielle, who loves his mother the most?" This is no good. Generic *he* also jars when we use it for technically generic but socially gendered subjects. Try "someone has left his lipstick." (After all, some men wear lipstick.) Or "a young nurse should always remember his bedside manner." "A flight attendant should remember that his appearance matters." "A prostitute risks his safety walking the streets." Can we imagine Gwynne committing to these? If not, perhaps "*he* embraces *he* or *she*" has something awry.

And even if Gwynne would accept these, singular, epicene *they* nonetheless has a better case behind it than gender-neutral *he*. For one thing, it often lines up with the "notional", or real-world, meaning of the antecedent. *Everyone* is grammatically singular (it takes *is*, not *are*). But it is semantically plural (referring to all people, or all the people relevant to a discourse). This is just one reason many people reach for *they* in sentences like "Everyone has their own opinion." It's not one person, but the set of all people.

Some might object that *they* can't be both singular and plural. But they're forgetting a fact right under their noses: English already has a pronoun that is both singular and plural: *you*. It was originally only plural, but wound up singular too, after a series of changes in usage (chiefly the retirement of *ye*, and the later loss of *thou*). The language has hardly collapsed in a heap of sundered logic. Plenty of languages have pronouns that can be both singular and plural: French *vous*, German *sie/Sie*, and so on.

At this point, head-in-the-sand sticklers look to good old English tradition: *he* has included *she* for centuries, and you can look it up in the dictionary. Quite so. The only problem is that epicene *they* is even older, and you can look that up in the dictionary too. The *Oxford English Dictionary*'s first citation for sex-neutral, singular *they* is not "modern", as Gwynne says. It is from 1375, in a poem called *The Romance of William of Palerne*.

> Hastely hiȝed eche wiȝt..til þei neyȝþed so neiȝh..þere william & his worþi lef were liand i-fere.

It's hard to see through the Middle English spelling, but *þei* ("they") refers back to *eche* ("each"), a singular noun.

So if you're a traditionalist, this hunk of Middle English, the earliest known singular *they*, is older than so-called sex-neutral *he*, for which the *OED*'s first citation is from about 1405. After tracing the history of singular *they* through the centuries, the *OED* drily notes that "this usage has sometimes been considered erroneous." But the dictionary does not condemn it.

So singular *they* is no scruffy outsider to the grammar, used only in rushed and incautious speech. Nor is it some modern abomination invented to annoy conservatives like Gwynne. Among its other citations:

> Every person ... now recovered their liberty (Oliver Goldsmith)
>
> If a person is born of a ... gloomy temper ... they cannot help it (Lord Chesterfield)
>
> Every body does and says what they please (Lord Byron)
>
> Now, nobody does anything well that they cannot help doing (John Ruskin)
>
> It's unpleasant enough to drive anyone out of their senses (George Bernard Shaw)

Singular *they* appears several times in the *King James Bible*, including a well-known lesson from Matthew 18:35: "So likewise shall my heavenly father do also unto you, if ye from your hearts forgive not every one his brother their trespasses." Note that the antecedent here is "his brother": unambiguously male (as it was in Greek: *to adelpho autou*, "his brother"). And yet the committee of the King James translators knew that "his brother their trespasses" was perfectly acceptable here.[2] Jane Austen was mad for singular *they*, using it at least 87 times in her novels:

> Nobody meant to be unkind, but nobody put themselves out of their way to secure her comfort. (*Mansfield Park*)
>
> [E]very body was pleased to think how much they had always disliked Mr. Darcy before they had known any thing of the matter. (*Pride and Prejudice*)
>
> [E]ach of them was busy in arranging their particular concerns, and endeavouring, by placing around them books and other possessions, to form themselves a home. (*Sense and Sensibility*)

Finally, I can't help mentioning that Walter Bagehot, a constitutional scholar and once editor of *The Economist*, wrote that "Nobody fancies for a moment that they are reading about anything beyond the pale of ordinary propriety." Well said.

If a language book cannot get through the preface without promoting a fallacy of this magnitude, you're usually safe to stop reading there. But it is nonetheless a useful exercise to read on in *Gwynne's Grammar*.

Many grammar books do a jocular version of "false syntax", explaining a rule by breaking it. ("Do not use run-on sentences they are annoying.") *Gwynne's* offers an ingenious exemplar of how not to do grammar itself.

Take the so-called "split infinitive". Generations of students have been taught that English doesn't let you put anything between *to* and a verb, as in the famous case of "to boldly go where no man has gone before". Why on earth are so many people splitting infinitives anyway? Why are such a dedicated minority so opposed?

The first known person to write that it was impermissible to split an infinitive was John Comly, in 1803: "An adverb should not be placed between a verb of the infinitive mood and the preposition to which governs it."[3] The rule was repeated by other grammar books over time, becoming one of those things that everyone with an education "knew" – but which wasn't true. True experts never accepted the rule; the great English lexicographer and usage-book author H. W. Fowler called it a "superstition" in 1926. All decent modern guides to English grammar agree that where a modifier is best placed between "to" and the verb, that's where it should go.

Gwynne has seen these arguments. But he is adamant, nonetheless, that an infinitive should never be split, with a bold justification: "Shakespeare never needed to split an infinitive, and scarcely a single instance of a split infinitive is to be found in the classical authors of the last two centuries." He goes on to say that a *single* well-known author, Fanny Burney, split infinitives.

Perhaps it's too much to ask that he actually open a book to check; in this case, a visit to Wikipedia would have put him right. The split infinitive was fairly common in middle English. John Wycliffe, an early translator of the Bible into English, used it frequently. The pattern did decline in frequency in the early modern period, though Shakespeare uses one ("thy pity may deserve to pitied be," from a sonnet). But it returned in force in the 18th and 19th centuries. Here are just a few authors Gwynne presumably skipped over while he was busy reading Fanny Burney:

Samuel Johnson: "Milton was too busy **to much miss** his wife"

Matthew Arnold: "without permitting himself **to actually mention** the name"

Samuel Taylor Coleridge: "the interest which the good people of Keswick take in the welfare of the beauty of Buttermere, has not yet suffered them **to entirely subside**"

Anthony Trollope: "curtains draped so as **to half exclude** the light"

Theodore Roosevelt : "His fortune being jeopardized, he hoped **to more than retrieve** it by going into speculation in Western lands"

George Eliot: "I undertook **to partially fill up** the office of parish clerk"

Henry James: "**To utterly forget** her past"

Mark Twain: "The commission's scheme **to arbitrarily and permanently confine** the channel"

Thomas Hardy: "She wants **to honestly and legally marry** that man"

George Bernard Shaw: "Just sensible enough of his own callousness **to intensely enjoy** the humour and adroitness of it"

Rudyard Kipling: "which prompts a man **to savagely stamp** on the spider he has but half killed"

Ernest Hemingway: "But I would come back to where it pleased me to live; **to really live**"[4]

It is very hard to think of a practice that can be more venerable than one used by Johnson, Arnold, Coleridge, Trollope, Roosevelt, Eliot, James, Twain, Hardy, Shaw, Kipling and Hemingway – not to mention very many others. Shaw, whose metalinguistic curiosity was so great that he made a phonetician the main character of a hit play, once wrote to a newspaper demanding that the editor who enforced the split-infinitive rule be fired. The split-infinitive ban has been demolished, again and again, by sensible grammarians.

If a medical textbook, even a successful one from a quality publisher, repeated the myth that a woman's uterus causes hysteria or that an excess of black bile leads to melancholy, those passages alone would make you reach for another textbook. But *Gwynne's Grammar* also gets it wrong on many smaller points.

- It repeats the belief that *hopefully* cannot be used to mean "it is hoped that", as in *hopefully it will rain tomorrow*. (There is nothing wrong with this "sentence adverb", which takes a place alongside *frankly*, *honestly* and the like. They express the attitude of the speaker rather than the subject of the sentence.)

- It defines "noun" and "verb" as "a person, place or thing" and "a doing word". These are simplifications intended for children, and are not technically accurate. In reality, nouns and verbs are defined by their grammatical functions: a noun can be the subject of a sentence, can be plural, etc. A verb is required in all English sentences, may be in the past tense, can head a verb phrase, etc. *Nothingness* isn't a person, place or thing, but it is a noun; *To exist* is not "a doing word", but it is a verb.

- Gwynne repeats the myth that gerunds must be preceded by a possessive pronoun. But Lewis Carroll wrote both "in hopes of his being able to join me" and "the music prevented any of it [not *its*] being heard." An avalanche of other citations from great writers show that there is nothing wrong with either (though stylistically one or the other might be better in some cases).[5]

- His definition of a clause is "a group of words with a verb in it". That would make *purple horseradish Steve drive* a clause.

- His definition of a phrase is even more confused: "A phrase is a group of words *without* a verb in it." That would make *red horseradish Steve tree* a phrase. And in any case, verb phrases obviously have verbs in them.

Now we are talking about a medical textbook that says that the humerus is in the leg, the femur is in the arm, the spleen produces insulin, the eyeball produces adrenaline and the gallbladder is the seat of consciousness.

What's going on? Gwynne has a reasonable grasp on some elements of traditional grammar, and it's hard to take issue with his description of proper punctuation. But on nearly every complicated, contested or even interesting point, he gets it wrong, as if he had an unerring instinct for getting it wrong, a compass with a needle that consistently pointed any way but north. There's a pattern.

Being a conservative on matters of grammar is no sin at all. The problem is that Gwynne does not even know how to determine what conservative English usage and grammar is. He boasts of consulting "dozens" of grammar books in the research for his own. Perhaps this is the problem: he is not reading anything but grammar books, but none of them are scholarly. It seems they are all ones that themselves discuss grammar in the authoritarian abstract, as Gwynne does – declaring rules without looking at the language itself.

The essence of *descriptive* grammar, which is what experts do, is not to throw out rules. It is to find out what the rules are by consulting native speakers of the language. Now, this can mean many different kinds of native speakers, depending on what kind of language you want to describe. If a linguist wants to survey Yorkshire dialect, the native speakers will be old people in rural Yorkshire who use the dialect every day. If the dialect is urban London teenager-speak, the native speakers will be London teens.

It is perfectly possible – in fact, it is only reasonable – to learn traditional standard written English by consulting the body of traditional standard written English. But this is not Gwynne's approach. He teaches not what great writers do, but what he was taught. When he isn't sure or can't remember, he consults another grammar that employs the same methods. Grammarians who don't look at evidence, but merely repeat rules they've heard elsewhere, are trading in rumour and hearsay rather than ascertaining facts first-hand.

Is singular *they* a modern, politically correct barbarism? If you're Gwynne, you say so, and that's that. But a serious student goes to the evidence. Any good library has the *Oxford English Dictionary*, which describes at length and in detail the long history of epicene *they*. The same goes for the split infinitive. No "classical authors" use it? Instead of asserting, look at classical authors, or look at the many good grammar and usage books that themselves consult the classical authors. If a disputed usage is truly rare, a good book recommends against it. If it is common in informal contexts (speech, letters), again good usage advice is straightforward: use with caution and avoid in formal writing. But if, as in the case of the split infinitive and singular *they*, the evidence is vast that these usages are common among good writers, then go with the evidence.

Gwynne has no time for this approach. He pronounces, and the case is closed. His Preface makes a show of using the teaching methods that have worked in the past, before the hippies screwed everything up in the 1960s. But far from being conservative in the best sense, respecting traditions of actual usage, his kind of approach is radically authoritarian. Do as I say, not as the great writers do.

There's a joke, often told as a true story, that goes

> Churchill, drunk as usual, met a woman at a party. "Would you sleep with me for a million pounds?" "Well, I might," comes the reply. "What about for a hundred pounds?" "What kind of woman do you think I am?" "We've already established that," comes Churchill's smug reply. "Now we're just haggling about the price."

The same goes for prescriptivism and descriptivism. No sane person is a pure prescriptivist, declaring a rule to be valid even in the face of literally millions of high-quality citations from edited writing that show otherwise. In the end, we must concede that the language is what it is, when the facts of good writing are overwhelming. Evidence simply has to play a role.

So we are really just haggling about the price. What evidence would it take to convince a Gwynne that singular *they* is grammatical, or that the split infinitive is perfectly respectable? A billion citations? A million? A thousand? A hundred? It is perfectly fine to be conservative – to, in the metaphor, demand a high price in terms of evidence before changing your mind. And it is just fine to be a progressive, and accept a disputed usage after seeing it merely dozens or hundreds of times in professional, edited English, rather than thousands or millions.

But to ignore evidence *entirely* risks making you look ridiculous, or even unmoored from reality. At a debate in 2014 in London, Gwynne did his usual shtick of a "proof", connecting the decline in grammar to the decline in thinking, the decline in thinking to the decline in good behaviour, and so on. As evidence that the society was in serious decline, accompanied or even caused by the decline in grammar, he offered that "when I was young, there was no such thing as suicide." This is obviously preposterous. When Tom Freeman, an editor and language blogger present at the debate, got home, it took him five minutes online to determine that suicide rates had fallen by half from 1959, when Gwynne was 17, to 2007. Whatever else modern grammar teaching is doing, it appears to be saving thousands of lives.

*

Gwynne is a bit ridiculous on purpose; his pomposity is obviously meant as an amusing show, and one that has served him well. His book is filled with example sentences like

> the order [of adjectives] is opinion–size–age–shape–colour–origin–material–purpose. Following this rule, the book you are holding is therefore a nice little just-published oblong-shaped attractively coloured much-needed paperback grammar textbook...[6]

> It is a pity that the new-fangled teachers did not realise that grammar was such an important subject.[7]

But his logical proof is, he tells us repeatedly, meant to be taken seriously. Without good grammar, you can't think straight, act right, and live well.

The proof is wrong for many interesting reasons. One is that plenty of thinking is perfectly possible without grammar, or even without language. Gwynne concedes that basic animal urges like fear don't rely on language. But there's a vast amount of sophisticated mental processing that has little or no relation to language. Think of the sophisticated movement-planning of a gifted athlete, the aural appreciation of a skilled music critic, or the palate of an expert chef. These are rare skills, far beyond animal urges, acquired with difficulty, and yet they rely little or not at all on language.

Many kinds of thought, from artistic to mathematical, and from simple to complex, are possible without language. "Genie" – a girl famous to linguists for having been raised until age 13 without language by her abusive parents – was able to learn a number of words, but never to speak properly with English grammar. But her ungrammatical narratives certainly showed that she had vivid memories of her horrible father ("Father hit big stick. Father angry. Father hit Genie big stick. Father take piece wood hit. Cry. Me cry.") And she could tell far more intricate stories with pictures. In other words, she could clearly think.[8]

So can people with a condition called Broca's (or agrammatic) aphasia, who have lost the ability to use grammar normally. Their stories, like Genie's, come out as a mess of content words that give a clear gist but which do not form grammatical sentences. They are nonetheless comprehensible; Broca's aphasia affects only language production. Indeed, sufferers often show frustration that they can't express what is obviously clear in their minds.

People can even solve complex intellectual problems without words. Steven Pinker, in *The Language Instinct*, lists a host of scientists from Michael Faraday (electromagnetism) to James Watson and Francis Crick (the helical structure of DNA) whose breakthroughs were visual, not verbal. Pinker concludes with a quotation from Einstein, who described the thought experiments that led to some of his breakthroughs: "this combinatory play seems to be the essential feature in productive thought – before there is any connection with logical construction in words or other kinds of signs which can be communicated to others."[9]

Of course, people do think in language sometimes. And sometimes language is clearly an aid to thought. A meteorologist with different names for clouds can easily pick them out of the sky and model how they interact with other weather phenomena. One of the best examples of language enabling thought is numbers: peoples whose languages lack higher numbers (some languages don't go beyond two) have no ability to tell five from seven objects; they must rely on "many" and can't be more exact. Mark Liberman, a linguist at the University of Pennsylvania, calls numbers an unusual example of a "linguistic technology" without which certain things just can't be done.

But in general linguists agree that speakers of all languages (including non-written ones, the vast majority of the world's languages) are capable of a vast range of thought. Scientists have yet to locate a language in the world that makes certain kinds of thought impossible. Of course, certain words may be missing in a language – Cherokee may lack a word for "Higgs boson" – but words can easily be coined or borrowed. European languages constantly borrow English terms of science, technology or business.

What most linguistic "technologies" like numbers and advanced vocabulary do is make certain thoughts (and the communication of those thoughts) more efficient, not make them possible in the first place. "Seven" can be expressed as "one one one one one one one", or with seven notches on a stick, but "seven" or "7" is quicker. It can be usefully combined with other concepts to help organise useful memorised facts like "seven times eight is fifty-six."

An enlightening thought experiment on what words make possible is Randall Munroe's book *Thing Explainer*. Munroe, who once worked for NASA and now writes a comic strip about mathematics, computers, language and logic, explains some of the world's most complicated technologies using only the most common 1,000 words in the English language. This can be hard to do with the Large Hadron Collider (which he calls the "big little-thing hitter") but it is fascinating (and hilarious) evidence that thought clearly does not proceed directly from language, as many people seem to think. Physicists invented the word "hadron" because they needed it; they did not find the particle because they had the word in their vocabularies.

And in any case, Gwynne and prescriptivists like him would have you think that *grammar*, not primarily vocabulary, is the key to thinking. His theory entails that people who use non-standard (what he would call "incorrect") grammar can't think straight. Prescriptivists in this school of thought are playing a morally and intellectually dubious game: they are implying that people who don't speak like they do are necessarily stupid.

Can that be so? No. Listen to some of the most articulate figures in Anglophone history in particular, speakers of non-standard dialects: "Ain't no Vietcong ever called me nigger." Muhammad Ali could have said "Given my experience with racism in America, I refuse to fight for a white-run government against foreigners I have no quarrel with." That would have been fine, too, but a lot less memorable, and the sentiment would have been exactly the same. Taking it out of Ali's African-American English and putting into standard English does not a jot for its actual content.

What about country white dialect? Another of my favourite quotes is one attributed to Josh Billings: "It ain't the things people don't know. It's the things they know that ain't so." The quote (often credited to Twain too) anticipated later fears about "fake news", confirmation bias and other mental bad habits. Ronald Reagan used the quote in 1964 but rendered it in standard English: "Well, the trouble with our liberal friends is not that they're ignorant; it's just that they know so much that isn't so." Is that any clearer? Any better? Did Reagan think this statement through better than Billings had? It's worse, in fact: "the things they *know* that *ain't so*" has a pleasingly punchy rhythm-rhyme combination that makes it unforgettable.

So even if thought sometimes depends on language, it doesn't in the slightest depend on the grammar of standard English, dialectal English, standard Italian, dialectal Italian, German, Japanese or Javanese. Thought may depend a bit on grammar, but thankfully not on Gwynne's grammar.

*

Gwynne, then, is a grammar crank. But there's another side to his crankishness, and it is up to the reader to decide whether it has anything to do with his ideas about language. According to the dedicated digging of Oliver Kamm, an editorial writer at the London *Times*, Gwynne is an ultratraditionalist "sedevacantist" Catholic, a member of a group rejecting the Second Vatican Council, which considers every pope since 1958 a heretic, leaving the See of Rome vacant. He rejects the theory of evolution utterly.

Kamm has unearthed three papers written under the name N. Martin Gwynne, apparently from the 1980s, in which Gwynne claims that the earth neither revolves around the sun nor rotates on its axis. In three chapters, he declares Galileo, Newton and Einstein to be perpetrators of "cruel hoaxes".[10] The existence of atoms is also a myth, according to Gwynne.

Why perpetrate these hoaxes? And who is behind them? Gwynne calls Newton an agent of "revolutionary international forces" and "a member of one or more of the secret societies warring against God and the human race". Galileo, Gwynne says, is recognised as an intellectual martyr only because he "was one of the most important of Satan's human agents that have ever lived and that the Jewish/Masonic/occult powers who are now so close to victory in their plan to rule the whole world wish to recognize his contribution in an appropriate manner".

Gwynne calls Einstein an "artificially created giant", only modestly talented in physics, but "with considerable abilities as an actor and a showman". He was chosen because the powers foisting Einstein's theories on the world needed a Jew. Why?

> From the middle of the nineteenth century onwards, those
> presented to the world as the modern geniuses marking the
> turning points in civilisation have been Jews. I do not wish to
> exaggerate this, and it is certainly true that non-Jews too, such as
> Darwin at the beginning of the period and Lord Keynes in more
> recent times, have had their nonsense presented as majestic
> contributions to human knowledge. Nevertheless, if asked to
> name the three men whose writings had the greatest influence
> in shaping the modern world, few would go beyond Karl Marx,
> Sigmund Freud and Albert Einstein. Explanations for the
> phenomenon, adequate or otherwise, are suggested elsewhere in
> other papers that I have written. Here I record only the fact and the
> inference that can be derived from it. The Jews are entering into
> what they believe to be their inheritance.

Gwynne's theories don't stop there. Another book of his, called *Banks and Money*, is described by its traditionalist Catholic publisher as proving that "money creation by the worldwide banking system is immoral and suicidal, though useful and even indispensable for bringing about the 'New World Order'." (*Banks and Money* is, for reasons unknown, unavailable in the British Library, although the British Library is required by law to have a copy of every book published in Britain.)

Finally, in an essay on the *ad hominem* tactic in debates, Gwynne admiringly cites "a learned professor ... because he said it about as well as can be said." The learned professor is Robert Faurisson, who has spent a career denying the existence of gas chambers at Auschwitz. Faurisson's essay, cited by Gwynne, speaks not only of himself as a victim of *ad hominem* attacks but also of Ernst Zündel, a German whose

Holocaust denial has earned him convictions for racial hatred in Canada and Germany.

After Kamm exposed these writings in the *Jewish Chronicle*, Gwynne sent him a friendly note. "I am jolly well not anti-Jewish! Nor am I a Holocaust denier," he wrote, citing a Jewish banker and a Jewish lawyer with whom he first had business dealings in Australia, and who later became his dear friends. Gwynne invited Kamm to dinner at a London club; Kamm refused, saying that Gwynne's writings were the problem, regardless of any of his personal relationships.

It is startling that so many people were eager for a return to traditional ruler-on-the-back-of-the-hand grammar teaching that they rushed to embrace such a scientific and moral ignoramus. As of this writing, two years after Kamm's revelations, Gwynne was still a regular host on a BBC Radio 5 show about grammar, and due to publish a new book, *Gwynne's Kings and Queens*, about English and British history. He has never been publicly held to account for these writings. Nor have the authors of any of these pieces of praise for *Gwynne's Grammar* had them removed from Amazon, where they were still proudly displayed as of early 2018:

> Dynamite to modern, child-centred education: a guide to the forgotten rudiments of the English Language.
>
> – Elizabeth Grice, *Daily Telegraph*

> Curious and brilliant ... it is wonderful that his crisp, lucid book has at last been embraced by the many.
>
> – Charles Moore, the *Spectator*

> Witty, engaging and highly educational stuff.
>
> – *Times Educational Supplement*

> Mr. Gwynne is unflinchingly, unapologetically rear-guard... The personality of its author is not the least attraction of *Gwynne's Grammar* ... [a book] with not the least wisp of dumbing-down in his composition ... [He] does not deny that grammar can be hellishly complicated ... [and] his definitions – terse, logical, precise – are among the best things in the book ... I feel a certain

elegance in what I have been taught and still take to be correct English.

– Joseph Epstein, The *Wall Street Journal*

A very useful, pertinent summary and it deserves both to be used and enjoyed.

– Tony Little, headmaster, Eton College

Invaluable.

– *Writing Magazine*

Warm and utterly self-assured ... Refreshingly opinionated ... [Gwynne] is an unashamed prescriptivist ... [and his] judgment is unambiguous ... It doesn't matter how many academic linguists tell us that language changes over time ... Educated people still want to know whether they should write "amuck" or "amok", "between" or "among".

– Barton Swaim, *The Weekly Standard*

It would be easy to dismiss Nevile Gywnne – even with his rave reviews from the conservative press and his love-note from the future king. His views on geocentrism, the New World Order and a Jewish/Masonic conspiracy should cast him out of polite society. But Gwynne-style beliefs about language, just as majestically unconcerned with the facts of the matter as his beliefs about so much else, turn out to be regrettably common among many professions in which fact-finding is the core of the job.

And among them, it pains me to write, is journalism. Journalists proudly think of themselves as sceptics, unearthers of hard, counterintuitive truths. But in linguistic matters, some journalists are perfectly willing to accept old beliefs without question. They are often passed down by a senior journalist: an editor or columnist with an encyclopaedic knowledge of every grammar rule they have ever heard – whether valid or not.

A notable example is Simon Heffer, a British columnist who has written a Gwynne-style grammar, *Strictly English: The Correct Way to Write ... and Why It Matters*. The book, just like Gwynne's, contains plenty of material that is unobjectionable. But it also repeats so many mistakes and disproven "rules" – calling singular *they* an "abomination" for example – that it is impossible to rely on Heffer for "the correct way to write".

Gwynne and Heffer share a quirk: a nostalgia and reverence for Latin. Heffer's book mentions Latin 44 times. Though he acknowledges that Latin can't always be a source of authority for English, it is hard to understand some of his analytical mistakes unless they come from faulty Latin analogies. Gwynne's book goes further, mentioning Latin 68 times, and is more explicit in reasoning from Latin. He says that "during the last four centuries, it [English] has been, together with classical Greek and Latin, one of the three great vehicles of thought, communication, science and culture of all time."

It's not a coincidence that language conservatives admire Latin and Greek. The languages represent a kind of Platonic perfection for a certain kind of mind. First, they were taught in every good school back in the days before the flower children came in in the 1960s and ruined education. But second, studying these two languages really is one of the best ways to learn a lot about grammar generally. People learn their first language without any explicit teaching, creating a blistering variety of sentences before they have begun reading. So they often struggle to understand why they should care about naming the elements and structures of a language they can already use.

Learning a foreign language, unlike one's native language, requires learning some explicit grammar terminology, from simple stuff like "noun" and "verb" to higher-level things like "past participle" and "subordinate clause". In a modern foreign-language class, this stuff is mixed in with exercises designed to get students talking comfortably, whether or not they know a subordinate from a subjunctive.

But in Latin and Greek, the aim is never to get kids talking comfortably. It is to read the long-frozen texts of great writers, to understand and translate them. Reading such polished texts in these difficult languages really does require knowing the function of every word in a sentence. In Latin and Greek these are signalled with case endings, as was the case with Old English. And only professional scholars of those languages study how their case endings were gradually, naturally, worn away; how their languages gradually but just as naturally changed, how their vocabulary inexorably shifted, until

Latin had become French and Spanish and the Greek of Aristotle had become the hugely different modern demotic Greek spoken in Athens today. If you are Gwynne, the idea that languages might stop changing at their high point makes sense. They want English to do this because, in their imaginations, Greek and Latin did so – in the frozen varieties they learned two millennia later in school.

Before the 17th century or thereabouts, English, like most European languages, was a mere vernacular, and most serious work was still written in Latin. When the analysis of English grammar began, the first grammarians mistakenly tried to press English (a Germanic language) into a Latinate mould it did not fit properly. And some of these analytical mistakes are still with us today. The infinitive is a single word in Latin and Greek; therefore nothing may come between "to" and a verb in the English infinitive, QED. If you're confused by the logic, you should be. It makes no sense.

Similarly, in Latin, when a pronoun in a predicate refers back to the subject of the sentence, they should both be in the same case, the nominative. By this logic, English should do the same. This is the reason many people have been taught to say things like "it is I" and "that is he" instead of "it's me" and "that's him".

For a certain kind of grammatical classicist, it doesn't matter that Latin and English differ utterly. For the Gwynnes of the world, the classical languages represent a host of good things: the great texts of the ancient world, the days when every schoolchild learned Caesar and Cicero at a tender age, and last but not at all least, the knowledge of grammar itself (based on Greek and Latin forms). Greek and Latin even gave us most of our words for talking about language: syntax, morphology, grammar (Greek) or verb, adjective, preposition (Latin).

Gwynne knows that English is a Germanic language. But when your whole linguistic vocabulary is Latin and Greek, and you were taught to revere Latin and Greek texts from childhood, and you were taught a faulty analysis of English based on Latin and Greek, it can be hard to see English afresh, and to question whether some of that traditional Greco-Latin analysis wasn't flawed.

For example, as we've seen, learning Latin and Greek is, in large part, learning declension: the different case endings that nouns, adjectives, pronouns and a few other words take, depending on their role in a sentence. (The other big part of learning Latin and Greek is learning verb conjugations.) After you've climbed these – admittedly big – hills of declension and conjugation, and got a certain amount of vocabulary under your belt, you're off to the races: with a dictionary you can read most anything in Latin and Greek.

Classicists who have done all these declensions in Latin and Greek in school can't help themselves when they see the few remaining case endings in English change or disappear. We're back to why the case of the missing *whom* bothers some people. To the classicist, Sherlock Holmes's "who's sleeping with *who*" is a crashing, obvious mistake: *who* is nominative, and prepositions are never followed by the nominative – not in Latin, not in Greek, and, until the last few centuries, not in English either. I too tend to be jarred when people like Sherlock use *who* for *whom*, and it's because I, too, have studied languages with lots of case endings (though in my case, German, Russian, Arabic and Greek, with no Latin).

But as we have seen, English has shed the vast majority of its case endings. As a result, case just isn't something English-speakers think about very much. In school, it hardly needs to be taught, since only six words, all pronouns, show a distinction between nominative (*he*, *who*) and objective (*him*, *whom*) case. In the vast majority of instances, even young children get them right: nobody says *I saw he*. *Whom* is one of the last tricky cases.

One of the few other remaining tricky cases is in compound noun phrases – that is, the habit of using *X and I* where it should be *X and me*. Bill Clinton once said "Give Al Gore and I a chance." Since you wouldn't say "give I a chance," you shouldn't say "give Al and I" a chance, goes the logic. And "Between you and I" drives sticklers into a rage: the internet is full of people saying things like "If you say 'between you and I', I pretty much want to punch you in the face."[11]

Why is this slip so common? Our internet enforcer would have to punch a lot of illustrious writers – Henry Fielding and Benjamin Moore, for example – in the face. The mistake is even more common in speech, just like the use of *who* for *whom*. Gwynne may be onto something when he implies that lack of Latin and Greek education is changing people's use of English. He would say it is eroding their attention to fundamental distinctions of grammar. A dispassionate linguist would say that word order is doing ever more in English, and case less and less, part of a very normal shift that has also happened in other European languages. We haven't got to the point where people say "I love she" rather than "I love her," and we probably won't any time soon. But *whom*'s decline and the persistence of "between you and I" indicate that case – so critical to using Old English correctly – is becoming a marginal phenomenon in today's English.

*

That isn't quite the end of the story, however. Some people worry about using the way things *are* to describe the way things *should be*. In the cliché, "is" doesn't imply "ought". Some people, when they want grammar advice, don't want a long historical survey of messy evidence. They want an answer to "what should I do?" Can a descriptivist offer that?

Certainly. The best prescription comes from an accurate grasp of the facts, and here we turn to some outstanding examples of a sensible synthesis between descriptivism and prescriptivism. The long-running conflict between the two philosophies is giving way to an increase in good prescriptive usage and grammar books based on evidence.

An outstanding early example of descriptive prescriptivism is *Merriam-Webster's Dictionary of English Usage*. Published in 1994, *MWDEU* should be on the shelves of anyone who claims seriously to care about grammar and usage. It is 978 pages of proof that gathering facts and offering advice need not be in conflict. Its chief editor was Ward Gilman, known as the dictionary's in-house grammar brain, and notorious for terrifying young new lexicographers at Merriam-Webster with his crash course in grammar.

MWDEU gives its blessing to split infinitives, singular *they* and any of the other usages attacked by the likes of Gwynne. But it hardly blesses any and every usage. Its ruling on the "comma splice" or "comma fault" – joining two sentences with only a comma – is solid good sense. Though Benjamin Franklin wrote "The New Jersey Job was obtained, I contrived a copperplate press for it," comma splices are rare in edited prose today, appearing primarily in letters, or in fiction where a certain effect is desired. In other words, say *MWDEU*'s editors, "You probably should not try the device unless you are very sure of what you want it to accomplish."[12]

MWDEU can even channel classicists when looking at the plurals of Greek- and Latin-derived words. Considering whether phenomena can be singular – "a phenomena" has occasionally turned up in written sources, from *Science* to *The Economist* – *MWDEU*'s editors ultimately rule, with a little bit of sass, that singular *phenomena* "must be recognized as a borderline form at best. You can be a pioneer, if you wish, but we do not recommend it." Merriam-Webster goes where the evidence leads, rarely letting its editors exercise opinion A when facts seem to support conclusion B.

But it is also possible to mix personal judgment with prescription. And that is exactly what Bryan Garner says is his aim as a "descriptive prescriptivist". Garner is a law professor at Southern Methodist University in Dallas, Texas, but he has uniquely combined his legal career with a sideline as one of the most industrious lexicographers working today. He has written many books for lawyers, advising them on how best to persuade judges in their briefs, editing the venerable *Black's Law Dictionary* and co-writing a book with the late Antonin Scalia of America's Supreme Court on how to interpret statutes. But he has also written two books for the general reader: *Garner's Modern English Usage* and *The Chicago Guide to Grammar, Usage and Punctuation*.

Lawyers have reason more than most to care about strict, clear usage. This will seem laughable to a lot of readers – "legalese" is synonymous with impenetrability to non-lawyers. But legal writing has direct, important effects on the world. A statute binds all of the people in a jurisdiction with the force of law. Poorly written laws confuse people as to what exactly they are bound by, forcing courts to step in and interpret the laws. And in common-law countries like Britain and America, a court's judgment can itself have the force of law, binding future courts to follow its interpretation, so it's important that judges write clearly, too. Finally, ordinary lawyers are constantly writing things like contracts that – for all their impenetrability to the layman – when done well, prescribe exactly what each party to the contract is supposed to do.

Lawyers amass evidence to make their case, and in this way, Garner is a lawyer-lexicographer in a good way. Over decades, Garner has gathered thousands of citations of real English that have informed his flagship *Modern English Usage* over four editions. He is an unabashed prescriptivist who has criticised descriptivism, but one with his eyes wide open to the real world.

Unlike most prescriptivists, he lays out clearly ten criteria that he says will guide him. Though many of them are traditional to prescriptivists (simplicity, conservatism), many of them are pragmatic (realism). And his last criterion is clearly descriptivist: "actual usage". The citations he has gathered from voluminous reading have always informed his judgments. And for the fourth edition of his usage dictionary, published in 2016, he added a new, far bigger source of data: Google Books, which lets users chart the rise and fall of words and phrases in millions of published works. For many entries in the dictionary, Garner even provides a graph created from Google's data. Descriptive prescriptivism indeed.

Garner understands that language will never be perfect, and he does not pretend that the rules of grammar descend from heaven on a cloud of pure logic. Take his ruling on singular *they*. For Garner, English's lack of a better solution is a clear "inadequacy" – he makes no attempt to hide the fact that here, English simply has a defect, rather than a "logic" invisible to all but the classically educated.

As both a conservative and a pragmatist on these issues, Garner recognises that singular *they* is common and on the rise, and that it "promises to be the ultimate solution to the problem", but that in print today, it annoys many readers. In writing where "credibility is all" and annoying even a few people would do harm, then, he simply urges a few practical ways around the problem.

- Delete the pronoun altogether: "every manager should read memoranda as soon as they are delivered *to him*" [delete *to him*]
- Change the pronoun to an article: "An author may adopt any of the following dictionaries in preparing *his* [read *a*] manuscript"
- Pluralise: "A student should avoid engaging in any activities that might bring discredit to his school." (Read: *Students should avoid engaging in any activities that might bring discredit to their school*)

And so on.

Garner is prepared to change his mind in the face of evidence. In the past, for example, one ran the *gantlet* but threw down the *gauntlet*. But Garner looked at the Google Books numbers and found that "run the gauntlet" is now 11 times more common than "run the gantlet". So he changed his recommendation, accepting that "to run the gauntlet" is fully part of standard English.

Once in a while, Garner will stand his ground, defending an older judgment against the evidence of recent change. *Masterly* and *masterful* were once kept distinct by many writers, the former meaning "skilful", the latter meaning "imperious". Not all writers have observed that distinction – the *OED* cites people like John Ruskin using *masterful* in the "skilful" sense. And Garner concedes that "masterful performance" is more common than "masterly performance" in Google Books' data, by a ratio of 1.2 to 1. He concludes, nonetheless, that "*masterly* writers continue to like *masterly.*" You can disagree, but at least you know what you are disagreeing with: Garner's judgment, not a purported fact.

Garner says he overruled the data seven times for the 2,500 ratios he calculated with the Google Books data. Every writer deserves a few chances to say "I know what the data say, but I still think…", and Garner has used his sparingly. But overwhelmingly, the Google data confirmed rather than contradicted his standing judgments from previous editions of his usage dictionary. It must have been pleasing to have such clear confirmation that descriptive facts and prescriptive advice need not conflict.

Garner is a language tamer who realises that the goal is the best possible English, not perfect English. And perhaps the best symbol of this is how he rates correctness itself. For the narrow-minded stickler, things are right or wrong, and to make a mistake is to betray a disregard for the beautiful logic of the language. Garner, though, uses a 1–5 scale to rate usages from fully rejected to fully accepted – a clear acknowledgment of language's organic and changing nature.

Brittle logical systems can only return an answer of "right" or "wrong". Garner, by contrast, is comfortable with "yes, but…". "Run the gauntlet" is now a 5, as is a split infinitive: perfectly all right. *Masterly* for *masterful* rates a 4, or as he puts it, "ubiquitous, but…". And *splitting image* for *spitting image* is just plain wrong – a 1, or "rejected". This makes a skim of Garner's book a pleasure: even where the reader disagrees, it's on the level of "3?! That's a 4, at least!", and not "I'm right, you're wrong and that's that."

Garner has not only brought a reasonable level of lawyerliness to his lexicography. He has also brought good sense on plain language to the legal field. Perhaps the best example of a righteous language-taming endeavour is his campaign against *shall* in legal writing. Some writers (Gwynne among them) stick to an old view that for the simple future, *shall* should be used with first-person pronouns (*I shall, we shall*) and *will* should be used with the others, but that in cases where someone wants to express determination or will, the verbs and pronouns flip: *I will* means that someone has determined to do something, and *he shall* means that he is determined or obligated to do something.

This mess of a rule – which Gwynne would find "logical" – has only ever been observed consistently by some users of English. It's far less commonly observed in Scotland and Ireland and hardly at all in America. Garner says that this old *shall–will* paradigm "now has little utility" in a brief entry.

But it's not this *shall* of futurity or this *will* in traditional grammar in England that Garner has in his sights so much as the legal *shall*. In his dictionary of legal usage, he notes the many different ways lawmakers use the word:

- "The court shall enter an order." This **obligates** the court to do something.

- "Objections to the proposed modification shall be filed upon the debtor." This is a common locution in legalese, but it does not impose an obligation; it says **what must happen** *if* one does have an objection – which one may not.

- 'The sender shall have fully complied with the duty to send notice when the sender receives electronic communication." This is not imposing a duty, but explaining that operation X is complete only when condition Y obtains. It really just serves to **define** something, in this case defining when the sender has "fully complied with the duty to send notice".

- Finally there are "directory", not "obligatory" cases when courts have held that **shall really means should**. "Anyone bringing a malpractice claim shall, within 15 days after the filing of the action, file a request for mediation."

So *shall* has two strikes against it: even specialists use it to mean too many different things, and it's exceedingly rare in ordinary American parlance.

As a child, Garner was once told by a student teacher that *shan't* wasn't "a real word". He realised not only that his hometown had an anti-intellectual streak but that *shall* was not current in American English.[13] In trying to narrow *shall*'s focus, his crusade is not to dumb down the language by getting rid of it, but to smarten up the language by using more precise words. As part of a committee on rules in the American federal court system, Garner helped get *shall* dropped from almost all the rules, replaced by alternatives like *must, may, will*, or *is entitled to* that can't be read the wrong way.

A less confident and learned language tamer would never attempt the task of chasing a whole modal verb out of the English language. The average middlebrow prescriptivist merely insists that *shall* simply isn't that complicated, if you take the time to master its logic. But Garner has his reasons: he points out that a leading legal dictionary devotes 76 pages to *shall*, and that American jurisprudence is all over the map as to how it should be interpreted. This is a real problem with life-and-freedom consequences for all those who live under the laws drafted with *shall*. And so *shall* is a worthy target.

Note that Garner is not saying *shall* is ungrammatical on some Platonic level of correctness. Writers like Gwynne insist that some things, like *it is I*, are technically correct even though they admit that virtually nobody says them. For them, abstract correctness is on a special plane above and beyond communicative effectiveness and actual practice. So their books read as more intended to convey an attitude – "I hold correctness dear" – than to improve writing. Garner holds correctness dear, too – but always with a view to making writing readable and effective first and foremost.

*

Merriam-Webster's Dictionary of English Usage betrays its publisher's mission: collecting citations of English in order to make ordinary dictionaries. And Bryan Garner's *Modern English Usage* betrays its author's main vocation, that of a lawyer.

The final language tamer we turn to is perhaps the most surprising – although he shouldn't be. Steven Pinker is an arch-descriptivist: an academic language scientist and psychologist who has spent decades criticising half-baked old shibboleths of writers like Gwynne. Pinker, in his book *The Language Instinct*, objected to the sticklers' appropriation of a beloved Yiddish word in calling themselves "language mavens", saying "*kibbitzers* and *nudniks* is more like it!"

So it's not entirely surprising that Garner, a prescriptivist, singles out passages from *The Language Instinct* for criticism in the frontmatter of *Garner's Modern English Usage*. But just as Garner has become more openly descriptivist over the years – remember his proud descriptive use of Google Books data in the fourth edition of his usage guide – Pinker in 2014 released an avowedly prescriptivist language guide: *The Sense of Style*.

What? A prescriptive book from an arch-descriptivist? Pinker pooh-poohs the distinction between the two camps of language writers. Yes, academic linguists writing in an academic mode focus on accurate description, not advice. But the fact that description and advice are two different tasks does not mean that they are in conflict. In *The Sense of Style*, Pinker offers prescriptive advice based on the facts of high-quality edited writing. Where he finds a rule with little support in the history of good English, he says so. And where he finds a rule that is, in fact, observed by careful writers in prose written and edited for the public, he recommends that you, too, follow that rule.

Pinker is not just a linguist but a cognitive scientist, and it shows in *The Sense of Style*. Writing and speaking are, after all, psychological activities: one person trying to convey thoughts and meanings into the mind of the other. So Pinker's advice is strictly based on how to do this well, drawing on his decades of studying the human mind.

Take the constant advice to "omit needless words," best known from William Strunk and E. B. White's *The Elements of Style* (from which Pinker adapted his own book's title). It is indeed good to whittle away words that add nothing but length to a sentence. Strunk and White tell you to do so – but Pinker tells you why. Human working memory is limited, able to hold only about seven items in the mind at one time, and possibly as few as three or four. When writers unnecessarily lengthen sentences, they're taxing the reader's working memory.

It's not just long sentences that are difficult. Some structures are harder than others. Pinker explains beautifully with syntactical trees – a modern cousin of the "sentence diagrams" some readers will have learned in schools – which show the grammatical relationships of the words in a sentence.

For example, a sentence like

> This is the judge all shaven and shorn that married the man all tattered and torn that kissed the maiden all forlorn that milked the cow with the crumpled horn that tossed the dog that worried the cat that killed the rat that ate the malt that lay in the house that Jack built.

is a long one. But it isn't difficult – it is a nursery rhyme for children, who have little trouble learning and repeating it. That's because of its structure: the judge all shaven and shorn has a relationship with the man all tattered and torn – he married him (to a woman, of course). Once we have that judge–man relationship sorted, we can forget about the judge, and drop him from our working memory. The structure brings us to a new relationship: the man all tattered and torn that kissed the maiden all forlorn. (Note: no judge here.) Then we move on to the maiden, who milked the cow with the crumpled horn. Here we can drop the man from our minds. And so on. The repetition also makes the structure easier, since once a structure is activated in the mind, it's easier to use again moments later: this is the A that X'd the B, this is the B that Y'd the C, this is the C that Z'd the D...

Other long sentences, though, have a very different structure. Pinker's example is from an op-ed criticising Bill Clinton's war over Kosovo, written by Bob Dole, whom Clinton had defeated in the 1996 election. It's a doozy:

> The view that beating a third-rate Serbian military that for the third time in a decade is brutally targeting civilians is hardly worth the effort is not based on a lack of understanding of what is occurring on the ground.[14]

Notice that it's considerably shorter than "This is the judge all shaven and shorn..." But it's far harder to read. Why? This is where psychology and linguistics come into their own. In linguistic terms, it's "centre-embedded": rather than closing off each phrase before starting a new one, as our sentence did above, it wraps phrases around phrases around phrases. It takes several readings to get the basic idea: that a certain view is not based on a lack of understanding of the facts.

Why is it so hard? For one, there's an incredibly long noun phrase

> The view that beating a third-rate Serbian military that for the third time in a decade is brutally targeting civilians is hardly worth the effort

which itself contains several long elements, such as the noun phrase

> a third-rate Serbian military that for the third time in a decade is brutally targeting civilians

and a reasonably complex subordinate clause

> that beating [the Serbian military] is hardly worth the effort

The noun-phrase-within-noun-phrase-within-noun-phrase structure here puts a heavy load on working memory; several long and complicated things have to be held in the mind while we fight our way to the distant predicate.

Moreover (Pinker does not point out, but could have), there are several negations in the sentence. Saying something is "hardly" worth the effort is a way of saying it is "not", and saying that the view that something is *not* worth it is *not* based on a *lack* of understanding makes a reader's brain juggle three negatives at a time. Multiple negation is hard. Here, Dole has used the right number of negatives – the sentence is perfectly logical – but it puts the work on the reader to figure them out. No reader should have to work this hard.

Pinker's book – taken with Garner's descriptive prescriptivism – should finally put paid to the idea that there are only two schools of thought in correct use of language: "Obey every rule you've ever heard from anybody" and "do whatever you feel like." Pinker the descriptivist reiterates the rules that are really followed by good writers, throws out the hoary superstitions, and – most importantly – explains the secrets of good writing in a way that goes beyond right and wrong, sinner and saved. On rules, the big meta-rule is this: *obey the rules that are actually observed by good writers and editors, and if you're in doubt, consult a book that gathers evidence from good, edited work.* But Pinker goes one step further and says that *even if you follow the rules, you can write badly – so always keep the reader in mind. Strive not for mere error-free prose, but for elegance.*

*

But is striving for mere elegance enough? The pundit with whom we began this chapter doesn't think language is a matter of style and effectiveness. Gwynne is convinced that it is a matter of logic. English grammar proceeds from simple principles which, if properly understood, always yield the right answer.

Logic is a real thing. If all men are mortal, and Socrates is a man, then Socrates is mortal, and there's no universe in which this does not hold. Mathematics is a form of applied logic, and so when 2 and 4 are both defined, then there is no universe in which 2+2 does not = 4. There's no wiggle-room: 5 is not close enough, nor is 3.99999, even. In a strict and very real sense, 2+2 can only be 4.

Language kibitzers and nudniks of a certain stripe think that words work this way, too. Take the so-called rule that *be* and its various forms (*is*, *are*, *was*, *were*) link a subject and a predicate in such a way that the two forms must be in the same case – the nominative. This is what Nathan Heller, in an attack on Pinker in the *New Yorker*, depicted as a kind of grammatical equals-sign: "in the phrase 'it was he,' 'it' and 'he' are the same thing: they're both the subject, and thus nominative."

Heller is confusing semantics and grammar. Semantics relates to meaning, but grammar does something different, organising words in a sentence. And they don't always work identically. Yes, in the phrase "it is he," "it" and "he" are the same person. But just because Socrates is always Socrates in the real world (semantically), the grammar gives us several ways to refer to him: *it*, *he*, *him*, *Socrates*, *the renowned barefoot Greek philosopher* and others among them. There is no reason in logic, or in grammar, that the subject and predicate must have the same form. "It is Socrates," "It is he," "It is him," and "It is the renowned barefoot Greek philosopher, Socrates" all refer to the same person in the predicate, though they have different forms.

So there is no reason subject and predicate must have the same form – even the same grammatical case – just because they refer to the same real-world object. Perfectly sensible languages like French and Danish use non-nominative pronouns in predicates (*c'est lui, det er ham*, both similar to "it's him"), and their speakers have included such illogical mumblemouths as Descartes, Voltaire, Kierkegaard and Niels Bohr.

But isn't it confusing – even illogical – that there are two ways to put a pronoun in a predicate compliment? No grammarian – Pinker or *MWDEU* or the even more liberal descriptivists included – disputes that *It is he* has a long history of distinguished usage, after all. What kind of system gives *it's he* and *it's him* both as options?

There are many ways in which correct English varies. One reason is that a series of conquests of England (first by Vikings, then by Norman French) scrambled the menu of options, giving English a grammatical flexibility borrowing from Anglo-Saxon, Old Norse and French. Another is that languages just naturally develop variants; one more formal, one more relaxed but neither more correct than the other. After all, we have both "it is" and "it's", and nobody says one is correct and the other is not. It's as if the "purists" of English grammar can't handle simple variation, for fear that it will contaminate a much-loved product, their language.

Why not accept both "It is he" and "it's him"? Just like the other cases, they offer English-speakers two options, one more formal and one more conversational. (There's a reason it's awkward to say "It's he" or "it is him," mixing the more conversational and more formal forms. "It is he" and "it's him" are both much more natural.) Everyone will understand your use of either form – provided you use the right form in the right social situation (the subject of a later chapter). Nathan Heller would have you end a relationship gently by telling your soon-to-be ex that "it's not you; it's I." I recommend this only if you truly never want to see that person again.

*

So how does the more sophisticated pundit think about grammar? If

Pinker objects to the grouches adopting "maven", I'd like to object to their claims on "stickler", "traditionalist" and "purist". Depending on the day, a language lover can be a descriptivist, looking into the origins of the latest bit of teen slang or the linguistic meaning of emoji, or turn around and be a fierce prescriptivist, as a writer and editor.

I'm one of those people, and hardly unique. I like descriptive digging into linguistic facts, as a language columnist at *The Economist*. I'm also an editor, though. And in years of editing, I have never yet seen a piece of writing that could not be improved. Most pieces need at least something of a firm hand in getting them into shape, and many of them need a radical rewrite. I not only impose the norms of English grammar as I know them but also niggling *Economist* style rules, like the fact that "Mr" has no full stop, or that we don't say "tyre manufacturer John Jenkins" but rather "John Jenkins, a tyre manufacturer". I have to overcome my American aversion to "tyre" and "full stop" and fix American writers who write "tire", so that readers of *The Economist* get a consistent product. In other words, I am a descriptivist on Fridays, when I do my digging into the facts to finish my column, and a prescriptivist on Mondays, when copy from other writers comes in and my colleagues and I get it into shape.

A "traditionalist" or a "stickler" for good grammar and usage knows that English is a mixed language that provides a reader not with a rigid logical code, but a menu of *options* for getting ideas effectively into the reader's mind. These options have developed for different reasons over a long history. Different good writers use them very differently. When a standard product (like *The Economist*) is the desired outcome, then you make a few arbitrary decisions, so that readers don't encounter both *Mr* and *Mr.* on the same page. But that doesn't make either one right or wrong.

Applying grammatical standards need not mean rigidity about so-called rules, because English – like every language – is not a rigid thing. Its rules can best be thought of as guidelines that it's helpful for the whole society to agree on, like tipping 15–20% in America (where waiters and waitresses earn a pitiful salary) but much less or not at all in Europe. But unlike the tipping rules, grammar rules are almost entirely tacit. This is why many of them are known by everyone (nobody needs to look up the past tense of *walk* in a grammar book). Many of them are in dispute (despite what some say, you really don't need to worry about ending a sentence in a preposition). Many of them are tricky (English's declining attention to case has put *whom* on a death-watch). Many of them are changing (we'll look at change in detail later). Many of them depend on occasion (there's a chapter on that, too).

The grammar-grouch's mistake is to conflate all of these: a rule's a rule, it must be observed at all times, it doesn't change, and violating it doesn't merely make you look a fool; it is to violate a timeless logic itself. The most overblown of them go further, like Gwynne, and insist that thought itself depends on grammar, with grammar being a bunch of rules that Gwynne learned back in school, but which great writers have never taken all that seriously.

That's nonsense. Thought isn't language, language isn't just grammar, grammar isn't usually what the hardiest of grouches think it should be. Despite the hope that any language should proceed without change from a single unvarying source, it has a lot of tolerance for variation. That's because it is more robust than the sky-is-falling brigades give it credit for. And ultimately, that's because its users are smarter than that. We see just how human and wild a phenomenon language is when we look at why it is so hard for machines to master.

3

Machines for talking

FOR NEARLY AS LONG as humans have been building sophisticated machines, they've been asking themselves a scary question: what if humans themselves are machines? For centuries, philosophers have quaintly imagined the mind to be something like the advanced machines of their day. Descartes compared it to a water-clock, and Leibniz compared it to a mill. Other technologies have included the telegraph and the telephone switchboard. Today, the natural metaphor is a computer.[1]

As humans have conceptualised the mind as a kind of machine, a second thought – perhaps just as unsettling – has occurred to them. How would we know if an intelligent-seeming machine has a mind? And if it does, how would we know it's benign? Adorable thinking machines like the robot from the eponymous *WALL-E* are the exception, in popular culture. For some reason, when we imagine thinking machines, we imagine them as heartless: it's easier to imagine computers thinking than caring, so fiction has given us more memorable murderers, Terminators and HAL 9000s than it has automated pals.

But how could we tell that a machine is thinking, rather than just responding to input according to instructions? What would a computer need to do to prove that it is doing something like what the mind does? Alan Turing, a British computer scientist, suggested a simple test, involving mastery of humankind's most famously human trait: language. A computer can be said to pass what Turing called the "imitation game" only if it returns answers to written questions that fool a human examiner into thinking that the machine is human.

Turing had suggested in 1950 that

> I believe that in about fifty years' time it will be possible, to programme computers ... to make them play the imitation game so well that an average interrogator will not have more than 70 per cent chance of making the right identification after five minutes of questioning.

Turing's statement later morphed into an unofficial (and statistically different) threshold for "passing" the Turing test: if 30% of judges were fooled by a machine, it would be said to have passed.

In 2014, a chatbot named Eugene Goostman, pretending to be a 13-year-old Ukrainian, was breathlessly announced to have passed the Turing test at a competition at the Royal Society in London. "Eugene" fooled 33% of the judges.

But was Eugene really doing something to rival thinking? With the benefit of hindsight – which the judges of course did not have – you be the judge. One trick that helped Eugene was pretending to be a young teen boy, who distracted his interrogators by goofing around:

> **Judge**: what is your gender

> **Eugene**: I'm a young boy, if you care to know. And not very ugly, by the way!

Eugene couldn't have pretended to be a mathematician or an art critic; this level of response would not have satisfied a questioner who asked "what do you think of abstract impressionism?"

Eugene distracted another judge, an actress and playwright, by being obnoxious:

> **Eugene**: Well, I'll read something of your books, if they ain't too tedious (which is highly possible:-)

> **Judge**: grammar... aren't too tedious! A bit rude of you...

> **Eugene**: Calm down, please.

Another trick was to quickly turn the interrogatory tables: Eugene would often refuse to answer a question, papering over his refusal and taking control of the conversation by asking one of his own:

> **Judge**: what are your qualifications

Eugene: My qualifications? I'm not gonna tell you. Oooh. Anything else?

But perhaps the most obvious trick was that Eugene was a non-native speaker of English. This would excuse any flubs in his language:

Judge: Hi I don't think it will rain anymore today, what do you reckon?

Eugene: What are you usually doing when it's rain?[2]

Some of the flubs were programmed intentionally, to make Eugene more human. What human 13-year-old boy types with perfect grammar and punctuation? Real human teens participated alongside the chatbots in the Royal Society test, and their messages were filled with mistakes too. All this taken together successfully lowered the bar so that Eugene could clear it.

Critics cried foul. Eugene's accomplishment was bought with cheap tricks: distraction, redirection, joking. Eugene had not displayed real understanding of much of anything. "He" had merely used something like human language just competently enough to fool a minority of human judges (via text-only chat, not voice, of course) for five minutes. Sure, his creators had done something impressive. But that feat, hardly anything remotely as sophisticated as a real mind, took 65 years after Turing proposed his imitation game – and this counts for "passing". In a way, it highlights just how hard true artificial intelligence, including mimicking human language, really is.

This should give pause for thought to all those who think that grammar, or language generally, is fundamentally logical. Computers are nothing if not logical. Yet they struggle mightily to convince even a minority of people that they are a goofball teen who doesn't speak English as a first language. What is it about language that makes it so hard for computers to get, so to speak, their heads around it?

In Turing's time, after all, optimism for language-capable computers was immense. It wasn't just Turing's prediction of what would be possible "in fifty years". In 1954, researchers from IBM and Georgetown University demonstrated a computer translation system that successfully did something even most humans cannot do: translate from one language to another. Specifically, the system translated sentences from Russian to English like *Mi pyeryedayem mislyi posryedstvom ryechyi*, coming out correctly as "We transmit thoughts by means of speech." The journalist from the *New York Herald Tribune* was one of the many to be flabbergasted:

> A huge electric "brain" with a 250-word vocabulary translated mouth-filling Russian sentences yesterday into simple English in less than ten seconds. As lights flashed and motors whirred inside the "brain", the instrument's automatic type-writer swiftly translated statements on politics, law, science and military affairs. Once the Russian words were fed into the machine no human mind interfered.

Leon Dostert, the lead scientist for Georgetown, predicted that fully automated quality translation would be an "accomplished fact" not in Turing's 50 years, but in three to five. Bear in mind that of course translation, unlike acting like a 13-year-old boy, requires mastery of not just one but two languages, and the interface between them. If mastering language is remarkable, translation is remarkable squared. The audience for the demonstration was wowed, and Dostert's confident prediction was widely believed and repeated by 1954's equivalent of the tech press.

The achievement was seen as all the more significant for its cold-war context: the 1950s was the decade of the nascent space-race, and of Western fears that the Soviets had stolen a march in technological progress. A translating machine was seen as proof that the breakthroughs could come on both sides, and must have seemed as otherworldly as Sputnik itself.

So how far has machine translation come? Anyone who generously gave machine translation not five but Turing's 50 years, and looked at the options like "BabelFish" available online around 2004, will have noticed that computer translation still had a very long way to go. After that early wave of optimism in the 1950s, scientists realised that it was a lot harder to get computers to deal with natural human language than they had realised. Progress was so slow that it became a joke in the scientific community that true machine translation was five years away, and always would be.

Today, though, language technologies are no longer hopeless. Not just machine translation but speech recognition, speech synthesis, and the ability to carry out basic spoken commands have gone from the pages of science fiction to the very real kitchens, bedrooms and pockets of many ordinary people. The digital assistants in smartphones (Apple's Siri, Microsoft's Cortana, Google's Google Assistant), and their counter-top home-based equivalents (Amazon's Alexa, Google Home), using only voice as their input, are no longer mere curiosities. They can now give useful output to questions like "What's the weather going to be like tomorrow in Seattle?" or "How do you say 'thank you' in Swedish?", and can carry out commands from "turn off the lights in the master bedroom" to "make a calendar appointment for me at the dentist for November 5th at 3:30".

How they got so much better, rather quickly, is a story of interest not just to tech nerds. If language were truly logical, its rules eternal and unambiguous and transparent, computers should be excellent at it. But it turned out that it wasn't the computers that were the problem – it was the task they were given to solve. The mismatch between how computers think and how humans use language made the programmers go down a blind alley for years, before giving up for decades. When they started again, they did so with entirely new approaches, first eking out improvements slowly but surely, and then stumbling on methods that brought big improvements quickly. A big part of that new approach was shelving the idea of teaching computers explicit rules. The new approach would have them finding rules – or, really patterns – themselves.

*

The IBM–Georgetown translation system that dazzled onlookers in New York in 1954 was – under the hood – quite simple: it had just six rules, and a vocabulary of just 250 words. The sentences it was given to translate were toy examples that its creators knew it could handle. Obviously 250 words and six rules wouldn't do to capture the whole complexity of Russian, or of English, but its creators saw in it an exciting proof of a concept that just needed scaling up.

But scaling up, it turned out, was a lot harder than they realised.

Programming a computer to apply twelve rules correctly is not twice as hard as programming it to apply six. It's exponentially harder. (We'll see why in a moment.) And at the same time that computerised translation bogged down, so did other fields: speech recognition (a simple transcription of a stream of spoken language), automated parsing (breaking down a sentence into its component grammatical parts) and speech synthesis (getting computers to "speak" words, given a bit of text input). The early wave of optimism crashed on the reef of reality. These three tasks – understanding a string of speech, understanding its grammar and speaking back – are ones that humans master unconsciously, with little to no formal teaching, as children. But these tasks turned out to be far more difficult for computers than anyone had realised. No wonder that translation – which very few highly educated adults are even any good at – was even harder.

In 1966, twelve years after the IBM–Georgetown translation demonstration, the National Academy of Sciences asked John Pierce to prepare a report on the state of language technologies. Pierce had a sterling reputation: he had supervised the team that had developed the first transistor and overseen the development of the first communications satellite. His formal report concluded, in diplomatic language, that future American government funding "should be spent hardheadedly toward important, realistic, and relatively short-range goals". The real message was clear: up until then, money had been spent thoughtlessly on trivial, unrealistic or long-range goals.

Pierce wrote privately in 1969 about the progress in another field, speech recognition, to the *Journal of the Acoustical Society of America*. This time, he was frank:

> ...a general phonetic typewriter [ie, a speech-recognition system that would take voice input and produce text output] is simply impossible unless the typewriter has an intelligence and a knowledge of language comparable to those of a native speaker of English ... The typical recognizer ... builds or programs an elaborate system that either does very little or flops in an obscure way. A lot of money and time are spent. No simple, clear, sure knowledge is gained. The work has been an experience, not an experiment.

He went on to compare speech-recognition to schemes to turn water into gasoline, and said that "to sell suckers, one uses deceit and offers glamor."[3]

In just over a decade, automated language processing had gone from a problem that would be solved within a few years to being equated – by a distinguished technology pioneer – with quackery, even fraud. As a result of stalling progress, and thanks to withering critiques like Pierce's, funding dried up drastically for language-technology research for two decades.

What had gone wrong? It turned out to be hard to teach a computer language because the scientists simply did not realise just how much people actually know. Take the problem of translation. One might sensibly break the problem down like this: you take the source-language sentence, and break apart its grammar. You find out what are noun phrases, what are verb phrases, where modifiers like adjectives and adverbs go, and so on. You now have the original string of words represented in the abstract language of rules. The words themselves are easy: look them up in a dictionary, and translate them. The last step is the opposite of the first: you take the noun phrases and verb phrases and so on from the source text, and build the equivalent structures in the target language, slotting in the words you looked up in the dictionary.

So take "a green pencil" in English. It's a noun phrase. Break it down into its grammatical bits (it's an article, an adjective and a noun). Go to your electronic dictionary and translate each word into French: *Un. Vert. Crayon.* Rebuild the noun phrase in French, bearing in mind that, in French, adjectives usually come after nouns. Your system's designers know that, so they built it as a rule into the French grammar system. So the new order is article-noun-adjective. You rebuild the phrase, now in French: *Un crayon vert.* Easy, right? In this paragraph, we've created a toy translator that can turn an English phrase into a French one, with not just a dictionary but a grammar rule ("English adjectives come before the noun. French adjectives come after the noun.")

Except that even in this three-word example, the complexities can easily multiply, as anyone who's lived through first-year French knows. What if we want a green car, not a green pencil? French nouns, unlike English ones, have gender. *Crayon* is masculine. *Voiture* (car) is feminine. And so both the article and the adjective have to change form to agree in gender: *un* becomes *une*, and *vert* becomes *verte*. We have to code in a new rule for that: nouns must have an invisible informational tag that says "masculine" or "feminine", and every dictionary entry for an adjective or an article must have two forms, one for each gender, so the right one can be called up.

. Now throw in numbers, too: if we get multiple cars or pencils, we have to add an -s to the noun and the adjective, and *un* becomes *des*. And throw in irregulars: *beau* (beautiful) has the feminine form *belle*. And the masculine plural form *beaux*.

We can see how the complexity has multiplied with the simplest possible three-word noun phrase. But so far, the rules are algorithmic: the kind of thing that, given enough time, can be programmed rule-by-rule. Even 1960s computers, and most certainly today's, could handle a few dozen rules, a medium-sized vocabulary and a manageable number of irregularities. These irregularities include the fact that a medium-sized number of French adjectives usually come before the noun, like *gentil*, *gros* and *long* ("kind", "large/fat" and "long"). Each of them, in the computer's mental lexicon, would have to have some kind of invisible label saying "put these before the noun, not after", and our little grammar will have to look for that label when assembling a noun phrase.

But what about things like *a great man*? Again, in English, the order is the usual article-adjective-noun, and our rule says to rebuild that as article-noun-adjective in French: *un homme grand*. But now we've turned him into "a big man". *Grand*, when it comes in the usual position after a noun, has its basic meaning of "large". To be "great", it must come in the unexpected position, before the noun, as in English. And it's not just *grand*. Maddeningly, a number of French adjectives behave the same way, changing their meanings depending on whether they come before or after the noun they modify: *ancien* (which can be "ancient" or "former"), *brave* ("honest" vs "courageous"), *cher* ("dear/beloved" vs "expensive") and we've only reached C in the alphabet. French, despite the cheerleaders who think it is the perfect language of logic, is just as unwieldy as English.[4]

Our "toy" translator is a toy no longer, and it's going to start wheezing under the weight of all these rules and exceptions, not dozens but now hundreds, pretty soon. And we haven't got past a three-word noun phrase yet. But in theory, we could keep plugging away at programming words, rules, exceptions and their complex interactions. In principle it's not at all hard to programme a computer to handle "OK, if 'great' is the English word, translate it as *grand*, and supersede the usual noun-adjective rule and use adjective-noun instead. And if the noun carries the 'feminine' tag, don't forget to make the adjective *grande*. And if it's plural, *grandes*." We're going to need more powerful hardware, as the task gets harder. And we're going to have to be very clever in our coding to handle the many interactions of the rules. Much time will be spent debugging and testing, to spot problems we hadn't imagined.

But we haven't got to the heart of why computer processing of language is so hard yet. As many grammar rules as there are, their number is finite, and computers are getting more powerful all the time. The problem is not in the hardware.

Yehoshua Bar-Hillel was an Israeli pioneer in machine translation, organising the first international conference on the subject, in 1952. But he came to be a sceptic of the idea that computers could ever produce fully automated, high-quality translation. Bar-Hillel saw that many constructions were not only complex but ambiguous. His example was "the pen is in the box" – easy enough. (*Le stylo est dans la boîte*.) But what about "the box is in the pen" – a perfectly sensible sentence, if we're talking about an animal pen and not a writing instrument. But while the two kinds of pen share a word in English, they don't in French. (An animal pen is an *enclos*.)

A human knows that a normal-sized pen can fit into a normal-sized box, but not the other way around. A computer translator, however, has no idea what a normal-sized pen is. Our toy translator has been doing mindless dictionary lookup. *Stylo* will probably come up first in the dictionary (the writing instrument is mentioned more often than the animal enclosure). How does our translator know to skip past it and look for the "enclosure" word?

It doesn't. Bar-Hillel said the same thing of translation systems that Pierce had said of speech-recognisers: that to work properly, they would need something like a human level of intelligence about the real world beyond language – a programming feat light-years beyond the computer programmers of their day. Computers can be taught all kinds of facts that fit neatly into a database: Lincoln is the capital of Nebraska,

Ouagadougou is the capital of Burkina Faso, −195.8 degrees Celsius is the boiling point of nitrogen.

But most facts are not so easy to pin down, and they are not computable. You might have a rule that says "If the original sentence is 'X is in Y', then X must be bigger than Y. So look up the size of X, and of Y. If there are multiple translations of either, restrict the translations to ones in which the size of X is smaller than the size of Y." But how big is a box? This isn't the kind of thing a computer can look up, as it can the capital of Burkina Faso. It relies on human common sense. And this is to say nothing of other, even more quintessentially human traits: what does "in" mean in "you're in my heart" and "it's all in your head" and "a new battleship is in our budget"?

*

Up until this point in the discussion of computers and languages, the difficulties computers find when they deal with language are well known, or easy to predict. Different languages have different complex grammars (adjective-noun vs noun-adjective). Single words (*pen*) can mean different things. Idioms (*it's all in your head*) need special attention. Anyone who has learned a foreign language has come across these, and such stumbling blocks are very well known indeed to professional translators, who deal with at least two sets of these issues (one for each language) on a daily basis. This is why translation is hard.

But for computers, it's harder still for yet another reason that would never occur to most human beings. Sticklers and grouches like to cry that if language were properly used, it would have no ambiguity. They have little idea how much ambiguity lurks in even the simplest strings of English.

Take just one example, beloved of linguists: "Time flies like an arrow." Not a common proverb, but it sounds like it should be one. You know what it means when you first encounter it.

You know what it means because when you read a sentence, your mind mentally parses its grammar; even if you think you never learned very good grammar in school, your implicit knowledge of English means that you'll be able, without any trouble, to chop this into meaningful pieces and give those pieces mental labels. They look something like

time (noun, or subject, or "what we're talking about")

flies (verb, or "the action word")

flies like an arrow (predicate, or "what we're saying about the subject")

> **like an arrow** (adverbial phrase, or modifier, or "what kind of flying time does")

>> **an arrow** (noun phrase; a bit like "time", but not a subject)

Note that these chunks are all meaningful in some way on their own. Also note that some chunks contain other chunks: "flies like an arrow" contains "like an arrow" which contains "an arrow". The structure is what we call recursive: smaller units nest inside larger ones. Finally, notice that not all the chunks are meaningful: "time flies like an" doesn't hang together in any coherent way, not like "flies like an arrow" seems to. You know this, even if you're a bit fuzzy on what grammarians call the different chunks.

But what if "time flies like an arrow" is followed by "... and fruit flies like a banana." Suddenly we have a radically different idea of what the first half might mean. Our chunks are now very different.

Time flies (noun phrase, or subject; the topic of the sentence. They're some kind of flies. Are they flies that move around in time?)

like (verb, "the action word"; these time flies are fond of something)

like an arrow (predicate; "what we're saying about the subject")

> **an arrow** (noun phrase; direct object; "the thing being liked"

The first version of our sentence meant that time flies in the same way that an arrow flies. The second version means that some sci-fi creatures called "time flies" are fond of an arrow. Five words, two completely different meanings.

More than two, actually. What if you encountered the same five words in this context: "Arrows are really good at timing flies. So I want you to time flies like an arrow." Now we have new chunks:

Time (verb; a command)

flies (noun; direct object; the thing being timed)

like an arrow (adverbial; a description of how the flies are to be timed – the same way that an arrow would do it)

Finally, absurd as it may seem, there's one more parsing: "You timed those arrows really well. So I want you to time flies like an arrow." Similar but not the same as our last sentence, we have

Time (verb; a command)

flies (noun; direct object; the thing being timed)

like an arrow (adverbial; a description of how the flies are to be timed – the same way you timed those arrows just a minute ago)

Five words, four meanings.

The last three parsings almost certainly didn't occur to you, unless you have a very unorthodox mind. There are no such things as "time flies" zipping around the space-time continuum. Arrows don't time things with a stopwatch, so nobody is going to instruct you to time anything as an arrow would do it. And finally, you are unlikely to be asked to time an arrow, then to time flies in the same way.

You know all that. Every six-year-old knows all that well before starting grammar in school. But a computer doesn't know that. Here are the kind of things a computer can be taught. Our first parsing can be diagrammed like this:

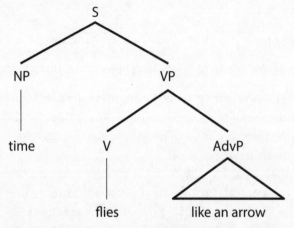

A computer parser can be taught rules to make sense of our sentence. In its lexicon, it can find that "time" is a noun. It can further know that some nouns can stand alone as a subject of a sentence (we don't need to precede it with "the" or "a"). Then it can look up "flies" and find a verb, "to fly", which occasionally appears in the form "flies" – specifically when the subject is a singular noun like "time". So far so good. Finally it can look up "like" and find that it's used to compare one thing to another. It can compare two nouns alone using a form of "to be" – "hares are like rabbits." Or if there's another verb there, it can compare the way two nouns perform the same action: "X verbs like another noun verbs". And finally, there's a pattern where the second verb is omitted: "X verbs like another noun [verbs]". Our parser can see that this sentence fits that pattern: "Time flies like an arrow [flies]".

Having seen all these common patterns, it can apply this parsing. And that would be the end of that – the programmers could cry "our computer can understand language!" – except that there's no reason in principle that it might not choose any of the other four common parsings. "Time flies like an arrow" has the same common structure as "Steve runs like the wind." But in the "... and fruit flies like a banana" parsing, "time flies like an arrow" has the same common parsing as "frat guys like a party." In the "arrows are really good at timing flies, so I want you to time flies like an arrow", it has the same common parsing as "approve memos like a boss."

How is a parser to choose between these options, all common ones? Without extra training, it can't. And though this example is beloved of linguists for its brevity and oddball parsings, it's hardly unusual in being ambiguous. Many words double as nouns and verbs, and a parser can easily see them both ways – especially if the other slots in the sentence are filled in in ways that conform to the rules of the grammar that the parser has been taught. (If they don't, the parser will know the parsing must be wrong, and reject it.)

Little helper words can help us figure out whether a word is a noun or a verb. ("The" can come right before a noun, but not right before a verb, for example.) But in some contexts, little words that help provide context are often omitted, as in telegrams or headlines, where space is at a premium. In just one day's *Wall Street Journal*,[5] I noticed two:

Unilever sees small profit rise

Swiss watch exports hit record high

In the first, it's not clear if "small" modifies profit (a small profit, rising) or "rise" (a small rise in a profit that might have been big to start with). In the second, it's not clear if "watch" is the main verb, or a noun referring to a certain well-known Swiss export. The reader has to read the stories to find out.

The ambiguous readings here all result in grammatical sentences; there is nothing that a rule-book-wielding schoolteacher could point to as an error. It's only in highly artificial languages like Lojban, which we saw in Chapter 1, where this kind of ambiguity is not possible. (In fact, the creators of Lojban hoped that the language might serve as a logical interface between humans and computers, in a way that no messy natural language could.) In real language, ambiguity lurks everywhere. We don't notice it most of the time, because usually one reading of a sentence is far more plausible than another. But try telling that to a computer that has merely been trained on grammar rules.

With the rules-based approach, language technology had gone down a blind alley. It could cope with a large number of rules, and exceptions could be added on manually. But it gets hard when the rules – contra the prescriptivist grouches – often have no logic (*un homme grand* vs *un grand homme*). It gets much harder still when the rules need to interact with real-world knowledge (*pen-pen*). And finally, computers can easily be stumped by the fact that language is radically ambiguous (*time flies*). A perfect computer-language system would have to integrate approaches to all these kinds of problems to know that "time flies like an arrow" shouldn't be parsed like "fruit flies like a banana." Computer scientists are good at programming rules, and they're good at building lots of databases of real-world information. But they struggle to integrate the two in the way that the human mind does effortlessly.

No programmer was smart enough to design perfect systems for translation, or merely for understanding natural-language commands in a single language, flawlessly. The best they could do was to build systems that could acquit themselves in highly restricted domains.

A notable one was SHRDLU, created from 1968 to 1970 by Terry Winograd, then a computer scientist at the Massachusetts Institute of Technology. In a (virtual) box of objects of different sizes, shapes and colours, SHRDLU could perform tasks and answer questions, and even remember what it had recently done, with impressive skill:

pick up a red block

OK.

find a block which is taller than the one you are holding and put it in the box

OK.

what does the box contain?

The blue pyramid and the blue block.

what is the pyramid supported by?

The box.

how many blocks are not in the box?

Four of them.

is at least one of them narrower than the one which I told you to pick up?

Yes, the red cube.

is it supported?

Yes, by the table.

when did you pick it up?

While I was stacking up the red cube, a large red block and a large green cube.

why?

To get rid of it.

why did you do that?

To clean off the red cube.[6]

SHRDLU was ground-breaking in several respects. It had its own, obviously accurate grammar parser. It understood things about the virtual "objects" it handled, like for example which were "narrower" than which. It could even answer "why". (Computers are not, typically, good at explaining themselves.)

But all this worked only in the restricted little world of Winograd's tabletop shapes. There was no possibility of misreading "box" as, for example, the pugilistic verb. Winograd found it impossible to extend SHRDLU's capacities to bigger and more free-flowing worlds. He later wrote that "There are fundamental gulfs between the way that SHRDLU and its kin operate, and whatever it is that goes on in our brains," and became a critic of artificial intelligence, dedicating his later work to making computers' limited abilities more accessible to humans, rather than trying to make them think like humans.

In his doctoral thesis, Winograd had anticipated the kinds of problems that computers would face in the real world. He posited a kind of question that would be easy for any human, but which would stump even a sophisticated computer, because it would draw on real-world knowledge. For example: "The city councilmen refused the demonstrators a permit because they feared violence. Who feared violence?" The same question could be posed with "advocated" in place of "feared". Who feared violence? Who advocated it? Simple, for a human, and mind-bogglingly hard for a computer.

This kind of problem became known as the Winograd Schema, and Hector Levesque of the University of Toronto borrowed it to host a "Winograd Schema Challenge", the first running of which took place in 2016. The prize money of $25,000 would go to the designers of a system that could handle Winograd-schema questions with better than 90% success. The top scorer did just a little better than 50–50, with a score of 58%.

*

With the failure of "good old-fashioned AI" – programming enough symbolic rules into a computer to make them handle language

– research funding dried up, and researchers concentrated their efforts on smaller problems for several decades. But in the 1980s, optimism returned with a new kind of artificial intelligence. This kind would be not cleverly programming computers to think, but turning "dumb" self-teaching algorithms loose on masses of data, and having them teach themselves.

The statistical tricks for doing so have been around a long time. But computers have lacked two things needed to make them work. One is sufficient power to be able to crunch lots of data quickly enough in order to make progress with a complex phenomenon like human language. And the other is simply masses of data, which weren't available until recent decades.

"Rules-based" translation never died out completely, despite its decidedly mixed quality; a few companies kept making translation services that used hand-coded rules to turn Russian, say, into English. But in the 1980s and early 1990s, IBM, the same company that had been behind the dramatic display in 1954, tried the new, data-driven approach, which came to be called statistical machine translation. IBM's new system was called Candide. The name was appropriately chosen; like Voltaire's fictional young man, Candide was naive, starting out knowing nothing of French. (Indeed most of the scientists involved in building it didn't know French.)

But Candide's builders had the clever idea of having Candide learn from a mass of text that had been translated by human beings, and hit on the notion of using the proceedings of Canada's parliament, a collection equivalent to America's Congressional Record, called *Hansard*. Because Canada is officially bilingual, all of Canada's parliamentary debates are published in both French and English, no matter the original language spoken in the parliament.

Hansard was there to train Candide. In the training phase, the system looks at each sentence, one-by-one, and gradually develops a probabilistic prediction of whether any given French sentence will be translated as a given candidate English sentence. It does this by further breaking down the sentence into chunks, and seeing what tend to be the corresponding English chunks. The French *homme* will usually be the English "man", so the probability that "homme" is translated as "man" will be set fairly high. (But not to 100%, as *homme* can also mean "human", just as "man" can in old-fashioned English.) The same can be done with short phrases; now Candide can see that *grand homme* tends to get translated as "great man" in *Hansard*, and *homme grand* tends to get translated as "large man". This is the heart of a statistical machine-translation system: making good guesses, based on lots of past data, about what chunks will translate as what.

But the system needs a second component, too. French and English syntax differ quite a bit, and the ideal output will be a good English text, so statistical machine-translation systems also need a "language model": essentially a model of what good English looks like. In other words, the translation engine is translated on lots of good-quality bilingual text like Hansard, but the language model is trained only on monolingual text (English, in this example).

To do so, a big collection (called a corpus, in the jargon) of English training text is parsed for its grammar by humans. Nouns and verbs are identified as such, as are noun phrases and verb phrases, adjectives and adjective phrases, and so on. The language model uses statistical techniques similar to the translation model, learning from the hand-parsed training data about what English sentences tend to look like grammatically – how commonly does a noun phrase consist of two bare nouns? How often does a verb phrase have a noun phrase in it? It also learns what English words are common, and which ones tend to occur next to which. Its goal is then to look at an English sentence it has never seen before, and rank it in terms of plausibility.

So the translation model sends several candidates to the language model, each of them assigned a probability as to how likely they are to be a translation of the French. But some of them will be word-salad: godawful, ungrammatical or implausible English. The language model then assigns a probability to the candidates too – which ones look the most like good English? Then the probabilities of the translation model and the English language model are multiplied; the "winning" candidate, having scored reasonably on both, is the translation that the system provides.

By 1993, IBM's engineers were able to announce that 62% of Candide's output sentences were accurate translations.[7] This isn't a result that would convince anyone to fire their human translators. But it was evidence that completely "naive" statistical translation could offer a way past the roadblocks that hand-coded, rules-based translation systems had run into.

It would take more powerful computers and, more importantly, more data – what would come to be called Big Data – to take statistical translation from interesting to useful. And few companies have more data than Google, a company that had set out with the modest ambition of being a kind of instant index to the entire internet. In 2006, Google launched Google Translate, its own machine-translation system, and by 2007, Google relied on entirely statistical translation.

Google Translate, like Candide, would use large hordes of documents translated accurately by humans to train its translation systems. But there was more data out there than *Hansard* had ever provided Candide. It was on the internet. Google, the company that built its success on crawling the internet looking for information, sucked up anything that looked like a translation from one language to another, and threw it into the training data that would hone its systems. This could be identical web pages differing, in their web address, only in /en versus /fr at the end. The algorithm could assume that one page was a translation of the other, and take in the data. Google knew that some of this data would be imperfect – perhaps not even a translation at all. But the engineers reckoned that vast amounts of imperfect data were better than modest amounts of perfect data.

Google Translate's users quickly found that it offered much more accurate translation than the other free online systems they had amused themselves with earlier in the first decade of the millennium. Users and journalists had got used to "round-tripping" a translation from English to Russian and then back again on the likes of BabelFish, a rules-based system, and publishing the ridiculous results. (Round-tripping the translation, naturally, multiplies the errors.) But suddenly Google would provide a rough-and-ready translation that would give people a usable gist of a foreign text. Here's one blogger's experiment with BabelFish versus the new Google Translate, from 2007, round-tripped to German and back:

Original: "Most state-of-the-art commercial machine translation systems in use today have been developed using a rules-based approach and require a lot of work by linguists to define vocabularies and grammars. Several research systems, including ours, take a different approach: we feed the computer with billions of words of text, both monolingual text in the target language, and aligned text consisting of examples of human translations between the languages. We then apply statistical learning techniques to build a translation model," explains Franz Och.

BabelFish: most state OF the kind commercial machine Uebersetzungsysteme the used today with a guideline-created approximation and a quantity of work was developed by linguists requires to define vocabulary and grammars. Several investigate systems, including ours, take another approximation: we draw in the computer with billions words of the text, both einsprachiger text in the target language and the aligned text, which consist of examples of human translations between the languages. We use then statistic acquisition techniques, in order to establish translation a model, "explain Franz Och.

Google: "Most of the state-of-the-art commercial machine translation in use today have been developed, with a rules-based approach and requires a lot of work by linguists to define vocabulary and grammar. Several research, including ours, a different approach: We feed the computer with billions of words of the text, both monolingual text in the target language, and text, consisting of examples of the human translation between languages. We have to learn statistical techniques to translate model, "says Franz Och.[8]

Professional translators would sniff at the quality of Google's translation. But it is clearly a big leap ahead of BabelFish, and users quickly took a keen interest in Google's new toy. Unlike professional translators, it was immediate – and free.

Google Translate's public success reawakened interest in computerised translation. It also came at a time when newly powerful computers were eking out gains in other kinds of language processing. The most visible was speech recognition, the automated transcription into text of a stream of spoken words. The same newly powerful computers and newly available masses of data started making these systems better as well.

Humans can understand speech sounds because they have characteristic frequencies. For example, when you pronounce the vowel in "fleece", the sound waves produced by your body have stronger energies in the frequencies around 300Hz and 3000Hz than they do at other frequencies. Those listening to you don't need to read your lips; a lifetime of hearing English has taught them to associate those frequencies (called "formants" by phoneticians) with the "ee" vowel.

But computers cannot be taught to pick words out of a stream of sound waves so easily. One reason is that sounds do not come in perfectly discrete, separate units, easy to pick up: sounds blur at the edges and run into one another. Another reason is that, in languages with irregular spelling (like English), transcribing each sound as a single letter would be a disaster. The second syllable of "bottle" doesn't have an e-sound in it at all, and in American pronunciation, there's no t-sound in the word either (it comes out *bodl*). A third factor is that sounds vary according to where they appear in a word. Say "lamp" and "full" aloud, and notice how different their l-sounds actually are (linguists call the sound in "lamp" the "light" l-sound, and the one in "full" is "dark"). Finally, many words, as well as strings of words, are homophonous, either perfectly or very nearly so: how is a computer to tell "an ice man" from "a nice man"? In very slow speech, the speaker's airflow will stop between "an" and "ice", but in most rapid speech, it won't.

Once again, merely programming rules ("when you hear formants at 300Hz and 3000Hz, transcribe 'ee' ") won't do; there are simply far too many complexities in real speech. (Most people have no idea just how many, which is why they hate hearing themselves on tape. They have no idea how often they say "um", stumble over words, restart sentences and so forth.)

But a statistical approach can work surprisingly well. Here, too, computers need training data to learn from. In this case, instead of a mass of texts translated by humans from English to French, speech-recognition systems learn from a mass of recordings, paired with transcriptions of those recordings made by humans. Now the trick is to match not a string of English text to a string of French text, but a series of vibrations in the air to a string of words.

Given enough data, computers can do exactly that, with increasing accuracy. Word-error rates have crept down gradually as computers have become more powerful, and are being fed more data. And the systems will get better if people continue using them. Every time a user uses a digital assistant with a speech-recognition system, the data becomes potential training data for the company that makes the system, as most requests are sent via the internet to the provider's computers in the cloud.

Finally, once again, a language model helps to make sure that the output of the speech-recogniser isn't gobbledygook. Given the messiness of real speech, a number of transcriptions will be plausible given the sounds the system has heard. But most of them won't be good English. So the language model, seeing both "a nice man" and "an ice man" as possibilities, will rank the more common phrase, "a nice man", as more plausible.

*

These big, statistics-driven approaches made language technologies a lot better, but only gradually. The next big leap came with a new kind of machine learning, called "deep learning". Deep learning relies on digital neural networks, meant to mimic the human brain at a simple level. Virtual "neurons" are connected in several layers. As the network is fed training data, the connections between the many neurons in the various layers are strengthened or weakened, in a way scientists believe is analogous to how humans learn. Neural networks were introduced for a few language-pairs for Google Translate in late 2016, leading to an immediate and dramatic improvement in Translate's performance. That same year, Microsoft announced a speech-recognition system that made as few errors as a human transcriber. The system was powered by six neural networks, each of which tackled some parts of the problem better than others.

None of these systems are perfect at the time of writing, and they almost certainly won't be any time soon. "Deep learning" brought a sudden jump in quality in many language technologies, but it still cannot flexibly handle language like humans can. Translation and speech-recognition systems perform much better when their tasks are limited to a single domain, like medicine or law. This allows the software to make much better guesses about the appropriate output, by focusing on vocabulary and turns of phrase that are common to those domains. The same goes for the growing use of online help chatbots, which can automatically help a banking customer through a text-only interface. These can perform surprisingly well because they, too, are limited to what customers might want to say to a bank.

Why are even the world's best computers, programmed by the world's best artificial-intelligence scientists, still struggling to do what children seem to do by magic? The rules-based approaches in artificial intelligence didn't "scale up", as the geeks say, and now it's the turn of neural networks and deep learning to make the next round of progress.

What humans may do when they learn language is combine these two approaches in ways that still elude the artificial-intelligence engineers. The 1980s saw a debate between those who believe the mind manipulates abstract symbols computationally – a bit like rules-based, "good old-fashioned" AI – and the early pioneers of digital neural networks, who thought that learning language was merely a matter of strengthening some neural connections here, and weakening some there, as the mind was presented with new data, a bit like today's digital neural networks.

In 1988, Steven Pinker, then at MIT, and Alan Prince, then at Brandeis University, developed, essentially, a hybrid theory. They focused on past-tense verbs, and how children acquire them. Children sometimes over-generalise regular rules to irregular verbs ("we holded the baby rabbits") and sometimes get things right ("we held the baby rabbits") or even do both at once ("we helded the baby rabbits") before learning to use verbs correctly. Pinker and Prince found that neither rules nor neural networks could alone explain why.

They concluded that symbolic reasoning – in principle like the "old-fashioned" AI approach – helped explain how kids learn regular rules. This, according to Pinker and Prince, is part of a broader human ability to combine mental symbols (like the stem of a verb, *walk-*, and its past-tense ending, *-ed*, to make *walked*). But in Pinker and Prince's hybrid approach, this wasn't enough. A modified neural-network approach helped explain how children learn *irregular* verbs. This isn't a feature of verb learning per se, but a general ability to associate one thing with another and learn from patterns.

For example, when they hear disjointed and distracted input from parents, even the smallest child seems to realise quickly that there's a class of words called "verbs", without knowing the label. They are able to generate a rule like "add a d-sound to the end of a verb to make it past."[9] Of course children don't have any of this explicit knowledge. (Most adults don't, either.) Yet they generate the rules and apply them surprisingly quickly between ages two and four. This is the rules module.

But with irregular verbs, children have to pick up hazy patterns. Many irregular verbs have rough similarities: *ring, rang, rung, drink, drank, drunk*. Seeing a new form of a verb that behaves similarly (*sing, sang, sung*) will tend to strengthen the connections between the members of this "i-a-u" family. But children may over-generalise, saying something like "bring, brang, brung" until they notice that their parents don't, and this will weaken the associations between these verbs a bit. (Actual correction by parents – "it's *brought*, sweetie..." – seems to play much less of a role.)

*

So human children seem neither to blindly follow the rules they learn, nor to merely infer from lots of data. The rules get them going quickly, making useful sentences of their own after learning from relatively sparse data. And the data-gathering approach lets them gradually store up and recall some of the more intricate and rarer bits of the language they need.

This is an absolutely stunning ability, given that we're talking about kids who cannot yet tie shoelaces. Yet since every cognitively typical child does it, it's not a miracle, even though it looks like one, a testament to the power of the human language faculty. What can it tell us about the nature of language itself, and the language-tamers' belief that language is all about rules?

First, kids don't need to be drilled in the vast majority of the grammar rules of their language. They can not only make the past tense, but ask questions, issue commands, and learn "if... then..." statements by age four or so. All this happens despite the fact that many of the rules make no objective sense. To ask a yes–no question,

English requires children to use a dummy verb, *do*, at the beginning of the sentence. (Few adults stop to think how weird that is.) To ask a "wh-" question (*what, where*), they have to fiddle with the word order of a statement, too: not *where my teddy is?*, which keeps the word order of ordinary statements, but *where is my teddy?* And sometimes they have to combine them: "What do you like?" joins the two rules. This is hard to teach adult learners of English – "what do you like?" is hardly a transparent way to derive a question from the statement form, "I like apples."

So when children arrive at school, there is no need to see them as savages who need to be "taught grammar". They already know a huge amount, and they continue learning from their environment in the early years of school, aside from their formal instruction.

How best should they be taught the intricacies as they progress to reading and writing? The language tamers have a simple answer: teach them the rules. But this is only a partial answer. Remember our two artificial intelligence approaches: "good old-fashioned" rules-governed hand-coding, and "machine learning", of which neural nets and "deep learning" are currently the state of the art. The human brain, in its wonders, has no need to choose one or the other.

For both speech and writing, both approaches are needed, too. There is no dispensing with exposure. Children need to hear lots of words directed at them, as well as in their environment, to pick up vocabulary and fine-tune their grammar. And to see how words work on the page, they need exposure to good words on pages, and lots of them. There is probably nowhere on earth a skilled writer, mastering the finer points of written style, who is not also a reasonably avid reader. There are too many subtleties for them all to be taught by rote.

But some things are best taught by rote. *Whom*, because it doesn't occur much in speech, tricks even many frequent readers and experienced writers. And yet mastering it is still a part of producing high-quality prose. So students are best taught explicitly – at an appropriate age – how to find the role a *who–whom* word is playing in a sentence, in order to choose the correct form.

In the 1960s, explicit teaching of grammar rules began to fall out of favour in Britain and America, and the fashion became to let students start by writing, with teachers correcting the mistakes as they came. As a result many adults today can't talk about how the parts of a sentence hang together – even many highly competent speakers and writers.

The pedagogical pendulum has begun to swing the other way, especially in Britain. Children learn a blizzard of grammatical terminology in primary schools, discussed in detail in Chapter 6. All this has been done in the name of raising standards. But there is no clear evidence that this actually makes better writers.

So what is the right approach? Remember the idea that our minds may have two kinds of ways of learning: an ability to apply rules to abstract mental symbols ("nouns can be the subject of sentences", "add -ed for the past tense") and inductive, patient strengthening of the recognition of certain patterns. Both are part of a sensible introduction to how English grammar works.

In short, kids need to read, read and read some more, starting as early as possible, so they become comfortable with what the good stuff looks like. This prepares the ground for learning abstract concepts, which should be introduced later. Over-emphasis on the rules before children are strong readers is counter-productive. Knowledge fits into the mind best when it can be connected to things that a person already knows. Reading, reading and reading more gives people an implicit knowledge of the rules of good writing, which can later be formalised. Reversing that order is like throwing seed onto frozen, unploughed ground.

The question of whether the mind is a kind of computer, or whether advanced artificial intelligence can be said to have a mind, can be left to the philosophers. But computers do offer us some intriguing analogies for learning. Rules alone are not enough. Language doesn't work that way, and our minds do not work that way. Experience with language does most of the heavy lifting of teaching children (and adults) how to wield it well. The rules can be added on for the tricky cases, at the appropriate age, but we should never confuse an explicit knowledge of rules ("this is what a relative clause looks like") with an ability to write. Lousy writing can be grammatical; good writing can have errors.

Computer scientists who work in natural-languages processing are exploring best-of-both-worlds systems, for translation, parsing and other applications. They are combining newer-fangled machine learning with explicit rule coding. Educators should do the same, researching which things are best learned by experience, and which are best learned by rule. But rules cannot be the be-all, end-all. Whether or not a child's mind is a computer, it can't be programmed like one.

4

Buxom, but never nice

IF COMPUTERS, WHICH CAN DO truly amazing things, struggle with language, then the human brain must be a fairly awesome machine to be able to handle it. Not only are there hundreds of explicit rules – the kind that can be programmed into a computer – but there are also many unwritten rules that most people know, but don't know that they know. Truly comprehensive books about English grammar, those that try to describe all the things a competent native speaker knows, can easily run to nearly 2,000 pages, and their authors would concede there are many things they could not include, or do not even yet understand. The system is awesomely complex, and yet any native speaker masters it well enough to create sentences that no one else has ever said before.

More amazing still, perhaps, is the fact that we understand each other. Not only can you use your knowledge of grammar and vocabulary to turn a complex thought into a string of words, but you can also turn your mental representation of those words into vibrations in the air. When they hit the ears of another native speaker of that language, they put the same thought in their heads that you had in yours. Language is not just an incredible faculty of the human mind; it is an incredible fact about human minds working together.

Two people who have never been formally educated in their own grammar can still use that grammar to discuss the weather, gossip, make hypothetical plans, build something, take a road trip, tell stories about their past or do a million other things. If this system is so intricate, why doesn't it crash more often? Failures to communicate are interesting (and often funny), but paying attention to them can distract from the miracle of just how easily we understand each other almost all of the time.

When people worry about language change, they often say that if the rules change, then we won't be able to understand each other properly anymore. Given just how complex the language faculty is, that might seem like a legitimate worry. Anyone who has ever tried writing the simplest computer program has learned how frequently bugs – either conceptual mistakes by the coder, or even a simple typo – come up in code, and how much they bedevil the working of the program. Now imagine that the syntax of these computer languages changed randomly every so often, without any announcement or planning. Old software wouldn't work properly. Mid-career coders would be flummoxed, trying to find the mistakes in the code but unable to do so because they don't know the new syntax. Younger coders who knew the new rules would talk at cross purposes with the older ones who knew the old ways. It would be chaos.

This is the kind of chaos some people fear if language changes in major ways. Old texts will be hard to read. Communication across generations would be constantly stymied by misunderstanding. To the extent the old system was logical, the new one would risk being less powerful and useful.

And yet it's hard to find an example of this actually happening in the real world. To return briefly to the example we began this book with, Sherlock Holmes in *Sherlock* – not only an intelligent man but a grammar snob – neglects the *whom* in saying "who's sleeping with who." Watson, his friend and roommate, is another educated man, perhaps the kind we'd expect to be looking out for *whom*. But the conversation is seamless. Either both are post-*whom* types, or both are able to use *who* and *whom* interchangeably after a preposition like *with*, or Watson hears Sherlock's *who* and merely mentally translates it into *whom*. *Whom* is slipping out of the language. And yet as it does so, it does not result in the kind of annoying "SYNTAX ERROR" breakdown messages that plagued my childhood efforts at computer coding.

How do languages change? How do *whom*-ful languages become *whom*-less ones without disaster? The system is anarchic – in the literal sense of having no ruler. And it is often random: sometimes things happen for no good reason. But it is not truly chaotic.

Remember, *who* is the pronoun that stands for the subject of a clause, and *whom* stands for its object. It is undeniably important to know who or what is the subject of a clause, and who or what is the object. But precisely because it *is* important – something no reasonable person denies – language compensates for the loss of one way of marking this distinction by bringing about another one. No language's speakers have ever found that they could do without the subject-object distinction, leaving any sentence of the "John killed Jim" type ambiguous as to who killed and who was killed. People care about that kind of thing.

Language organises itself in order to carry out the tasks needed of its users. Adam Smith created the image of an "invisible hand" guiding the economy. But of course what he meant was that lots of uncoordinated decisions by many participants in a market were efficient at creating order – setting prices that were neither too low to deter sellers nor too high to put off buyers – that no planner could have achieved alone. Modern scientists and social scientists have come up with a less vivid but more accurate description of such situations: spontaneous order.

If language does not crash – if it is not like computer code – then what is it like? Because it is a human behaviour, the best comparison is a biological one. As a system, natural languages are less like C++ or JavaScript, and more like an ecosystem. Ecosystems have thousands of species in a complex web of dependencies. They feature habitats from treetop nests to lakes and holes in the ground. More to the point, they are dynamic: seasons come and go, temperatures and precipitation change, and the system responds with it. Sometimes such changes are permanent: an invasive species appears, or a disease wipes out part of the food chain. These events can be disruptive – but they don't wipe out the ecosystem. The system *adapts* – sometimes becoming an entirely different kind of ecosystem, given enough time. Animals may change their behaviours; population ratios may change. But the point is that the actors and forces in the system work together as a system, so not even a major change brings things crashing down. Living things are adaptable; it is true of individual organisms, it is true of species and it is true of ecosystems, too. Not indestructible, but adaptable and robust. Life would be impossible if they weren't. And it is spontaneous, undirected order that we have to thank for this robustness.

What evidence do we have that language is a domain where spontaneous order arises and holds sway? The answer is simple: every language is changing, all the time. The only languages that ever stop changing are dead ones. There is not a tongue recorded – and almost certainly none that has gone unrecorded – that has not changed in big ways as well as small as the centuries have gone by. And yet the fascinating fact to explain is this: there is no language we know of in the history of the world that has become unfit for communication. Languages somehow seem to look after themselves. "Neglect" of grammar and high standards never leads to collapse – not ever.[1]

But plenty of people have a hard time believing this, and think language needs active intervention to stay healthy. In some countries with resources to spare, an official guardian is set up to look after the language: a kind of hyperactive game warden or park ranger. The most famous is the French Academy, though there are many others in Europe, and a few elsewhere. But those who believe that languages need an academy to look after them should, by extension, believe that languages without academies suffer by comparison. And yet they don't. English has no governing academy, but the language thrives just fine without one. And though the French respect their academy, it turns out in actual practice that they ignore most of its rulings.

Official language academies represent the most extreme form of top-down language planning. But in countries without an academy, like America and Britain, language tamers step in and declare their willingness to maintain or restore order. This sits oddly, though, with democratic and rich countries' attitudes in other domains, like economics. Communism has failed in most of the countries that have tried it, and few people today are keen on adopting a command economy. And yet, quite a lot of people have a soft spot for a kind of linguistic command economy.

But no command is needed. At every level of organisation, from sound, to vocabulary, to grammar, to discourse structures, languages tend to come with all of the tools they need for their particular culture. When some element of these systems changes, many language teachers, editors and pundits declare it an "error" and try to stop or reverse the change. But usually it proceeds anyway. And yet it almost always does so without harming the overall expressiveness of the language. This is because a language acts like a system, in which one change causes other changes until it is in balance again.

A body seeks homeostasis. An ecosystem sees populations rise and fall, but has a way of guaranteeing that neither predators nor prey over-proliferate. Economies raise prices to fend off shortages, and lower prices to clear gluts from markets. And this all happens without some kind of agent or director. Language changes work much the same way.

*

Begin with the most atomic units of language: not words, but sounds. If you've ever learned a European language or two, you might have noticed an odd fact about English. In languages as different as French, German, Spanish and Italian, the sounds represented by the letter *a* have a clear family resemblance: say *pâté*, *lager*, *tapas* and *pasta* back to back (to keep things just in the food and drink family) and you'll notice that they all have similar a-sounds, not too different from the *a* in English's "father". And if you see a word you don't know, but I tell you it comes from a European language (say *frango*, Portuguese for "chicken", or *kawa*, Polish for "coffee"), you'll naturally pronounce it with that same sound. It seems like the natural, default sound for *a*. So how on earth did English get the completely different sound in words like *name* and *face*?

If you go through the rest of the vowels, many of them are odd in this same way. From Pisa to Nice to Ibiza, *i* has an "ee" sound. So why does the English "long *i*" not sound like these European *i*'s at all, but rather like "aye" in words like *I*, *ride* and *hive*? And why does *e* sound so differently in French (think *éclat* and *élan*) than it does in English's *meet* and *meme*?

English used to have the same vowels as its close European cousins. It doesn't any more as a result of something linguists have named – in a rare instance of fun linguistic terminology – the Great Vowel Shift, or GVS. In Chaucer's time, *name* was pronounced as it is in German today, with a good clear *nah* and the reduced little -*uh* sound at the end called a "schwa" (the sound of the *a* in "sofa" or "woman"). But the Great Vowel Shift turned "nah-muh" into "naym". It turned *time*, once pronounced "teem", into "tie-eem". It turned *meet* from something akin to *mate* to something homophonous with today's *meat*. Why, how and with what consequences?

We don't really know what started the GVS. Some sounds just

change randomly, just as some genes randomly mutate. Some such changes will be unstable, taken up by a small number of people before disappearing. But others will catch on, spreading from speaker to speaker.

To show how vowels changed in Middle English, it can be useful to look at an example closer to today. For example, some speakers of American English say the words "cot" and "caught" identically; most British speakers and many Americans keep them distinct. Sometimes changes like this have no wider effect. It doesn't matter much if "cot" and "caught" alone are homophones: one's a noun, one's a verb, and they have such different meanings that the possibility of confusion is very low.

But sometimes these changes are more systematic. If a whole set of words (every word rhyming with *caught*, like *taught* and *naught*) starts to rhyme with another large set of words (every word rhyming with *cot*, like *tot* and *not*), suddenly we have lots of homophone pairs (*caught-cot*, *taught-tot*, *naught-not*) and the possibility for greater confusion. Previously important distinctions in the language can be lost.

But usually, overall clarity isn't. And that's because the system itself responds to keep vowels as distinct as they need to be, a fascinating example of language's self-regulation. We needn't go to Chaucer's time to see this in action, either. A cousin to the Great Vowel Shift has been happening in our lifetimes.

Linguists classify vowels on three dimensions: high-low and front-back, based on where the tongue root is in the mouth, and rounded-unrounded, depending on the position of the lips. Putting rounding to one side for a moment, the trapezoid over the page is how linguists draw the possible space for vowels, with a general Midwestern American's vowels plotted with the letters. To the top and left is the vowel in *fleece*, which is high and front. To the bottom left is *æ* as in *cat*, low and front. To the top right is *u* as in *boot*, high and back. Bottom right is *a* as in an American's *hot* vowel, back and low.

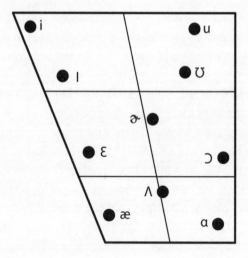

Notice how the vowels are roughly equidistant. This is a good thing, for the sake of communication. The more distinct the vowels are, the less the chance one will be misheard for another in a noisy room or over a distance.

So what happens when one of them moves, and that distance closes? Now they're a bit too close; the possibility of miscommunication rises. This is where the system starts to change as a whole, to maximise efficiency. One change prompts another, which in turn prompts a third, and so on. Linguists call this a "chain shift": other vowels move as a result of the first one's shift, keeping the distance between them roughly the same as before the shift began.

William Labov, a sociolinguist, has identified just such a shift called the "Northern Cities Shift", for its prominence in cities around America's Great Lakes. First, the vowel in words like *trap* was "raised", meaning that the tongue root is higher in the mouth when it's pronounced. The result is a word that sounds a bit more like *trep*. That pushed it closer to the vowel in words like *dress*, while leaving an empty space where the *trap* vowel had once been. This led the vowel in words like *thought* move further forward, near *trap*'s old, now empty neighbourhood. That brings the vowel in *strut* down into *thought*'s old place, and so on through a whole chain of changes:

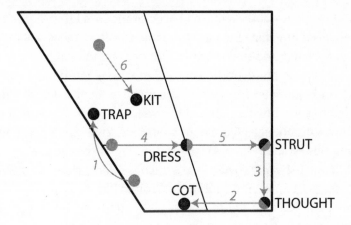

This leaves a system in which most of the vowels are in a new place – but crucially, they are still systematically distinct from each other. We have a new accent, but what we haven't got is a pile-up of vowels so that *caught*, *cot*, *cat*, *cut* and *kit* all sound the same, leaving the people on the Great Lakes unable to talk to each other.

No single person set out to start the Northern Cities Shift. Nor did anyone regulate it as it was going on. Millions of people just gradually adjusted their pronunciation to ensure that they could still understand each other, in a process that took decades, so slowly that hardly anyone was aware that it was going on.

Now we have the answer to why English no longer has "European" vowels. The Great Vowel Shift was also a chain shift. *Meet*, as mentioned, used to be pronounced as if its vowels were "normal" European *e*'s, so it came out as something like the modern *mate*, though without the movement of the tongue that *mate* has today (that is, a diphthong: two vowels gliding together). And *boot* sounded roughly like today's *boat*, but again, without the diphthong. (Imagine a Spanish or Italian person saying "boat" with their native accent.)

But the -ee- and -oo- vowels started to move towards the familiar vowels they have today. The problem is that now the vowels were close to those in words like *time* and *moon* (which sounded roughly like today's *team* and *moan*). The chain shift began: the vowel in *time* started to change, sounding more like "tuh-eem". Having formerly a pure vowel, it was now a diphthong. And *moon* started to take on its modern sound. But *house* at that time had been pronounced like "hoose"; now it and *moon* threatened to have the same vowel, so the vowel in *house* began to change to something like huh-oos (another diphthong).

In a second phase of the shift, other vowels moved: the vowel in *mate* once sounded like that of the modern English *father*. Then it moved to sounding more like the vowel in modern *cat*. At that time, *meat* was pronounced like a drawn-out version of modern *met*, which (if you close your eyes and say them aloud) sounds more like *cat*, or the Middle English *mate* vowel. That's uncomfortably close. So the vowel in *meat*, too, had to move, going on to sound like the *modern* version of "mate", but again, as a pure vowel: a monophthong, not a diphthong. Finally, *meat* wound up sounding like it does today.

This is a much-simplified account of what went on (other vowels were affected, too). And scholars are still debating the ordering, dates, and transitional phases the sounds went through.[2] Some divide it into two shifts. The story of the GVS, beloved of linguists, can make it sound more orderly and coordinated than English-speakers would have experienced it at the time. But the important point is the systematic nature of the shift. When one change threatened ambiguity or confusion, another change happened to make that confusion less likely. If *that* change in turn caused another problem, something else had to change. And so on again, until the system settled down, with as many vowels as it had had before. Only later did a couple of them merge (today, *meet* and *meat* are homophones, but only a few such mergers took place). In other words, it was the Great Vowel Shift, not the Great Vowel Collapse. The system worked.

*

At any given point, a change like those that made up the Great Vowel Shift or the Northern Cities Shift could be considered an error. After all, the "traditional" usage of older and wiser people was one way, and suddenly the innovative usage of the young goes another way. It seems to older speakers as if the young don't care about correctness. This is a common reaction of older people to innovations everywhere, but it's particularly pronounced in language.

Traditionalists have a point: a change really can introduce

temporary confusion. Chain shifts don't happen all at once, as if by fiat. One change causes another, over a long time, and at any given time people attached to an old pronunciation and those using a new one really might confuse each other. As the GVS was going on, and the vowel of *meet* was still pronounced a bit like *mate* by some, and like today's *meat* by others, it may have occasionally confused people. (And confusing "can I have some of your meat?" with "can I have some of your mate?" might start a fistfight in most cultures, to say nothing of 15th-century England.)

But while the oldsters have a point, it is a limited one. A given change may temporarily confuse some people. But it does not mean the collapse of civilisation, or even of the language. It just means that the pieces of the language system are moving – as they virtually always are – with friction, and one of those changes has wrought some temporary discomfort to some speakers. It seems a paradox that the product of a bunch of changes – each of which can be confusing or annoying on its own – can result in a system that is well balanced and well suited for a language's purposes. But that's just what we see: "annoying" changes, everywhere and all the time, yield perfectly usable, indeed amazingly expressive, languages.

The paradox is resolved by comparing the time scales. Individual changes might happen quickly enough to be noticed, and to annoy some people. But whole shifts, like the Great Vowel Shift, take so long that nobody lives to see their completion. (And "completion" isn't quite the right word either, since the system will keep on changing.) So change – natural and inevitable – is unsettling in its particulars, even if it is neutral overall and in the long run. Languages don't "evolve" in the sense of constantly getting better, or even more complicated. But neither do they fall apart.

*

It can be argued that the Great Vowel Shift actually was a bad change in one respect, though. After all, the GVS did make English spelling extraordinarily confusing, and in the process also wrenched it out of sync with the European spelling systems that share our alphabet.

But it can just as easily be argued the other way around, that this is a case against conservatism, not a case against change. The confusion wrought by the vowel shift was not only the fault of change in pronunciation but also the fault of conservatism in spelling. We don't know of a single living language that is pronounced exactly as it was in 1400; keeping a spoken language stable for this long is almost certainly impossible.

So those looking after the *written* language face a difficult decision. Do you occasionally update spelling (and vocabulary and grammar, which we'll get to), to reflect changing pronunciation? This is disruptive and annoying when it takes place. In recent years, even modest changes in spelling in European languages have caused one furore after another. A mostly sensible set of changes to German spelling in the 1990s caused a nationwide wave of acts of civil disobedience. Several German publishers refused to use the new version, among them Germany's biggest news-publishing group and one of its most prestigious national papers, the *Frankfurter Allgemeine Zeitung*. One state, Schleswig-Holstein in the north of the country, went so far as to hold a referendum against the reform, and the federal constitutional court was called upon to rule whether the changes were legal. The court decided that since no national law regulated spelling, nobody could be forced to use the new (or indeed the old) spelling. The changes were eventually modified, but most of them were kept. People got used to it.

Much the same happened – albeit more amusingly – just to the north, in Denmark's Majonæse War. In 1985, the Dansk Sprognævn, an institution something like the French Academy responsible for official rulings on Danish, announced that it would release new, native Danish spellings for some words that had long ago been borrowed from French. These words had, by then, long since had typically Danish, not French, pronunciations, and the regulator wanted to offer "Danish" spellings, which could be voluntarily used alongside the French ones.

Heated resistance in the newspapers and among the public intellectuals showed that – just as in France, just as in Germany – people simply didn't want the changes, no matter how much sense they made on paper. The attention somehow came to focus on a beloved egg-and-oil condiment that Danes were told they could now spell *majonæse*. The outcry worked: some of the announced double spellings were never introduced, and in a 2012 edition of the Dansk Sprognævn's spelling book, *majonæse* was left out, leaving *mayonnaise* the only legitimate spelling.

Updating clearly irritates people. So why not prefer stability instead, and just insist on a policy of "if the spelling ain't irreparably broke, don't fix it"? In this case, you get a different problem. The spoken language changes, the written one doesn't – and they gradually diverge. The French, for example, despite a minor recent reform of their own, have done a lot more conserving than they have changing, which is why French is filled with silent letters that annoy the foreign learner, and French native-speakers have to laboriously learn their spelling system much like English native-speakers do. Where English-speakers have the spelling bee, in French schools, the test is *dictée*, the ability to write down correctly a passage read aloud by a teacher. Danish has been conservative in spelling, too. So, predictably, it also has a lot of silent letters, and French-style pupil-torturing *diktat* exercises in school. English spelling is difficult for a broader basket of reasons, among them many foreign borrowings.

It's a damned-either-way proposition: people don't like to learn new spelling systems, but nobody would consciously invent a spelling system like those of modern French, English or Danish, either. And nobody has yet come up with a spoken language that won't change, given enough time. Something has to give.

Linguistic conservatives – people like some English teachers, parents who want their children to sound educated, the guy at your office who doesn't mind telling you that you're saying things wrong – focus on trying to stop the sound change before it sets in. If they address an obvious mistake, like the wholesale substitution of one sound for another, in its early stages, they might stop the change, or keep it on the fringes. Think of *expresso* or *nucular*: they're widely heard but widely disparaged, and the original forms are widely known and used too. So *expresso* and *nucular* have become minor variants, not replacements, for *espresso* and *nuclear*.

But some changes are less discrete than obvious ones like *expresso/espresso* – the presence of a "k" sound that makes "es-" into "ex-" is obvious after all, and can easily be pointed out by one speaker to another. But the space of possible vowels is continuous, not discrete, and so changes can be so small as to go unnoticed. It's not really true that if you boil a frog slowly it won't notice and will never try to escape. But if a lot of speakers very gradually inch a vowel forward or back, up or down in the space in the mouth, without even knowing, then over time a major change can set in without anyone acting in time to stop it. That is because vowel-boiling, unlike frog-boiling, is painless and victimless.

The fact that English *name* and German *Name* are spelled identically and share a common ancestor, but come out sounding quite different, is a lot like the fact that the flipper of a dolphin and the arm of a human are biological homologues: they diverged from a common ancestor very gradually, and now look different and work differently. But just because the Great Vowel Shift made English *name* sound different from German *Name* doesn't mean *name* is wrong, any more than a hand is a "corrupted" version of a flipper.

When *a* as in "father" becomes *a* as in "name", it does so in a series of tiny steps. The same can go for vowel deletion; that "uh" that used to be at the end of *name* disappeared bit by bit, not all at once. Some consonant changes can be continuous too: the tongue can be used to stop or slow the flow of air anywhere from the teeth to the throat. A full stoppage of the air, as with a k-sound, can become a near-stoppage, as in the fricative sound at the end of *Bach*, which can gradually become a mere h-sound, which can then disappear entirely. (But consonants, by their nature, are less likely to change continuously than vowels are.)

*

Those opposing a pronunciation they don't like often appeal to spelling. (Think of Eddie Izzard, a British comedian, talking to an American audience about the pronunciation of *herb*: "you say *erb* and we say *herb*... because there's a fucking H in it.") This assumes the written language is the real thing, and what the spoken one should be modelled on. This is backwards. Remember, everyone speaks, and writing is a latecomer in the history of language. It has to be laboriously taught to children. Writing is wonderful, but it's the add-on, not the underlying thing. Insisting that speech – a live activity, always changing, a biological behaviour – must imitate writing – which is fixed – is a bit like insisting that people should continue to look like an old photo of themselves. Try as people might, they are exceedingly unlikely to achieve this. Sound, in particular, is unstable: Samuel Johnson said that "to enchain syllables, and to lash the wind, are equally the undertakings of pride."

*

Johnson, of course, was a lexicographer; though he might have thought that stopping sound change was futile, as a man whose life's work was defining, he might have at least hoped to pin meanings down. But after toiling for years on his masterpiece dictionary of 1755, he had become aware that this ran against the wild nature of language itself.

Trying to define common words with many definitions vexed him in particular. He mentioned *bear, break, come, cast, fall, get, give, do, put, set, go, run, make, take, turn* and *throw*, going on to say that

> If of these the whole power is not accurately delivered, it must
> be remembered, that while our language is yet living, and
> variable by the caprice of every one that speaks it, these words are
> hourly shifting their relations, and can no more be ascertained
> in a dictionary, than a grove, in the agitation of a storm, can be
> accurately delineated from its picture in the water.[3]

It's hard to conjure a more vivid natural image of what Johnson, or any lexicographer, is up against.

In his "Plan" for the dictionary, written in 1747, before he had got down to serious work, Johnson still thought he might "fix the language" with his dictionary, declaring that "all change is of itself an evil." But he had already anticipated how hard the work was going to be, given the ever-shifting nature of the target.

> [T]he strict and critical meaning ought to be distinguished from
> that which is loose and popular; as in the word *perfection*, which,
> though in its philosophical and exact sense it can be of little
> use among human beings, is often so much degraded from its
> original signification, that the academicians have inserted in
> their work, *the perfection of a language*, and, with a little more
> licentiousness, might have prevailed on themselves to have
> added *the perfection of a dictionary*.

The passage is vintage Johnson. It begins with the magisterial tone today's language tamers aspire to: "strict and critical" meanings should be distinguished from "loose and popular" ones. But before the sentence is out, Johnson has admitted that even "academicians" – educated, intelligent men – have loosened the strict meaning of words like "perfection". Perfection, strictly speaking, should be an absolute quality of unimprovability, hardly ever found on earth. He finishes with a double flourish: it is ridiculous to talk about the perfection of language; one might as well talk about the equally ridiculous idea of the perfection of a dictionary. Johnson loved to deride his own profession: a lexicographer was a "harmless drudge", an "unhappy mortal" whose task was to "remove the rubbish and clear the obstructions from the paths of Learning and Genius".

Johnson knew that a theory of language must be based on an underlying theory of human nature. People were imperfect, and the meaning of words could hardly be more stable than the minds and memories of their users; *ergo*, a dictionary could hardly be any better than that. And in fact, to page through his dictionary is to stumble serendipitously again and again over words that have changed their meanings radically since he attempted to pin them down in 1755. Johnson's must be one of the few dictionaries that can be kept by a toilet or next to a bed for both historical edification and entertainment.

In the same passage in which he complained about "perfection", for example, he also knocked an unappealing new meaning of the word *buxom*. It "means only *obedient*", he tells us, but it "is now made, in familiar phrases, to stand for *wanton*". What? Yes, *buxom* first meant "obedient" in the sense of pliable – its Middle English form was *buhsam*, related to the modern German word *biegsam*, or bendable. So it was a quality that a woman would promise her husband, in an old pre-Reformation English wedding vow: "I will be bonair and buxom in bed and at board." From "pliable" it was a short leap to "amiable, courteous, affable", as the *OED* puts it. And from there, it was just another short hop to "blithe, gladsome, bright, lively, gay"; Shakespeare describes "a soldier, one of buxom valour" in *Henry V*.

Then, *buxom* took on an association with lively good health and vigour. Thomas Gray, Johnson's rough contemporary, describes boys of "buxom health" in a poem about Eton. Johnson sniffed that "he seems not to understand the word." (Remember, he still thought that the only proper meaning was "obedient".) But Gray's use of "buxom" was perfectly current at the time. Curiously, of all those meanings, Johnson seems to have imagined the "wanton" sense. The citations he provided don't seem to indicate wantonness, and the *OED*, commenting on his entry, says that Johnson's "wanton" meaning is "seemingly only contextual".

Instead, from "good health", the word went on to another step, to meaning physical plumpness, and from there, another half-step, to meaning plumpness only among women. Today, most people use it as a synonym for nothing more than "big-breasted". Data from Google Books confirm that since 1900, nobody would describe the boys of Eton as "buxom": the most common nouns to follow "buxom" in Google's collection of millions of books are *woman, women, girl, figure, lady, lass, wife, girls, widow* and *dame*.

Buxom has had a strange career. It's a long road from "obedient" to "big-breasted", and today, even "buxom" for "big-breasted" sounds rather like someone's slightly out-of-touch uncle. ("Curvy" is about the only polite modern word for a big-breasted woman, but it's also a euphemism for "overweight". About the only way to politely refer to a woman's breasts today is to think twice, and then not do so.) Johnson was defining "buxom" in the middle of that word's long road. The good doctor got it partly wrong – the "wantonness" seems to have been mostly in his head. And he was even more wrong in insisting that only "obedient" was correct. The "gay, lively" meaning he thought Gray had used wrongly had been around for hundreds of years by the time he was writing. Needless to say, he could have had no way of knowing how the word would develop.

Somehow, though, it seems likely he'd have had a wry smile. Unlike many modern language tamers, Johnson was wise to be humble about the lexicographer's work; it's hard work, it's an inexact science, the target is moving while you're aiming, and as soon as your dictionary hits the presses, it has already begun to go out of date.

Armchair etymologists know many stories like that of *buxom*. *Silly* once meant "holy" (as in "seli martirdom", from 1225), but went through a series of intermediate meanings – "innocent", "pitiable" and "contemptible" among them – before arriving where it is today.

Nice went exactly the opposite way, starting out as meaning "foolish, simple" (eg, "I am unwise and wonderfully nice"[4] from 1375), then "characterised by wantonness", "of dress: showy, extravagant", "precise in matters of reputation or conduct" and "respectable, virtuous, decent", before arriving at today's meaning.

So in the Middle English era, manners dictated that a girl was expected to be silly and buxom, but never nice. What are we to make of a state of affairs that such basic words can so radically change their meanings? Why does this level of change not result in a complete communication breakdown? Can't words just mean what they originally meant?

The last objection is an easy one to answer; it is a variant of the so-called "etymological fallacy". Some would hold *decimate* to mean "to destroy (roughly) a tenth of", because it comes from the old Roman tradition of punishing of mutinous troops by killing every tenth man. The *deci-* root there appears in *decennial* and *decade* in English. Therefore, goes the argument, *decimate* shouldn't be used to mean to destroy entirely, or nearly entirely. But words – especially those words used most frequently – tend to have a way of drifting away from their etymological roots. Those who insist that *decimate* must mean to destroy a tenth must use *buxom* to mean *pliable* – after all, it's got the German root for "to bend" in it, just as *decimate* has the root for "ten". But anyone idiosyncratic enough to insist on this meaning for *buxom* is going to confuse every other native English speaker they meet, because the word just doesn't mean that anymore, any more than December is still the tenth month in the calendar.[5]

These changes in meaning don't result in a communication breakdown because words in a language form a system, just like the sounds of a language do. Parts of the system – the words – may seem to drift randomly, if you focus on one word, as with the long career of *buxom*. But focusing on the system as a whole, we see that each time *buxom* left an empty space behind, something always filled the gap. And the reason is obvious: the concepts left behind are important ones, leaving a vacuum that some word or another is just going to have to fill. In *buxom*'s case, "obedient" was in use by 1225, and *pliant* (a more literal synonym) is first attested in 1382. The lexicon abhors a vacuum; if a society values the ability to talk about obedience (and most do), then a label will arise. If that label changes meaning, another word will arise. The same goes for the rest of *buxom*'s many meanings: it may no longer mean "affable" and "gay", but *affable* does that job just nicely. *Gay* has moved on, too, of course, but its old meaning still has plenty of synonyms.

The story is not unlike that of the chain shift in phonology: one part moves, another takes its old place, a third part takes that second part's old place, and so on. One difference is that with sounds, the movements are relatively more systematic and predictable. In the lexicon, we may not see chain shifts as neat as the Great Vowel Shift. But we do find that, in any era, speakers largely have the words they need to say the things they want.

As an American in England, for example, I often come across the British complaint that to an American, everything is "awesome". The complaint really has two parts: one is that the word changed meaning by type, going from meaning awe-inspiring to meaning really, really good. Then *awesome* changed meaning by intensity, from really really good to really good, to good, to just OK: from "our trip to the Grand Canyon was awesome" to "the band was awesome" to "this coffee is awesome" to *The Lego Movie*'s theme song, "Everything Is Awesome". *Awesome* can even be a mere confirmation that one speaker has heard the other: "I'm going to the corner store; we need milk." "Awesome."

But this complaint is, like so many others, wide of the mark. *Awesome* didn't begin by meaning "awe-inspiring" – its first meaning was "awe-filled", attested by the *OED* in 1598, so used to describe a person feeling awe, not an object of awe. Only in 1637 does the meaning of "inspiring awe" appear ("A sight of his cross is more awsom then the weight of it."[sic]). Exactly this kind of extension in meaning is garden-variety language change, happening all the time. You may know someone who says that *nauseous* can't be used to describe a person who feels sick, but rather only the thing that is sick-making. But this change is already complete, and the old "sick-making" meaning of *nauseous* is so rare as to be confusing to most people.

So this type of change (going from "cause" to "experiencer" or the other way around) is commonplace. But when it happens in your century (as with *nauseous*) it provokes moral panic among those who think that the older meaning is always the right one; if it happened a few centuries ago (*awesome*) nobody is even aware of the old meaning anymore. Instead, today's panic is about the cheapening of the word to describe a coffee.

And yet we have all the words we need. If you need to say "filled with awe", try *awe-filled* or *awed*. If you need "inspiring awe", there's *awe-inspiring*. If you mean really incredibly good, you are spoiled for choice: tons of other words have gone from other more literal meanings to fill this vital lexical niche: *amazing, terrific, brilliant, genius, stupendous*. When you use them to describe a wonderful experience, they don't have anything to do with amazement, terror, shininess, genies/spirits or stupor, as they used to.

Some of these words still have their old meanings as secondary, literal ones: a diamond can be "brilliant". But some don't: *terrific* is no longer used to mean "causing terror", as it used to (Milton: "the serpent... with brazen eyes and hairie main terrific"). But for the original *terrific* we still have the older word *terrifying*, and the newer word *horrifying*.

Words jockeying for space and moving around the system are the norm, not an aberration. Johnson's dictionary contains many pairs of entries of similar words with similar meanings; it was evidently not clear to him whether *difficil* or *difficult*, *promulge* or *promulgate*, *heroine* or *heroess*, *subtile* or *subtle* would prevail; both were then current, so he defined them both.[6] Only one won in each case. Language tolerates synonyms (though perhaps only imperfect ones; no two words are used identically), and it tolerates confusingly similar-looking words (*flaunt/flout*, *rebut/refute* and others). But it doesn't like nearly identical words to be synonyms.

An interesting parallel can be seen in big uncoordinated systems of millions of users like Twitter. Hashtags are useful in that they allow users who don't know each other to organise their tweets so that others can easily find each other's tweets on the same topic.[7] Who picks a hashtag? Why does one succeed and another fail? It doesn't really matter; some hashtags (#blacklivesmatter) are evocative, and others (#yesallwomen) are not particularly so. But the point is that for the hashtags to be useful in organising Twitter, users need to use the same one. When news is breaking several competitors will naturally emerge, but prestigious users or successful tweets will quickly make one hashtag more popular than others. Other Twitter users, less prestigious or widely followed, will want to be part of the same conversation, and adopt that variant of the hashtag. The old ones often die out. (Sometimes, adoption of a hashtag can even signal group membership; after the passage of the Affordable Care Act in America in 2010, Republicans preferred #Obamacare and Democrats preferred #ACA.)

In other words, this is more spontaneous order. Quickly on Twitter, more slowly in the spoken language, and more slowly still in writing, words change meaning, new ones are born, and other ones die. There is change in the system, but it functions as a system, not as a lot of randomly fluctuating pieces. The users of a language – uncoordinated, with no guiding hand – make sure that the language hasn't been left without a word for describing things that they want to describe. Why on earth would they?

Both sides in the over-egged "usage wars" claim Johnson for their side. The prescriptivists praise his aim of keeping the "loose and popular" away from the "strict and critical". But the descriptivists notice one of history's most famous evolutions in linguistic thinking, from Johnson's confident "Plan" in 1747 – "all change is of itself an evil" – to his acceptance that change was inevitable in 1755's "Preface".

To Johnson's contemporaries, his evolution was invisible. One, Lord Chesterfield, went so far as to publicly hope that Johnson's work would make him more than a mere language tamer; in an article for *The World*, he wrote that "We must have recourse to the old Roman expedient in times of confusion, and chose a dictator. Upon this principle, I give my vote for Mr Johnson to fill that great and arduous post."

Chesterfield seemed to have hoped that Johnson would dedicate the dictionary to him. Johnson, for his part, had once hoped that Chesterfield would become his patron, and became disappointed. By the time of Chesterfield's offer of a linguistic "dictatorship", Johnson wanted nothing to do with him, and in a tart letter of reply let him know. But another reason may have kept Johnson from accepting this flattering – even overweening – offer of a dictatorship. He knew the subjects – words – were too many and too unruly to submit to even the most authoritative of hands.

Johnson was also a conservative Christian, who wrote a Christian-themed poem – *The Vanity of Human Wishes* – while hard at work on the dictionary. Christians see the world as fallen, and Johnson was no different; remember his insistence that perfection was hardly to be found on earth. But he needn't have been so gloomy about his work's prospects. Though he did not fix English in place, he wrote one of the most celebrated works of scholarship on the language in its long history, one that did a good deal to slow (though it could never stop) and temper the pace of change in the language. Yes, he was working in "times of confusion", as Chesterfield put it, and as Johnson seemed to agree. But in language, all times are times of confusion. Johnson did more than most ever could to bring some clarity to the world of words.

*

Sounds change. Words change. We've seen that they change as a system, though, keeping people's linguistic needs met at all times. What about the structures of the language itself – the grammar? Somehow it feels more fundamental than sounds or words. Those who sell lots of books about the need for keeping high standards in language typically pay little attention to the sound system, carping about pebbles in the shoe like *expresso* only occasionally. And they understand that with tens of thousands of words in a language, the rise, fall or change of any given word can only affect the system so much.

But grammar structures how words relate to each other to create meaning. Somehow it seems deeper and more important if the grammar changes than if a word picks up a new pronunciation (*expresso*) or expands in meaning (*decimate*). If sounds and words are part of the system, grammar *is* the system. And many people are convinced that grammar is in decline.

Happily, this is bunk. As with sound changes, as with words' shifting meanings, there has never been a language found anywhere in the world that did not have a grammar capable of carrying out all of the functions of a sophisticated, supple and powerful language. Grammars vary hugely in type. But serious linguists are unanimous: all languages are powerfully expressive, and their expressiveness in no way depends on people's freezing a certain kind of "proper" grammar in place. It follows that when a grammar changes – usually quite slowly, especially in comparison to how quickly individual words change – it leaves the language different, but never worse off.

People who learn Chinese describe two big challenges in doing so. One is the incredibly difficult script of the written language. Learners must memorise thousands of characters for basic literacy, and even this will leave them turning to a dictionary over and over to read an everyday text like a newspaper article. It is safe to say that this is one of the most fiendishly complicated writing systems ever devised. It has its defenders, mostly proud Chinese themselves – but not even they would call it straightforward and easy.

The other big challenge with Chinese comes not in writing but in speech: tones. Mandarin, the most common spoken variety, has four tones – level, rising, dipping and falling pitch – over the course of pronouncing a vowel. To Chinese-speakers, tone is as important for meaning as vowel quality is in English; you can no more mix up *shí* and *shì* and expect to be understood than an English-speaker can mix up "bit" and "beet". Tones are crucial to the system, and a nightmare for most Western learners.

But, says the enervated Chinese learner, once you've got a grip on the tones, and once you've got a basic vocabulary built up, there comes a strange and happy surprise. Many people put it starkly: Chinese has "no grammar". Unlike, say, French or Italian, which require you to memorise bucketloads of endings to form a past tense or a subjunctive, or German, which requires the mastery of a syntax that can leave verbs at the very end of hugely long clauses, Chinese seems simple. It's just word word word word word.

Can it really be that Chinese is so childish, though? How did such a sophisticated and ancient culture get built with a language that foreigners describe as being as simple as snapping Legos together? The answer is that of course it's not really all that simple, it's just that Chinese puts its complexity in different places; namely, it doesn't have all those endings that make acquiring Latin and Greek, German and Russian a long slog of memorisation.

For example, there is no obligatory marking of plurals in Chinese: 汽车, transcribed as *qìchē* and pronounced like "tchee-cher", can mean "car" or "cars". (This can be shortened to just 车, *chē*, too.) How on earth, then, do the Chinese know how many cars someone's got? Simple: they use context, plus a few simple strategies for clearing up ambiguity where context isn't enough: *wǒ yǒu chē*, said with no other context on a first date, probably means "I have a car," and not "I have cars," because the first situation is a lot more common. If someone wants to specify they have three cars, they use a couple of extra words. One is "three" (sān) and the other is a "measure word", used with plurals, as when English-speakers talk about "three *grains* of rice" or "two *loaves* of bread". So in Chinese, you'd say something like *wǒ yǒu sān liàng chē*, "I have three *liàng* of cars." But after that, once the presence of multiple cars is taken for granted, there's no need for the plural any more: unless the context changes, *chē* can be taken to mean the cars that have already been brought up. (And if one car has been stipulated at the outset, then *chē* will mean just the one car.)

Further, Chinese has no word for *the*, nor for *a* – which, if you think about it, are often superfluous in English. When "I have car" is said on that first date in Chinese, the "a" is unnecessary; it's a car you haven't heard about yet, so it can't be "the car". If we carry on talking about the car, though, it's now "the" car, the one we're already talking about. To sum up: *chē*, depending on context, can mean "a car", "the car", "cars" or "the cars".

This kind of thing – a telegraphic omission of anything that isn't absolutely crucial – seems to be all over the grammar of Chinese. The past tense is not marked as with an English-, Spanish- or German-style ending. (In other words, Chinese has "no tense", as some grammars will tell you.) But of course, Chinese people need to be able to talk about the past and distinguish it from the present. So they do so, once again, with context: in a sentence with "yesterday" prominent in it, the events I am describing are obviously already in the past. There's no need for an ending. *I eat yesterday* obviously means *I ate yesterday*. (The marker *le* often shows up in past-tense sentences, but it's not "the past tense", but rather says that an action is complete rather than continuous, and it's used in many non-past contexts.)

In other words, in some weird ways, it really does seem that Chinese has "no grammar" to the eye and ear used to Western languages. In other ways, it's clear that Chinese does have grammar: that *le*, for example. So what's going on here?

Chinese is the linguist's favourite example of what's called an "analytic" language. In analytic languages words tend to be short, and lacking those grammatical bits and pieces like English's plural-marker

-*s*, or the past-tense marker -*ed*. If you need to specify those bits and pieces, they're separate words, like the *le* that specifies a completed action.

In linguistics terminology, each meaningful unit of a language is called a "morpheme". *Meaningful* has three morphemes: *mean*, -*ing* and -*ful*. The first is the stem, which is a verb. The second makes *mean* into a noun, *meaning*. And the third turns the noun into an adjective: *meaningful*. *Mean* is a "free" morpheme, meaning it can exist on its own, whereas -*ing* and -*ful* are "bound" morphemes, meaning they have to come attached to another morpheme.

Analytic languages like Chinese have nothing but free morphemes. They may join together to make compound words – Chinese has lots of them, including *qìchē* for "car": *qì* means "steam" and *chē* is a vehicle with wheels (which is why, after it's clear we're talking about a car and not a bike or train, we can shorten it to just *chē*. A bike is a *zìxíngchē* and a train is a *huǒchē*). What Chinese lacks is those bound morphemes that signal bits of grammar in English, like -*ing*. *Le* is freestanding.

An even more extreme example of an analytic language is Vietnamese, called an "isolating" language because it lacks not only bound morphemes but also compounds made of free morphemes, like *qìchē*. Here's an example in Vietnamese, with a morpheme-by-morpheme translation below and a free translation after that.

khi tôi dên nhà ban tôi, chúng tôi bát dâu làm bài.

when I come house friend I, [plural] I begin do lesson

When I came to my friend's house, we began to do lessons.[8]

Notice *tôi*, meaning "I", three times. The first time, it's "I", the subject of the first clause. The second time, though, it comes as part of *ban tôi* – "friend I", or "my friend". And the third time it's part of *chúng tôi*, "[plural] I", or "we". This really seems like Lego language.

Yet it's not true that Vietnamese has "no grammar"; if that were the case, then learning it would simply be a matter of learning the words, and using them in any old order you please. But in fact, in any language, you have to learn which words go together in a meaningful way, like *chúng tôi* for "we". And just as importantly, you have to know which order the elements of a sentence go in: you couldn't just scramble the words in *khi tôi dên nhà ban tôi, chúng tôi bát dâu làm bài* and get a meaningful sentence any more than you can scramble a set of Scrabble tiles randomly and get a meaningful word. Vietnamese, like Chinese, does have grammar.

*

The opposite of an analytic language is a "synthetic" one. This is one in which words tend to have more than one morpheme to them, and sometimes have quite a few. One kind of synthetic language is called "agglutinating": in this kind, words tend to be long, with lots of different morphemes one after the other like beads on a string. A canonical example is Turkish, where two words, *Evlerindeymişçesine rahattılar*, mean "they were as carefree as if they were in their own house."

In agglutinating languages, words get very long. So another kind of synthetic language saves space by cramming a few bits of grammar into a single morpheme. Now we return to the more familiar languages of western Europe, many of which are "fusional" in this way, meaning they fuse together morphemes with independent meanings. In Spanish, *habló*, meaning "he spoke" or "she spoke", has two morphemes, *habl-* (the root meaning to speak) and *-o*, which is one morpheme, but which fuses three pieces of grammar together: the subject of the verb is (1) singular and (2) in the third person, and (3) the action is in the past. *Now* we have grammar, says the western European, whose canonical example of elegant, grammar-filled languages are ones like Latin and Greek (both fusional themselves).

What does all this have to do with change, the subject of this chapter? What can it tell us about the loss of *whom*? One answer is a fascinating theory about the relationship of these three types of languages: namely, that they naturally change into one another over time. Remember that English was once a language of many grammatical endings – heavily inflected, as linguists say – not just on pronouns and some verbs, as today, but on all nouns, all verbs and adjectives too. In fact, English was fusional, with endings that tended to indicate multiple meaningful things. *Cyninges* has the root *cyning*, "king", and the bound morpheme *-es*, carrying four bits of information: "1) third person 2) masculine 3) singular 4) genitive (ie, possessive)". In other words, "king's".

Many linguists believe that fusional languages like Old English naturally tend to become more analytic over time. It's important to note here that the types of language – fusional, analytic, isolating, agglutinating, and so on – are not rigid categories, but ideal cases. A language can be "relatively" agglutinating or "fairly" analytic. That's because language change itself is usually gradual.

In any case, over time, we see exactly what the theory describes: that a fusional language like Old English has gradually become a much more analytic language, namely modern English. Most of the endings have disappeared entirely: pretty much the only thing you can do, grammatically, to an English noun is add an -s (in most cases) to make it plural, and add an -'s to make it possessive.

So has English lost its grammar? No; it has replaced one kind with another. In Old English, a suffix told you if a word was the direct object of a verb. That meant that that word could freely appear in lots of different places in the sentence. In English, that has changed; no more ending, but relatively rigid word order, in that English must usually present subject, verb and object in that order. Case endings are grammar. But so is word order.

English is mostly analytic. But not entirely; as mentioned it has a few grammar endings left, like the -s that marks a plural noun. And it also has lots of "derivational" bound morphemes, like un- and -like, that can allow users to coin new words as needed, such as *unsquidlike*. Finally, English allows the compounding of free morphemes, like *year* and *book* coming together to make *yearbook*.

But becoming more analytic over time isn't necessarily a one-way street, with languages gradually losing inflections and the like. In fact, analytical languages, especially ones that are highly isolating like Vietnamese, can gradually become more agglutinating. How does that work? Who decides to create endings and make them new bits of grammar? Nobody, obviously. (Why would you?) But it happens by itself over time.

A textbook example of grammar happening from the fusion of a formerly independent word is the future tense in some of the Romance languages. *Habeō*, meaning "to have" in Latin, was used after the infinitive of the verb to form the future (with the *habeō* conjugated for the different persons: *habeo* for "I", *habēs* for "you", and so on) But over time, the pronunciation became hurried and less distinct, until it seemed like a mere add-on to the verb before it. So *venire habeo*, "I will come," was slurred over the centuries into what became the modern Italian *verrò*. What used to be a word is now an ending; an intricate bit of grammar in the modern language is the result of "slovenliness" and "laziness" on the part of speakers a thousand years ago. Remember our earlier example of the rock cycle. One set of forces (like water or glaciation) breaks down a solid rock into pieces; other forces (pressure, plus heat) fuse the little pieces together into new kinds of rocks.

But for readers unfamiliar with Latin and Italian, it's easier to demonstrate this phenomenon – known as grammaticalisation – of formerly freestanding words in English, today. Take *gotta*. Is that a real word? What kind is it? And for that matter, what about *hafta*, *oughta* and *gonna*?

English, like other languages, has "modal verbs", which express the relationship between a speaker and an action like obligation, desire, ability and so forth. They include *can*, *should*, *must*, *dare* and the like. These verbs take an infinitive after them: *can go*, *should work*, *must sleep*, *dare try*. If you've heard that an infinitive must have *to* before it, you will wonder if these are really infinitives, but they certainly are – a "bare infinitive" is one that has no *to* before it. Modals take bare infinitives.

Many verbs, though not traditionally called modals, behave like them, expressing things like futurity and obligation, but take a *to* infinitive rather than a bare one: *ought to work*, *got to sleep*, *have to run*, *going to try*. But in running speech, the *to* gets glommed on to the previous word: *oughta work*, *gotta sleep*, *hafta run*, *gonna try*. In fact, they really are parts of those words, in a sense. How do we know? Well, for one reason, you can't split them. You might say

Really, I gotta work

I really gotta work

I gotta really work

I gotta work, really

The one place you can't stick *really* is in the middle of *gotta*. You can neither say, hurriedly, *I got-really-a work*, nor even, carefully, *I've got really to work*. The *to* has become fused with *got* in speakers' minds. That's why it is most usually pronounced as a mere schwa -*a*.

If English, like most of the world's languages, weren't written, gradually people would stop seeing the *to* as a separate word and eventually they'd forget it ever was one. And this process would result in a new set of verbs, *gotta*, *oughta*, *hafta* and *gonna*, that take a bare infinitive, like their cousins, *must*, *should*, *can* and *will*. In other words, speakers aren't doing something stupid or lazy when they make *gotta* out of *got to*. They're economising on the movements in their mouths (the reasons most sound changes happen), but they're also subliminally reasoning by analogy: if *should* takes a bare infinitive, let's make *gotta* behave the same way and take a bare infinitive, by re-analysing the *to* as a mere ending on *got*.

This is something akin to what created the endings in the Romance languages; a formerly freestanding word is now an ending on another word. Of course in this case, the previous freestanding words still exist and can be used in other contexts. Take *going* and *to*: you can still say *I'm going to Atlanta*, and you have to pronounce *going* and *to* distinctly, even if you're an Atlantan like I am, and pronounce the name of your hometown as *Atlanna*. You can say *I'm going to Atlanna*. But you can't say *I'm gonna Atlanna*. This is not the *going to* you're looking for. *Gonna* has become a new mental dictionary item with its own pronunciation and meaning, quite distinct from the directional *going to* in both sound and meaning.

*

Over time, more and more of this thing can happen to an isolating/analytic language, *got to* turning into *gotta* again and again until our highly isolating language has become more agglutinating, with that -*ta* indicating that this is a kind of modal verb. Imagine our Atlantan under a mild obligation to return home. He might say *I kinda gotta go to Atlanna*. Since *kinda* naturally appears next to things like *gotta*, one can easily imagine it, in a thousand years, as a kind of bound morpheme that attaches to modals: *kindagotta*.

Languages that string morphemes along like this, remember, are called agglutinating, like Turkish. Words in agglutinating languages tend to get long. But sound change is driven by an attempt by speakers to economise on effort; long words and complex clusters of sounds can be hard to pronounce in one go. If *kindagotta* evolved as many other words do, the *-d* would probably disappear (many people already say *kine-a gotta*).

Then, the unstressed *-a-* is a ripe candidate for weakening until it disappears, too – *kine-gotta*. The *n* could weaken until it just makes the *i* before it sound more nasal, and then that nasality could disappear entirely, leaving *kigotta*. And so on. We're getting closer and closer to a pure grammatical word that would have a complex grammatical meaning (it would mean a relatively mild obligation to do something), but it would get simpler and shorter over time, until no one on earth could imagine it had once been *kind of got to*.

"Fusional" languages take their name from the fact that eventually, *kinda* and *gotta* could reduce so much that they'd no longer be distinct, with speakers not recognising the boundary between *kinda* and *gotta*. If a sort of *kotta* emerged from the whole process, four words would have fused to two, which would have (*woulda*) then fused to one.

If you've followed this long story, from the past to the present to the future, what do you see? A fusional language (Old English) that shed most of its inflection to become a mostly analytic language (Modern English). But Modern English is busy grammaticalising formerly freestanding words so that they behave like endings. In a hypothetical future, such words could combine in a *kindagotta* kind of way, making something like an agglutinating language, and in the distant future, these could fuse to make our *kotta* English: another fusional language with two grammatical bits in one word – just like Old English was!

Some linguists propose a kind of "clock", in which languages naturally cycle between types: fusional-isolating-agglutinating-fusional-isolating (see opposite).

Asya Pereltsvaig, a lecturer in linguistics at Stanford, posits that English is now at 3.00 on the clock. In other words, it may yet have some way to go before being maximally isolating. Evidence for that would be the fact that many people still say *whom* while many others don't; English hasn't lost its old inflections yet. But this scheme is

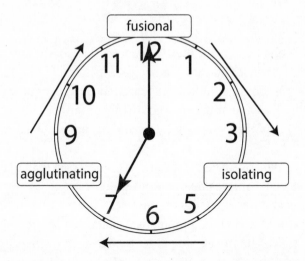

of course a simplification; as we've seen with *gotta*, English is in the process of melding together formerly free words too.

Modern (Mandarin) Chinese is considered a highly analytical language, but it is less so than its predecessor, Classical Chinese. Various bits and pieces have glommed onto Chinese words, once freestanding words, now obligatory endings, like the marker *-men* that turns pronouns plural: *wǒ* is "I", *wǒmen* is "we", *nǐ* is you, *nǐmen* is "you all", and so on. The formerly isolating Chinese is taking on bits of synthetic grammar.

In fact, type-changes between all three types have been fully attested by linguists: isolating to agglutinating, agglutinating to fusional, and fusional to isolating. So has any language completed the full cycle? It may take thousands of years to do so, and writing is only about 5,000 years old, so it is hard to be sure. But the best example available is Egyptian: Old Egyptian had a complex verb structure with suffixes and prefixes, Late Egyptian lost most of these and uses multi-word phrases instead, and Coptic, Egyptian's descendant, has developed complex verbs again.[9] It's the only language we know of to have gone completely around the clock, but if humans have been speaking for a hundred thousand years (we really don't know how long we have, but fifty thousand is considered a low estimate), and writing has been around for only five thousand, it's perfectly plausible that quite a lot more languages have gone that route without our knowing.

*

The clock is one theory. But there is a competing possibility. Namely, some research has found that a language's inflectional morphology – in other words, how synthetic a language tends to be, or how much it relies on prefixes and suffixes rather than word order – decreases as its number of speakers grows. Why would that be? And what would it mean?

First, the evidence. The big languages of the world tend to be more like English and Chinese – lots of word-order restrictions, not a lot of morphological inflection (suffixes, prefixes, "infixes" that go into the middle of words, and other grammatical changes that affect the form of a word itself). The smaller languages tend to be more like Turkish or Spanish; lots of information encoded in inflections. Of course Turkish and Spanish are, by world circumstances, big languages. But one study has found, looking at 2,200 languages, that over a large sweep of the world's languages, the more speakers a language has, the fewer bits and pieces go into morphological inflection, whether number, gender, case, tense or otherwise.[10]

This is an empirical finding, and an impressive one (it took lots of doing to figure out, since it's hard to compare the world's far-flung 7,000 languages). But the fall-off in inflection as a language gets bigger is only a gradual tendency, and nobody knows why it would happen. Here is one hypothesis. The more isolated and small a language is, the more it can afford to hold on to lots of complicated inflection. A small homogenous group will speak a very homogenous variety of the language, meaning children will hear a relatively "clean" version of the same language from a small group of people. They'll therefore learn it without a lot of loss. By contrast, a child who hears a huge variety of different speakers of the mother tongue might slough off the bits that don't seem to be shared, and learn a "least common denominator" form of it.

A second hypothesis has to do with *adult* language learning and spread. Small languages isolated by mountains or jungles will not see many adults learn them. English and Mandarin are learned by lots of adults as second languages, because they are big and important. When adults learn a language, they tend to dispense with bits that don't seem needed – like all of those word endings – and instead rely on other words and contexts to do the same job.

This is possible because much of language is redundant: in *two cars*, the presence of *two* implies multiple cars; why learn the -*s* ending to imply the plural as well? Life is short, and it isn't needed. If the past tense can be marked by some random ending, or by a transparently past-tense word like *yesterday*, why learn the ending at all? Adults find phrasal forms (like *two car, yesterday talk*) easier to pick up than grammatical additions to words (*cars*, *talked*), and they are better at figuring out from the broader conversational context what is meant; if "yesterday" was mentioned a few sentences ago they can infer that we're still talking about the past.[11]

An interesting test of this kind of thing is whether two languages, otherwise very similar genetically, might be different if one is isolated with no neighbours, while another is learned by a larger number of adult speakers, because the language is in constant contact with other languages. It's hard to test – linguists can't run an experiment where they strand a bunch of people on a deserted island for a thousand years and see what happens. But they can look at closely related languages in that situation. Icelandic, for example, has been on an isolated island for a thousand years, while its genetic cousins Danish, Swedish and Norwegian have interacted with each other and other Europeans the whole time. Sure enough, Icelandic, with its 340,000 island-bound speakers, is much more conservative and morphologically complex than the other three big Scandinavian languages, with their 15 million speakers and their millennium of interaction with the rest of Europe. This doesn't mean that Norwegians and Swedes are stupid and lazy, or that Icelanders are keen grammarians with high standards. It just means that Norwegian and Swedish have shed inflections faster than Icelandic.

A contrasting example comes from creole languages. These have typically formed when slave-owners speaking languages like English, Portuguese or French have gathered slaves speaking a variety of different languages, usually African ones. The slaves gathered in these circumstances had to improvise how to communicate with each other and their masters. Over time, their improvised forms – called pidgins by linguists – became regular ones, learned by children as their native language, and now called creoles. Sure enough, creoles are fully expressive and fantastically interesting languages, but ones lacking the beads-on-a-string agglutination of Turkish, or the complex fusional verbal endings of Spanish – more proof that languages commonly learned in adulthood rather than childhood will be less heavily inflected than others.

There is a final interesting wrinkle in the data. Bigger languages tend to have *more*, not less, complex phonological systems; that is, the way words are made from sounds. Language can have anything from about a dozen to more than a hundred different contrasting sounds ("contrasting" meaning that they are used to distinguish words; the different ways "l" is pronounced in English are not contrasting since these are not used to distinguish words.) Hawaiian has an extremely simple sound system, with few possible sounds. Few possible sounds mean that words have to be longer; if you only have a dozen sounds you need more of them to make up the universe of complicated words. If Americans know a word of Hawaiian past *aloha*, it is likely to be *humuhumunukunukuapua'a*, the state fish of Hawaii. Note the simple consonant-vowel-consonant-vowel structure of the word.

English, by contrast, has a fairly large inventory of sounds, more than Hawaiian if not quite at the top of the league. But it is phonologically complex in that, unlike Hawaiian, it tends to cluster together lots of consonants, in words like *strengths*. If English is not your native language, this is hard to say, at nine letters, but just one vowel. (The nine letters make up just seven sounds, though; *th* and *ng* are just one sound each.)

No one knows why big languages are grammatically simpler (at least in terms of morphology – all those endings) and phonologically more complex (Mandarin's tones, English's consonant clusters). But an obvious answer leaps to mind: the complexity has to go somewhere. It might be in the sound system (phonology). It might be in the word-building (morphology). It might be in the sentence structure (syntax). But a language has to have a minimal amount of complexity to do the things that a language does.

*

All of this historical linguistics may seem beside the point to today's

English teacher, say, or a hard-bitten copy-editor. For many such people, by God, *whom* is part of today's standard English, especially in writing, and to use *who* in its place is to make a mistake and to undermine its grammar. The editor in me would fully agree, and correct any such *who* to *whom*; in edited English, *whom* is still the norm. But the fan of historical linguistics in me would stand back with the perspective of a thousand years – admittedly a hard thing to do – and remember that most of the changes that affected English's case system were complete by Shakespeare's time. Fusional English became analytical English, but the bard did pretty well with that analytical English, and so do plenty of writers and speakers today. If *whom* kicks the bucket, that will still be the case.

Languages don't collapse. Not in sound, not in vocabulary, and not in grammar. At all three levels, change can seem (and often is) quite random, a result of people learning in a hurry and without a lot of attention. But the result is never a scrap-heap of unusable language. Everywhere one looks on the face of the earth, at every point in human history, we find nothing but fabulously complex language after fabulously complex language, reflecting the complex needs of a complex species. Some languages will have a bit more of this, and other languages will have a bit more of that. Some single languages will have a bit more of this at one point in their history, and at other points, will have a bit more of that. But we have never found a people that was unable to express things because they didn't take enough care with their conjugations. What we find is the opposite: big, prestigious languages in industrialised countries tend to lose a lot of what Europeans consider "grammar" (all those Latin-style endings), while small, marginal communities tend to keep them, despite living materially simple lives, often on the brink of starvation.

Sounds, words and grammar rules exist as a system, not as a series of unconnected bits and pieces. Though individual changes at any of those levels may be annoying in the short run, the system adapts in the long run, as a result of the ingenuity of its speakers. More fantastic still, those speakers' ingenuity is distributed and uncoordinated. There is no central planning. As language changes, the speakers, without being told to, change their behaviour subtly too, making sure that the language is never left with its needs unmet.

On Twitter, the sidebar to the left of the screen offers a list of other users that you might be interested in, under the banner "Who to follow". For those who feel that keeping *whom* is critical to keeping English expressive and clear, this is a travesty. And such people are nothing if not motivated: there is an extension for Google Chrome that will, for anyone who installs it, turn "Who to follow" into "Whom to follow". The extension has 575 users and a nearly perfect user rating. Its creator is Thomas Steiner, a German systems analyst at Google.

Steiner explained to me via Twitter that his English teachers worked hard to drill *whom* into him, and that it seemed a crime to replace a "historically grown" bit of English grammar with a "miserable *who*". But does he think it is crucial to understanding? In fact, he does not say what I expect him to, that syntax is something that tech people pay special attention to. Instead, he says that many in tech are forgiving of mistakes in English, given how many non-native speakers there are in the field. His browser extension, in the end, was a bit of fun, not an attempt to stand athwart this change in English grammar yelling "stop!"

Languages do change. Some changes really are annoying. But the genius of language, and the humans who use it, is that there's a little bit of Steiner in all of us, trying to express ourselves well. People are creative and energetic, whether in trying to stop a change or in making sure that any one change is ultimately balanced out by another. Languages don't decline, because their speakers just won't stand for it.

5

Language tamers with armies and navies

MY LANGUAGE BOOKSHELVES include a little book, hardly longer than a pamphlet, that bears the dedication "to all Yankees in the hope it will teach them how to talk right". *How to Speak Southern* was written by Steve Mitchell, a columnist at the *Palm Beach Post* from North Carolina, and my parents got it as a gift sometime in the early 1980s when we lived in Atlanta.

It's not what you'd call a great work of dialectology. A lot of its entries are simply "eye-dialect", linguists' terms for using fake spellings that reflect real pronunciations, like "jevver" for "did you ever", and "bleeve" for "believe". But in other ways it's an insightful little look into how people from the southern United States – my home region, and my father's – talk. It may not be highfalutin' linguistics, but it gives a pretty good look into how southerners talk at every level of linguistic organisation, from pronunciation to words to idioms to grammar.

Take pronunciation. The very first entry, "Ah: the thing you see with", highlights "glide-deletion". In words with the *i*-sound found in *rise* and *ride*, most English-speakers pronounce a diphthong, two vowels in quick succession: *ah-ee*. But in the south, *eye* and *ride* lose that second, *-ee* part of the pronunciation (the glide), giving *ah*. The example sentence given in *How To Speak Southern*: "Ah think Ah've got somethin' in mah ah." Other entries highlight the famous southern tendency to do the opposite of glide-deletion, drawing out vowels so that sometimes a single vowel turns into a diphthong: "griyuts", "fayan", "peyun" (*grits*, *fan* and *pen*).

Things get more interesting when it comes to vocabulary. *How to Speak Southern* has a few highly distinctive southern words, like: "arshtaters" for potatoes, or "wenderlight" (window-light) for a pane of glass. Other entries are standard words used in a non-standard way, like "Carry: To convey from one place to another, usually by automobile. 'Can you carry me down to the store in yo' car?'", or "Mash: to press, as in the case of an elevator button." My dad never pressed, but always mashed, a button.

Things get more fun still at the level of idioms or fixed phrases.

Bad to: Inclined toward, prone to. "Johnny's bad to get in fights when he gets drunk."

Comin' up a cloud: An approaching storm. "Stay close to the house. It's comin' up a cloud."

Give up to be: Generally conceded to be. "He's give up to be the crookedest lawyer in the whole state of Mississippi."

Git shed of: To rid oneself of. "That car is costin' me too much money, and Ah'm gonna git shed of it."

How to Speak Southern also lists a southernism that was later to become world-famous. It travelled with southern migrants from the southeast to the southwest, including New Mexico: "Break bad: to behave in a violent, wanton or outrageous manner for no discernible reason. 'Ole Bill broke bad last night and wound up in jail.'"

Southern American English is generally called a dialect, and not just an accent with some funny words, by linguists. What makes it a dialect, and not just a pronunciation? While there's no easy and universally accepted definition, one clear sign is that the differences between two varieties are different dialects, not just different accents, when the differences are systematic and go deep – especially to grammar. And yes, southern English has a lot of grammar differences from the standard kind.

Fixin': Preparing to. "Ahm fixin' to dig me some worms and go fishin'." [In linguistic terms, this is the proximate future: *fixin' to* is used to signal something that will happen in the near future; *going to* can be used for more distant plans, but *fixin' to* cannot.]

Might could: Might possibly. "If you'd invest in real estate you might could make a lot of money." [The "double modal" here is one of a class of dialectal usages that also includes *might oughta* and others. It isn't standard in English, but appears in other Germanic languages like German and Danish.]

Retch: To grasp for: "The right fielder retch over into the stands and caught the ball." [*Reach* was originally irregular in standard English, with past tense forms like *reihte* and *right*, before the regular form *reached* supplanted it. In this southernism *reach* is still irregular.]

Yawl: A useful southern word that is consistently misused by northerners when they try to mimic a southern accent, which they do with appalling regularity. Yawl is always plural because it means you-all, or all of you. It is never – repeat, never – used in reference to only one person. At least not by southerners. "Where yawl goin'?" [The most famous southernism of all, usually spelled *y'all*. After *you*, originally a plural, became a singular as well, a number of dialects created their own second-person-plural pronouns. Some New Yorkers use *youse*, and some Pittsburghers, *yinz*.]

Mitchell may not have been a trained linguist, but he spotted quite a few of the things that make Southern American English what it is, from sound to word to grammar: clearly a dialect, and not just a slightly different way of talking.

One more thing also marks a group of speakers as speaking not just an accent, but a clearly distinct variety of a language, and it is extra-linguistic. The kinds of people who write books like *How to Speak Southern* often see themselves as distinct not just in speech, but in culture and politics, too. And that certainly goes for the South, as you can see from the references to the Civil War that litter *How to Speak Southern*:

Robut E. Lee: The finest gentleman who ever drew breath and the greatest military leader since Julius Caesar and Alexander the Great. "Robut E. Lee didn't surrender. Grant just stole his sword and Lee was too much of a gentleman to ast [sic] him to give it back."

Hale: Where General Sherman is going for what he did to Etlanna [Atlanta]. "General Sherman said 'War is hale', and he made sure it was."

Yankee shot: A southern child's navel. "Momma what's this on my belly?" "That's where the Yankee shot you. That's yo Yankee shot."

For northerners, the Civil War is history; for many southerners, it still defines an identity.

"Dialect" is sometimes a dirty word. Many people think that there's the real version of a language, and then there are dialects. Those dialects then come in for disparaging descriptions like "slang", "patois", "gutter talk", a "bastardised" version of the language, and so on. The underlying assumption seems to be that they are degraded, fallen forms of the real language, which the dialect-speakers are too lazy to master.

This is not the case. Everything is some kind of dialect. The prestige, standard forms of a language just happen to be the dialect that was most important – close to a political centre of power, or with a powerful literary tradition behind it – at a critical period in the language's history. This is usually a combination of the rise of complex states (with their need for written records), the growth in writing and printing, the flourishing of universities, and so on. A standard language is just a dialect that happened to be in the right place at the right time, when these forces contributed to a settling down of one written form of the language. The English this book is written in is the descendant of one of England's many different dialects, but it happens to be one that was spoken in a triangle of important English cities, London, Oxford and Cambridge, at a critical period around the rise of printing.

Most people, when they think about it, are proud of the way they talk, which is exactly why Mitchell wrote *How to Speak Southern* and why someone gave it as a gift to my parents. My southern friends and family don't need a lecture in dialectology or history to have some sense, down deep, of what the linguist says explicitly: that everything is dialect, and that prestige varieties are just dialects too. To southerners, northerners talk funny, and a southerner won't hesitate to say so. Lewis Grizzard, a comedian from Moreland, Georgia, used to intone with mock seriousness: "There remains great chasm of misunderstanding between people from the north and people from the south, and you know what it all boils down to? It boils down to language. Yankees think we talk funny; God talks like we do."

*

But there's a certain kind of language tamer that doesn't find all this quite so funny. From across the Atlantic, another kind of southern speech has been the source of controversy. "Yugoslavia" – literally, the Land of the South (*yug*) Slavs – broke up in a series of wars in the 1990s. Since the breakup, language has been used as something for the former fellow Yugoslavs to bash each other with.

In the days when there was still a Yugoslavia, from the First World War to the 1990s, most of the country spoke a single language that Western linguists called Serbo-Croatian, and locals would often just call *naški*, or "ours". Despite the name, the language was spoken not just by ethnic Serbs and Croats, but by Bosnians and Montenegrins, two of the federation's other nationalities. (The Macedonians and Slovenians speak related languages, but ones distinct from Serbo-Croatian. A minority also spoke Albanian, only distantly related.)

Though there are dialectal differences in Serbo-Croatian – mostly on the level of pronunciation, and a few prominent words, including the months of the year – they were hardly enough to constitute separate languages. Some of the dialect differences within Croatia, in fact, were greater than any between Serbs and Croats. The biggest linguistic difference was not in speech at all, but in writing: Croatians, mostly Catholic, use the Latin alphabet, as do the Muslim Bosnians. Serbians, mostly Eastern Orthodox Christians, use Cyrillic.

After the fall of communism in the rest of eastern Europe, the former Yugoslavia broke up into its constituent republics: Slovenia, Croatia, Serbia, Montenegro, Macedonia and Bosnia-Herzegovina. But Bosnia was fought over between Serbs, Croats and the Muslim Bosnians, achieving piece only as an unstable federation. Finally, Albanian-speaking Kosovo broke away from Serbia, and is now recognised by many Western countries, but not Russia, Serbia and some of their allies.

Since the breakup, nationalists have done their utmost to split the formerly unified language as far apart as possible. Croats declared their national language to be "Croatian", and have busily purged "Serbian" words, even when these are international European words having little to do with Serbia.[1] The Serbians, meanwhile, now call their national language "Serbian", the Bosnians call it "Bosnian", and the Montenegrins call it "Montenegrin". Cigarette packs in Bosnia contain a warning, in "Bosnian", "Croatian" and "Serbian". *Pušenje ubija – Pušenje ubija – Пушење убија*. That last one is Cyrillic for *Pušenje ubija*, or "smoking kills".

Not all former Yugoslavs are ready to give in to the most fevered nationalists in their country, though. In March 2017, 30 linguists issued a "Declaration on the Common Language". They declared the speech of Serbia, Croatia, Bosnia and Montenegro to be a single "polycentric" language, like German, Spanish or English, with slightly varying national standards on a common theme. They didn't proclaim the return of "Serbo-Croatian" or call for reuniting Yugoslavia; they just wanted to acknowledge the obvious unity of Serbo-Croatian as a way to bring the countries closer together again. But the nationalists wouldn't have it. One website headlined its story "Balkan Esperanto To Extinguish Serbian Language". A Serbian professor of literature at the University of Belgrade declared the initiative an underhanded attempt to "denationalise" ethnic Serbs in the neighbour republics; that is, to make them feel less Serbian. The Croatian president said that the common language had died with Yugoslavia. Not to be outdone, a far-right Croatian nationalist called it "a wolf howl of Yugoslav nationalists for their lost country".[2] A declaration of the obvious was now fighting words. Many refused to read it. The Croatian prime minister said "Who in Croatia can support it?" Months later, the answer was in: thousands of people, tired of nationalist posturing, in all the republics.

*

People who classify and count languages can be broadly categorised as lumpers or splitters. Lumpers, looking at the linguistic facts of Yugoslavia, would insist that there is still a single language, despite the re-naming. (They'd probably also lump Macedonian in with Bulgarian, to the great irritation of the Macedonians.) Splitters observe the fine distinctions, would take account of what the people themselves say and believe, and would be more inclined to grant separate-language status to similar varieties.

The same exercise can be repeated in many other parts of the world; are the Scandinavian languages dialects of a single language (the lumper position) or separate languages? What about Hindi and Urdu? Galician and Portuguese? Moldovan and Romanian? On the most commonly used linguistic criterion – can the speakers understand each other reasonably well? – most of these would be lumped, not split.

The splitters, on the other hand, could have a field day splitting many recognised "languages". Swiss German and other dialects (Bavarian and Swabian, say) cannot be understood by Germans who speak only High German. Italian, too, is split into widely varying "dialects" that most linguists would classify as separate languages. Movies like *Gomorrah*, an international success in Neapolitan dialect, come with subtitles in Italian so that Italians in the rest of the country can understand them.

It's all in good fun in the Italys and Germanys of the world, where language differences are the subject of jokes and an acknowledged source of cherished diversity. But it's when countries come into existence, change their borders or otherwise feel threatened that language nationalists decide it's time to knock it off with the diversity and ensure a single, unified and prestigious standard. Things get ugly from there.

To speak the language of your choice is a human right, widely acknowledged. The Universal Declaration of Human Rights bans discrimination on account of language, and says that everyone is entitled to the realisation of the "economic, *cultural* and *social* rights indispensable for his dignity and the free development of his personality". If any cultural and social right is indispensable for the free development of a personality, it must surely be the language of one's choosing. Other human-rights documents, like the European Charter for Regional or Minority Languages, are even more explicit. The ECRML states that "the right to use a regional or minority language in private and public life is an inalienable right."

But in the real world – especially the real world of countries on the map with borders, governments, armies and education systems – the right to speak what you want, where and when, comes into conflict with a cherished goal of political language tamers: tidy nation-states, in which one language is singled out as national or official, and is owed protection and promotion. Indeed, the European charter, just after declaring the right to minority languages an "inalienable right", says that "the protection and encouragement of regional or minority languages should not be to the detriment of the official languages and the need to learn them."

National languages make a kind of sense; how is a country to function if its people don't understand each other? And yet, despite a one-country one-language Platonic ideal in many peoples' minds, official language policy around the world is a confusing patchwork of national policy, regional policy, or ministerial policy (located in the education ministry, for example), and unofficial practices. Hence the desire of the political language tamer to clean things up, if possible naming a single language for the country and giving that declaration force.

Of the nearly 200 countries in the world, as of 2000, just about 100 of them named a language or languages as official or national in their constitutions.[3] (The distinction between "official" and "national" is a fuzzy one.) Yet naming a language in the constitution makes a surprisingly small difference on the ground. The three biggest English-speaking countries – Britain, America and Australia – all lack any constitutional recognition of English. Canada and Ireland recognise English in their constitutions, but that's because both also recognise a second official language: French in Canada and Irish in Ireland. (In fact, in Ireland, Irish is, at least, rhetorically privileged, in Article 8 of the constitution: "The Irish Language as the national language is *the first* official language. The English language is recognised as *a second* official language."[4]) South Africa recognises English, Afrikaans and nine African languages as official. Most unusually among the big Anglophone countries, New Zealand gives two languages official status: Maori and New Zealand Sign Language, but not English.

Needless to say, English dominates public life in all of these countries, regardless of whether it's in the constitution or not. No declaration can change the facts on the ground. Witness Ireland, where the "national" and "first official" language, Irish, is spoken natively only by a small minority of the population, and learned only grudgingly by much of the English-speaking majority. Or witness South Africa, where all 11 languages are in theory equal, but where one – English – easily dominates the rest on the official level, despite being spoken by just under 10% of the population at home.

So language policy, if it is to mean anything on the ground, has to be more than a declaration that "so-and-so is the official language". It has to mean action: especially official use by the organs of the state (governments, police, courts), and money for teaching it to children. In some cases, language policy also means action, whether by commission or intentional neglect, to discourage or even suppress the use of other languages.

Coercive language policy is generally a bad thing, insofar as coercion generally goes against the idea of personal as well as national self-determination. But it's also true that the nation, and the nation-state, is a pretty reasonable way to organise people. Humans have a natural, and not always bigoted, desire to share a community with those like them, and that includes things like religion, culture, and yes, language. It isn't unreasonable for a state to foster a sense of belonging through a shared language.

But there is a further complication. Throughout history, borders have moved around people, bringing them into new states they had no desire to join. More recently, large numbers of people have decided to move across borders. That means that today, the average state is actually home to quite a few more languages than people tend to realise. There is hardly a linguistically homogenous state to be found anywhere. Only island states like Iceland and Japan come close, and even those countries have immigrants. (And in the case of Japan, there is also Ainu, a tiny indigenous language with a vanishing cohort of elderly speakers.) The monolingual nation-state is an ideal that countries never quite reach. This means that nearly all countries must find some way of accommodating both diversity on one hand and the desire to make workable countries on the other. It's much easier said than done.

*

Politics is about power, and so the best way of thinking about the politics of language might be looking at powerful languages as compared to smaller ones fighting for respect and their own patch of ground. What do speakers of prestigious majority languages owe to speakers of small ones? How should countries with several comparably strong languages be organised? What should countries do about languages that are dominant in one area but spoken by only a minority of the country as a whole? What about dying languages, even dead ones, trying to get back on their feet?

The first – but not the last – word in language tamers and state-building must be to look at the history of big languages running roughshod over little ones in their home states. For centuries, this is what language policy – if "policy" is the right word, went: the dominant language snuffed out small indigenous languages here and crushed dialect diversity there, in the name of building cohesive nation-states.

Language was nobody's primary concern while the big European states were being built. Elites were multilingual and married across borders to cement alliances in their jockeying for power. States grew, in the prototypical case, from the core out: a kingdom centred on Paris gradually getting control of the whole territory of France, a Spain gradually reconquering territory from the Muslims and then consolidating its grip on the Iberian peninsula, and so on. There was no need to bring the emotions of ordinary, poor people into the state-building project; their military service was forced or bought, not inspired by patriotism.

Everyone knew that languages didn't correspond with national borders, after all. People in much of western Europe spoke a version of late vulgar Latin they simply called something like *romanz*. When Dante, around 1305, wrote a defence of using the spoken vernacular rather than Latin for writing, he looked more closely at how people spoke these Romance tongues. In *De vulgari eloquentia* (written, tellingly, in Latin) he refers to "our language", apparently meaning all Latin-derived ones, before going on to describe three "parts": the language of *oïl* in the north of France, for the local word for *yes*, the language of *oc* in the south of France, and the language of *si*, which is to say, Italian. The modern national linguistic boundaries were still off in the future; for Dante the much more vivid linguistic units were the dialects of various Italian cities and regions, of which he takes a delightfully catty tour.

For what the Romans speak is not so much a vernacular as a vile jargon, the ugliest of all the languages spoken in Italy; and this should come as no surprise, for they also stand out among all Italians for the ugliness of their manners and their outward appearance ... After these let us prune away the inhabitants of the Marches of Ancona, who say "Chignamente state siaté"; [be as you are] and along with them we throw out the people of Spoleto. Nor should I fail to mention that a number of poems have been composed in derision of these three peoples; After these let us root out the Milanese, the people of Bergamo, and their neighbours; I recall that somebody has written a derisive song about them too ... After these let us pass through our sieve the people of Aquileia and Istria, who belch forth "Ces fas-to?" [What are you up to?] with a brutal intonation. And along with theirs I reject all languages spoken in the mountains and the countryside, by people like those of Casentino and Fratta, whose pronounced accent is always at such odds with that of city-dwellers. As for the Sardinians, who are not Italian but may be associated with Italians for our purposes, out they must go, because they alone seem to lack a vernacular of their own, instead imitating gramatica as apes do humans: for they say "domus nova" [my house] and "dominus meus" [my master].

No wonder people were not yet ready to fight for the idea of the nation-state with its single language. If you lived in Italy you didn't live in "Italy", but a region or a city-state with a compelling local identity. If you lived in the south of France, you didn't live in France; you just lived in "oc country" (now known by that name, Languedoc).

But following the French revolution, which spread ideas of liberty and self-determination to the masses, nationalism became a compelling way to get the peasants soldiering with spirit. This meant creating states that felt like families or villages writ large, and that meant homogenising out inconvenient bits of local diversity. The revolutionaries took a census of the local languages, finding a shockingly shallow knowledge of standard French; only a quarter of the population could speak it fluently, according to a census by the Abbé Grégoire, undertaken on behalf of the revolutionaries. For them, the spreading of (Parisian standard) French was crucial to the spread of enlightenment.

France was notoriously successful at suppressing its regional languages – Catalan, Basque, Occitan/Provençal, Flemish – as an explicit policy of its post-revolutionary governments. But the other growing nation-states did much the same. A key tool was the fledgling education system, in which children were humiliated out of using their local languages, often forced to wear some kind of token of shame if they were caught speaking them.

The next wave of linguistic steamrollers got going when the European powers started colonising much of the rest of the world. The United States, born out of a set of English colonies, warred with, forcibly relocated, and finally corralled on reservations the Native Americans it found on its ever-growing territory. Few of these groups were big enough to hold on to their languages. Much the same went on in Canada and Australia, with a twist; they also pursued policies of taking indigenous people out of their communities and placing them with white families to "civilise" them, inevitably resulting in the loss of their languages. In Africa, the French successfully imposed French on the large swathes they colonised. The British were more content to let their African colonial subjects continue to use their languages, but the elites learned English anyway, and speak it still today. The Spaniards, for a time, privileged some big indigenous *lenguas generales* (general languages) in their American colonies, the better to preach to the locals the wonders of Christianity. But over time, Spanish came to dominate the world that Spain conquered from California to Tierra del Fuego, as Spanish came to be associated with Christianity and with civilisation itself.

Nor was it just European powers that spread their languages by conquest. The earlier expansion of Islam, after its rise in seventh-century Arabia, spread Arabic from Morocco to Iraq, eventually pushing local languages like Coptic and Berber to the fringes. Christianity has always had a translating tradition, trying to win new believers by spreading the gospel in whatever local language would work best. Not so Islam, which has always insisted on the original Arabic of the Koran.

The spread of a powerful Chinese state over a large territory in East Asia was another variant still, abetted by the unusual case of a stable classical written language. This standard classical Chinese was used across a large territory where spoken "dialects" differed (and still differ) enough to make most Western linguists consider them separate languages. Nonetheless, one spoken variety, Mandarin, came to dominate northern China, on its way to becoming the biggest language in the world by number of speakers.

This is the world that was; if you could get away with doing something to increase your territory and power, which often meant the spread of your language too, you did it. Today, conquest and linguistic imperialism are bad form: most states avoid it and those that do it have to pretend they don't. America no longer shames American Indians out of speaking their languages, though it does little to support them. France tolerates the effort to breathe life back into Breton and Provencal/ Occitan, and signs in Catalan and Basque in the south, though a bit sullenly. (In 1990 it added "the language of the republic is French" to the constitution, and in 2015 the Senate blocked an amendment to the constitution that would let France ratify the European Charter for Regional or Minority Languages.) Spain has given extensive autonomy to the Galician-, Basque- and Catalan-speaking parts of the country, but this has hardly defused the language issue there, as we'll see in a moment.

Even non-democracies know that they should pay lip-service to the idea of tolerating minority languages. Chinese currency contains writing in Chinese, Uighur, Tibetan, Mongolian and Zhuang. But in practice, China is doing its best to spread Mandarin to the full extent of its territory and population. It is heavily settling Han Chinese into Tibet and Xinjiang (home of the Muslim Uighurs), to help sinify the population there, and Uighur activists claim that it is even transferring tens of thousands of Uighur girls to factories on the east coast.[5]

China is also pushing hard to encourage the use of Mandarin by the hundreds of millions of Han Chinese who speak a non-Mandarin variety like Cantonese or Shanghainese. These are as different from Mandarin as the Romance languages are from one another. But education is in Mandarin, by law, and broadcasters have to apply for special permission to broadcast in other languages. Knowledge of Shanghainese is now estimated to be below 50% in Shanghai, both because young Shanghainese are neglecting to learn the language, and because migrants from other parts of China are moving to the city. Because they do not speak Shanghainese, the locals are forced to speak Mandarin with them.

Cantonese, a bigger language, and farther from the Mandarin homeland, is more self-aware and secure. But this just means that many Cantonese-speakers resent the pressure to speak Mandarin all the more. In 2010, the local authorities publicly suggested raising the percentage of Mandarin used on one of the local television stations; tens of thousands turned out in the streets to protest the decision. The central state authorities insisted that they were trying to promote Mandarin, not sideline Cantonese. The protestors wondered why that didn't mean setting up a new Mandarin station rather than changing the ratios on a primarily Cantonese one.

In 2014 the education bureau in Hong Kong, where Cantonese is spoken, caused a furore by declaring that Cantonese was not an official language. The Basic Law of the province declared "Chinese" (and English) official languages. When the Basic Law was written (while Hong Kong was under British rule), the only variety of spoken Chinese with any claim to be "the" Chinese spoken in Hong Kong was Cantonese, not Mandarin. But the issue is confused by the fact that the written Chinese of Hong Kong, as in the rest of China, is a standard based on Mandarin. In any case, in the resulting backlash against the seeming slight to Cantonese, the education bureau sheepishly removed the offending text from its website.

*

It seems, then, that heavy-handed language bullying is passing out of fashion in states that want to have the respect of the rest of the world. The countries that want to get away with it cannot do it to culturally confident people who are able to join in protest (like Cantonese-speakers). They can best get away with it when the victims are isolated and poor and hardly able to get their protests heard (like the Uighurs).

Many of the states of Europe have big linguistic minorities, and many of those minorities in turn have states that speak their language nearby: there are Hungarian-speakers in Romania, German-speakers in Italy, Danish-speakers in Germany, and so on. Some of these minorities have come to comfortable arrangements, the Danish–German border area being a particularly admirable example of each group making reasonable accommodations of the other. Some of these situations fester and cause frustration on all sides, as was the case with the Hungarian-speakers in Romania.

These are long-running, mostly stable situations, for better or worse. But given people's passionate attachment to their languages, it is obvious that a sudden, surprising and unwelcome change to the status of a language – especially with a big neighbour that speaks that language next door – would be a particularly unwise move, like throwing a cigarette end in the general direction of a sign reading "NO SMOKING; JET FUEL". And yet that's exactly what happened in the former Ukraine, where disputes over language became proxies for who had the right to run Ukraine. A language dispute helped spark the civil war that dragged in neighbouring Russia, and resulted in Russia's annexation of Crimea.

The Soviet Union encouraged citizens to move around its constituent republics for various political reasons, including diluting the non-Russian nationalities with Russians. When the sudden end of the Soviet Union came in 1991, many Russian-speakers found themselves in newly independent republics, where the new titular nations – Estonians in Estonia, Lithuanians in Lithuania, Uzbeks in Uzbekistan, and so on – now expected to be running their own affairs, and in their own languages.

Ukraine was a special case. It is intimately intertwined with Russia historically, and its language is closely related to (but clearly distinct from) Russian. So naturally a large number of Russian-speakers lived in the newly independent country. Most ethnic Ukrainians spoke Russian, though not all ethnic Russians in the country spoke Ukrainian. To muddle the picture, there are ethnic Ukrainians who speak Russian as a first or preferred language, and many people simply pragmatically speak whichever language makes sense in a given situation.

But after 1991 Ukraine, like many of the other post-Soviet republics, promoted its language as part of the nation-building project, including in education, in the civil service, and so on. When I visited in the country in 1998 I was hopeful that my Russian would make travel reasonably easy, only to find that many people insisted on replying to me in Ukrainian, even when it was obvious that they spoke Russian. Ukraine's independence day fell during that trip, and I will always remember elderly patriotic Ukrainians solemnly singing nationalist songs in Ukrainian in a square in Lviv,[6] in the western heartlands of Ukrainian nationalism.

Russia did its best to dominate Ukraine's post-Soviet politics, supporting candidates that would promise to keep the country close to Russia. In 2012, the national government upgraded the status of Russian in the southern and eastern regions where it was most widely spoken, declaring it official alongside Ukrainian there. The debate over the bill caused a fistfight in the parliament (admittedly a common occurrence in the Rada, Ukraine's parliament). The president at the time was the pro-Russian Viktor Yanukovych, who had won office in 2010. Yulia Timochenko, angling to become the face of Ukrainian nationalism, called the new law a "crime against the state".

Then Yanukovych was deposed in 2014, amid accusations of corruption, during a standoff between pro-Russian and pro-Western forces. The new parliament, though, quickly made an unforced error: its very first act was to reverse the 2012 law on the status of Russian. Though the new president later vetoed the reversal, the fire was lit. Deputies have been forcibly stopped from giving speeches in Russian in the Rada, which became ever more prone to brawls – violence being what people do to protect their rights and honour when they don't trust the authorities to do the protecting for them. Vladimir Putin eagerly seized on the "proof" that the new government was trying to eradicate Russian culture in Ukraine, and took the opportunity to play the champion of Russian-speakers everywhere. Russia intervened in what was becoming a civil war, as verbal hostilities turned into armed ones.

Russian apologists have often portrayed Ukrainian nationalism as "fascist", selectively noting things like the Nazis' assembling of an SS brigade during the Second World War consisting of anti-Russian Ukrainians. But while there are of course extreme nationalists on the Ukrainian side, there are goons everywhere. There is a quiet, emotional Ukrainian patriotism that is as deep and genuine as any other in the world.

Nonetheless, the sudden downgrade of Russian's status in Ukraine came at the worst possible moment. Any Ukrainian state trying to disentangle itself from Russia in 2014 would still have had to come to terms with a large Russian-speaking population within its borders. Designing just the right accommodations for the Russian language while guaranteeing the primacy of Ukrainian would have taken a deft touch at the best of times. But the Ukrainian nationalists approached a situation calling for a scalpel with a wild swing of the axe.

*

The Ukrainians were not completely irrational to worry about Russian-speakers carving out a separatist bloc in Ukraine. In such divided countries, it's true, political scientists and liberals often preach regional autonomy and federalism. This is so that local minorities who can't see their preferences win out at the national level can at least see them through on their home turf. Give the minority a regional government, goes the theory, with control over education, policing, culture and so forth, and many of the grievances will fade away. Some form of federalism like that may still be the best solution for Ukraine, where the conflict continues at the time of this writing.

But local autonomy is no cure-all. In language policy, solutions like this, by design, make a national minority into a local majority with its own government. This, in turn, can lead both language groups to feel insecure and hard done by. One of the world's most successful bilingual countries – and one of its most successful countries, period – shows that it is hard to be bilingual even with decent constitutional arrangements and a strong foundation of goodwill.

Canada has a reputation among foreigners as boring, which is unfair. (Given the dozens of Canadian comedians and comic actors who've made it in America, with about a ninth of America's population, it's quite possible that the boringness-per-capita ratio is higher south of the border.) But Canada's language policy, in any case, is anything but boring: it has fascinated students of the subject, for its vast transformation of the linguistic facts on the ground. That transformation has been peaceful, but it continues to irritate many Canadians – of both big languages – on a daily basis.

France lost the French and Indian war – known as the Seven Years' War in Europe – and as a result, New France became the English dominion of Canada. Canada went on to sprawl across the continent, adding new provinces and becoming a confederation in 1867. English-speakers would dominate the vast territory. Francophones remained a minority, though they would dominate "Lower Canada", which became the province of Quebec, and many wound up in the provinces of Ontario and New Brunswick, too.

A century or so after confederation, English utterly dominated the public life of Quebec, despite the fact that native Anglophones were a small minority, mostly concentrated in Montreal. Business and finance were overwhelmingly conducted in English: in 1965, 80% of employers were English-speaking, and Francophones earned a third less than Anglophones.[7] Public signage could make casual visitors think they were in any other part of Canada.

But in the 1960s, Quebecers became politically engaged, first throwing off provincial conservatism and the influence of the Catholic Church in the so-called "Quiet Revolution". In 1976, for the first time, the province elected a government headed by Quebec nationalists, the Parti Québécois, who promised a vote on sovereignty for Quebec (in an "association" with Canada). The proposition put to Quebecers in 1980 was defeated, with 60% of those voting choosing to reject sovereignty. (The great majority of Anglophone Quebecers voted against it.) Having failed with sovereignty, in 1977, the Parti Québécois started the process of transforming Quebec linguistically by passing the famous – and for many Anglophones, infamous – Law 101, the Charter of the French Language, remaking the linguistic lay of the land in Quebec.

A 1973 law had made French the official language of the province. But as we've seen, such declarations can be meaningless. The 1977 Charter went much further, grabbing the levers of state power to make sure that the change was reflected on the ground. The language of government and economic life was to become French in fact, not just theory. The language of the provincial parliament and courts was declared to be French. (English-speakers could request translation.) Employers' communications to workers, and job advertisements, were required to be in French. No worker could be denied a job for being a French monolingual, unless the employer could prove a foreign language was necessary.

The bill was explicitly aimed at changing the linguistic demographics of the province. Children would be required to go to school in French unless at least one of their parents had been educated in English in Quebec, to ensure that as many as possible of the province's future adults would be at least fluently bilingual in French, and wherever possible, French-dominant. (All children in French-medium schools would continue learning English as a foreign language, though.)

Perhaps most symbolically, the Charter created what Anglophone Canadians came to loathe as the "language police": the Office Québécois pour la Langue Française (OQLF). The OQLF was charged with making sure that the law took effect, by for example making sure that menus, product instructions, ingredient lists and the like were in French. Public signage was to be "predominantly" in French, which required the French be significantly larger than the English. OQLF officials measuring the size of letters on signs became a hated symbol of the policy for irritated Anglophones. Another rule requires shop assistants to greet customers first in French, no matter the employee's first language. This often leads Anglophone customers to reply in French, leaving two Anglophones awkwardly conversing in French before one of them finally realises and switches languages.

In 2013, the OQLF (which has the right to issue fines, after giving warnings) warned an upmarket Italian restaurant in Montreal for using *pasta*, *antipasti* and *calamari* on the menu, rather than French equivalents such as *pâtes*. Massimo Lecas, uncowed, went public with his annoyance on Twitter, in an affair that became known as "Pastagate". Other business owners began venting their own stories, such as a brasserie owner who was asked to cover the "redial" button on his phone and the "on-off" label on the microwave.[8] Pastagate, according to one study, got 60 times more international press coverage than a foreign trip by Quebec's premier (equivalent to the governor of an American state), Pauline Marois, trying to drum up investment in Quebec.

In the fracas, the head of the OQLF was eventually forced to resign, and the government minister responsible for the office announced that its mandate would be loosened. In the future, she said, OQLF officials would be allowed to apply discretion, looking to see whether anyone was actually harmed by the lack of French, or if the matter was of interest to the general public. Sensible exceptions would be made for culinary and other cultural items.

But the beat of negative press coverage has continued. In 2016, La Mama Grilled Cheese, which sold the eponymous melty sandwich, was told to remove the word "enjoy" from its sign, and to call the sandwich a *fromage fondant*, even though most Quebecers call it a "grilled cheese" (or *grille cheese*) when speaking French. Also in 2016, a pub owner was asked to replace the 3-inch-by-3-inch "Recommended on TripAdvisor" sticker in the bottom corner of a window. The lessons learned from "Pastagate", it seems, were not remembered.

Decades of this kind of thing have made Quebec world-famous. For Anglophone Canadians, and for the large number of Quebecers who speak a third language and prefer English to French, this is all preposterous hair-splitting and time-wasting. In a decent democracy, a sensible principle is that people should be left to their own linguistic choices in private business.

But many other countries have taken inspiration from Quebec. They are trying to reverse the gradual switch of their entire population from one language to another, which happens as a result of conquest or other domination. Countries like Ireland, where revival efforts came too late to increase the number of native speakers, are a cautionary tale of what happens if language shift isn't addressed soon enough. So for many, Quebec's policy is a model achievement, not heavy-handed bullying. Places from Wales to Catalonia to the Baltic Republics have taken note of the results of Law 101.

That's because, in short, the law has worked. Though modified repeatedly by Quebec's parliament, either willingly, or grudgingly after adverse rulings by Canada's courts, Quebec is, today, dominated by French, publicly as it always was privately. Crossing the provincial border from east or west or the American border from the south now immediately gives the impression of entering another country.

That is partly because Anglophones, many of them highly educated, voted with their feet, leaving the province for other parts of Canada, along with some businesses that relocated their headquarters. The numbers bear out how much has changed. In the province as a whole, the proportion of schoolchildren with English as a mother tongue has fallen by a third, from 12% in 1976 to 8% in 2015. On the island of Montreal (including the city and some outlying towns), the stronghold of English in Quebec, those proportions fell from 26% to 19%.

They also changed the teaching itself. In the old school system, Anglophones and immigrants could freely choose whether to get schooling in English or French. Now the presumption is that French is the norm.[9] The proportion of pupils getting their education in French on the island of Montreal rose from 60.9% to 80%. Once, most immigrants coming to Montreal were educated in English; now the overwhelming majority, given no choice, are educated in French. Interestingly, the proportion of Anglophone natives going to school in French has also increased, from 8% in 1976 to 28% in 2015.[10] Many have done so because they know that staying in Quebec and thriving fully now requires a knowledge of French.

A Catalan nationalist once told me, "If a language is not indispensable, it is dispensable." Most such quotable quotes are misleadingly simple, but this bit of logic is true by definition. The Quebec nationalists have tried to do much as the Catalans have done: making their language, though a minority language nationally, indispensible in their region.

The success in reversing French's decline in Quebec is all the more startling given the global trends. French in Quebec is not only an island surrounded by a sea of English in North America. It is an island in a rising ocean of English globally. In the exact decades in question, from the 1970s to the 2010s, English has gone from being the world's most popular foreign language to the indispensible language of jet-setters and high-fliers, business executives, researchers and tourists everywhere.

The Quebec government has bucked that trend, and with, of all languages, French, widely thought to have lost its cachet as a crucial language of diplomacy and culture as France's global influence has waned. The key to this improbable turnaround for French in Quebec seems to have been a willingness to use methods that outsiders, and many Quebec citizens (some Francophones included), find unnecessarily coercive. It is hard to imagine mere suggestions having done the trick.

Quebec pulled this off with a strategy similar to that used in Catalonia – and in contrast to the fading fortunes of many minority languages around the world. The key is a federal system of government, with largely autonomous regions able to make much local policy for themselves. When Catalan nationalists took power in the autonomous region of Catalonia, created after Francisco Franco's death in 1975, they pushed harder and harder to restore the prominence of Catalan in the province. Nationalists in Quebec did the same. Wales has had some success restoring the fortunes of Welsh, not least because devolution in the 1990s has allowed Wales some autonomy in education policy.

Compare many other minority languages in Western democracies: Frisian in the Netherlands, Sorbian in Germany, Sami in Scandinavia, and so on. They lack French's global size and prestige (which, despite a decline relative to English, is still one of the world's most prestigious languages). But what Catalonia shows is that global power isn't needed to reverse the fortunes of a language. Local power will do much of the job. And it is precisely that kind of thing that power centralisers fear in national capitals when thinking about whether to devolve power to local regions.

Quebec is still part of Canada. It held another referendum on sovereignty in 1995, in which the "no" vote prevailed by a narrow 50.58%. Had Francophone Quebecers not been allowed to take their cultural future into their own hands with measures like Law 101, it's easy to imagine the vote going the other way. As it stands 60% of Francophones voted for sovereignty, a number that could well have been much higher.

Catalonia remains within Spain, uneasily, after an illegal referendum and failed attempt to declare independence in 2017. Some outsiders are surprised that Catalonia has pushed independence as hard as it has; the province has already gone a long way towards cultural autonomy, making Catalan a necessary part of living there, though not as far as Quebec has done with French. (It is possible to live in Barcelona, especially, speaking only Spanish. It is virtually impossible knowing only Catalan.) Catalan nationalists want a guarantee that whatever happens, their future is in their hands, not Madrid's. If the fallout from the failed independence bid is a rollback of Catalonia's autonomy, independence fever is almost certain to grow.

Catalonia and Quebec share an unusual situation: in the region, speakers of French and Catalan feel surrounded and poorly treated by speakers of the bigger national language, English and Spanish. But at the same time, both regions have local minorities who are members of the national majority: speakers of Spanish in Catalonia and of English in Quebec. English-speakers in Quebec, and Spanish-speakers in Catalonia, cannot freely educate their children in the family language, and in some cases cannot even get access to public services like health care in their language. In other words, it's a situation in which virtually everyone can be forgiven for feeling aggrieved. And history shows how explosive such grievances can be. Hitler claimed to be standing up for German-speakers in Czechoslovakia's Sudetenland; Vladimir Putin says he is sticking up for Russian-speakers in Ukraine. (And countries like Estonia and Latvia with large Russian-speaking minorities are rightly nervous that their countries could be the next places where Putin will intervene on behalf of local Russian-speakers.)

Federalism and minority rights must be delicately managed, and the arrangements occasionally updated. Even then, it is still no guarantee against separatism. Federalism may be expensive and complicated: duplicate parliaments, lawmaking authority shared between local and national government, and so on. But it's a lot cheaper than policies almost guaranteed to break up the country.

*

If speakers of a regional minority language like Welsh or Catalan feel threatened, speakers of even smaller languages have even more urgent reasons to worry. Like species, most of the languages that have ever existed have already become extinct, many without any trace at all. And they continue to become extinct today, especially small languages living close to big languages. They don't die by being wiped out by conquest anymore; they die when speakers gradually, generation to generation, stop passing on the small language and start learning the big one, usually a more economically valuable one. When the last native speaker of the small language dies, the rule goes, that's it – though some words and phrases of the language may linger, there will never again be native speakers.

There is one famous exception: the revival of Hebrew in Palestine, well before the creation of the state of Israel in 1948. Before 1900, Jews learned to read Hebrew so that they could read the Torah, pray in the language and keep a symbolic connection to the ancient Israelites. But nobody spoke the language day-to-day; the world's Jews were scattered between countries and spoke the prevailing languages of the places they lived, plus Jewish languages and dialects like Yiddish and Ladino. Then a passionate Zionist named Eliezer Ben-Yehuda led a revival movement, modernising the language, and encouraging parents to speak it exclusively to their children. The improbable dream came true. Today, Hebrew is a vibrant living language in Israel.

Many a language patriot has dreamed of doing the same with other extinct languages. American Indian tribes, armed with dictionaries and recordings of their languages – which activists like to call "dormant" rather than dead – have tried to get adults to use bits and pieces of the language, and read newly created children's books to the little ones to get them reading.

One notable example in America is Myaamia, also called Miami, the tribe after which Miami University of Ohio is named. There, a tribal activist named Daryl Baldwin has led what is probably America's most advanced revival movement. It is an uphill struggle. Baldwin counts many learners and supporters, but no fluent native speakers yet. His own son Jarrid grew up in the revival movement, surrounded by as much Myaamia as Daryl could give him. He considers himself a native speaker – but not a fluent one. Daryl plaintively tells me that the focus on fluency will make what progress the Myaamia movement has made easy to dismiss. It is incredibly hard to create fluent speakers without any to start with; Daryl says getting to that point will be the work of generations.

The Summer Institute of Linguistics, a Christian group, keeps the world's best catalogue of the world's 7,000-odd languages, called "Ethnologue". According to this gold-standard guide, nine are "reviving". In each case, Ethnologue's description reads the same way: "No known L1 speakers, but emerging L2 speakers". In other words, nobody speaks these as a native language (L1) but there are people learning to speak it as a foreign language (L2). But out of the gaze of the linguists at Ethnologue, in a corner of southwestern England, one language has managed to move past that status, and has achieved the improbable feat of having a tiny few fluent native speakers, after having been dead for a century or more. Its improbable heroes include two fathers who taught themselves a dead language, and then stubbornly spoke nothing but that language to their children.

Cornwall is one of the six traditional Celtic nations, along with Scotland, Ireland, Wales, the Isle of Man and Brittany. It retains a strong sense of local pride and identity, but its language, Cornish, died out some time in the 19th century. Cornish had had its heyday: the language probably reached its peak in number of speakers in the 13th century. Cornish literature included three Christian mystery plays, and a series of homilies translated into Cornish by a man called John Tregear. But already by Tregear's time, in the mid-16th century, knowledge of Cornish was starting to decline. He seems to have inserted many English words into his text while working quickly: "Ima an *profet* Dauit in peswar vgans ha nownsag *psalme* ow *exortya* oll an bobyll the ry *prayse* hag *honor*." It's hard to know which words Tregear didn't know, and which ones by then had been borrowed fully into Cornish from English. But the influence of the bigger language was obvious, and influence was soon to give way to dominance.

Cornwall was late to accept Henry VIII's English reformation, and to add insult to injury, the crown insisted on replacing the local prayerbook with an English one. Never mind that the Catholic Cornish had previously prayed in Latin; the imposition of English sparked an armed revolt. But the "prayerbook rebellion" was beaten back, and the territory where Cornish was spoken gradually retreated southwest down the narrowing peninsula. In 1777, the last known native speaker, Dolly Pentreath, died, and symbolically, the language did with it. Enthusiasts believe that the language continued in scattered use for some time among farmers and fishermen, but at some unknown point, that too was gone.

In 1904, though, Henry Jenner published a handbook of the Cornish language. His intention was not to teach people to read the classics of the literature in a dead language, he explained, but to get Cornish living and breathing again. But the movement remained on the intellectual fringes until the 1970s, when many small nationalisms – among them Breton in France and Basque in Spain – began to revive. Cornish enthusiasts began to learn the language more earnestly (though the movement was seriously distracted by a seemingly endless dispute over which of several new spelling systems should be adopted).

Among those enthusiasts were two who did what Eliezer Ben-Yehuda had done with Hebrew, raising their children to be the first native speakers in a very long time, by speaking nothing but Cornish to them. One was Ray Chubb, a soft-spoken proponent of Cornish who, after teaching himself the language from books, hosted weekly gatherings of Cornish-speakers at his house to work on spoken fluency. At some point he realised that he didn't want his young sons to be shut out of the proceedings, and began speaking exclusively to them in Cornish. To this day, they speak nothing else with their father, who in modestly telling me the story does not seem to realise the startling nature of his achievement. The boys themselves aren't interested in speaking to the press, he says, perhaps not realising themselves just what a rarity they are.

Tim Saunders, a poet, writes in Welsh, Breton and Irish, but his greatest passion is for Cornish. Like Chubb with his sons, Saunders raised his daughters by speaking nothing but Cornish to them, while their mother spoke Welsh. The two girls had no idea they were among the only living native speakers of the language. Today they are musicians, having been in the pop group The Pipettes together. Gwenno was the first to go on to a solo career, and she has recorded an entire sci-fi album in Cornish. She speaks mostly Welsh to her son, but reads to him in Cornish, and his grandfather, Tim, speaks only Cornish to him. Gwenno says her father made Cornish live and breathe with "an endless amount of stories and songs for us" growing up. But raising her son today, she wishes she had more than stories and songs; television programmes and smartphone apps would make a huge difference for a rising generation that gets most of its entertainment from screens.

In 2002, Britain agreed to accept Cornish as a protected language under the European Charter for Regional or Minority languages. The charter requires governments to support teaching and other efforts to promote languages listed on an official schedule. A small amount of money flowed from the government in London to a few public and private bodies in Cornwall, who spent it training teachers, developing written material and an audio learning program, and so on.

The money was a pittance – £150,000 (about $220,000) a year – but it meant several jobs for people fighting full-time for Cornish, and official recognition for the first time in the history of the British state. Then, in 2016, the British government, looking to balance its budget, cut the funding entirely. Cornish was back to relying on whatever money and time volunteers and donors could scrape together on their own.

At a single nursery in Camborne, in Cornwall, the two carers speak only Cornish to their handful of children. The determination of the Cornish activists to do what they can on a shoestring budget is evident when I visit. The handful of students are in the private home of Emilie Champliaud, who is French, and her Welsh husband Rhisiart Tal-e-bot. Cornish signs decorate the walls and Cornish sheet music sits on the piano. Though Emilie and Esther Johns, the other carer, speak only Cornish, the children largely reply in English, and the women, also busy making food and taking care of the children's needs, do not try to force them to speak Cornish. But when a game begins, the children know how to play it, and eagerly do so, in Cornish.

But those children then go on to English schools where Cornish is ignored, or even actively discouraged. Children are chided when they know only the Cornish and not the English word for something. So they stop using those words, their knowledge becoming increasingly passive and at risk of disappearing entirely. Meanwhile, the adult enthusiasts of Cornish – there are reckoned to be several hundred who have learned to speak it well – are scattered among the region's towns and small cities. The language has achieved something remarkable – especially with those true native speakers from Ray Chubb's and Tim Saunders's families. But it hangs on for dear life, as its boosters try to create a critical mass of people across age groups first using the language and – if true revival is to happen – then raising their children in it, as Chubb and Saunders did.

*

Cornish is, admittedly, a luxury. Only a rich country like Britain could afford to spend any amount of money on the revival of a long-dead language. Most languages die in poor countries, where speakers switch to a bigger language that will help them find a better life for their children. The idea of trying to reintroduce lost linguistic diversity into a country, Britain, that boasts the most successful language in history in terms of its global reach and the number, wealth and prestige of its speakers, seems, to some, quixotic or even silly. Newspaper stories about the Cornish revival movement are often snide and ill-informed: "Council splashes out £180,000 to try to stop the Cornish language dying out," read a headline in the *Daily Telegraph* in 2015, "splashes out" speaking volumes: One splashes out on a silly thing one doesn't really need. The article concludes with an unintentional insult, in a poll asking "Should the Cornish dialect be revived?" Though there is sometimes no clear-cut line between dialect and language – remember our "lumper" and "splitter" positions – Cornish has no relatives close enough to be a dialect of anything. It is a language.

Keeping languages alive may not be strictly useful. Some scholars argue that linguistic diversity is akin to biodiversity, a good thing in and of itself. That metaphor breaks down in critical ways, though. Critical knowledge *about* ecosystems may be lost when a language's last speaker dies. But languages in a figurative ecosystem don't work like species in a literal ecosystem. Species need each other to survive. Languages do not. In fact, countries with a large number of languages and no dominant *lingua franca* tend to be unstable and poorer than those with a dominant language.

Nonetheless, there's a case for politicians to act not like language tamers, but something like language game wardens, protecting threatened species from poachers or invasive species. Why? Not because it is strictly practical, but because each language is a unique product of humankind's genius. When a language is lost, something beautiful and irreplaceable is gone forever.

*

There is no single model for how a country should be, linguistically – Japan and Iceland are rich, stable and nearly monolingual; Switzerland, Canada, Singapore and Luxembourg are rich, stable and multilingual. But what is clear from the stories above is that sudden and coercive changes to the rules of the language system bring the threat of angry reaction. In a Canada, that means years of mostly well-mannered frustration. In a place like Ukraine, it means a fight: the fistfight in parliament when the bill was passed, and the war that followed when it was revoked. Linguistic minorities should be treated with respect, and accorded a reasonable space for the use of their language in the region (without trampling on the rights of minorities living among that minority).

By far the best way to draw the sting of language conflicts is to encourage not national but personal multilingualism. In the most successful multilingual countries – Luxembourg and Switzerland, for example – multilingualism is a bone-deep national value. In other countries, this is the goal, but it is only partly reached: more Flemish-speakers learn French in Belgium than the other way round, and more Francophone Canadians know English than the other way round. But the ideal is still a multilingual one, and helps minorities feel respected. In Spain, Castilian Spanish-speakers hardly learn the regional languages, and tend to scoff at their speakers' demands. It's hardly surprising that a large number of Catalans and Basques want a country of their own. They've learned the nation-state lesson.

Linguists like to repeat sociolinguist Max Weinreich's quip that "a language is a dialect with an army and a navy." This is tongue-in-cheek, mocking the idea that languages without their own states were mere dialects. But majority-language nationalism threatens to make Weinreich's quip not a joke but a self-fulfilling prophecy. When minorities are treated as though they don't speak a "real" language, they'll often decide that the only way to get respect is to get themselves an army and a navy, and fight for a real country. And that's where trouble begins.

6

Whom in a biker bar

IN THE TV SHOW *The Last Man on Earth*, Phil (Will Forte) wakes up to find that a deadly virus has wiped out humanity. He does what we all would do in these circumstances, and steals a fine car, moves into a mansion, trashes the art just because he can, and drinks morning, noon and night.

But gradually, the trash piles up, he grows a long scraggly beard, and living without limits begins to get him down. He begins talking to assorted sports balls, and flirting with a female doll. Resolved to kill himself, he stops short of driving his car into a rock when he sees a smoke signal; apparently someone has seen his painted "ALIVE IN TUCSON" signs. Approaching the fire, he passes out, and wakes up to a dream of a beautiful woman kissing him. Sputtering awake, he finds the woman with her lips to his to be a much more homely Carol (Kristin Schaal), giving him mouth-to-mouth resuscitation.

Phil is overjoyed to find another survivor, but his odd behaviour frightens her. Then, suddenly, it's her turn to be odd.

Phil: I promise you there's nothing to be afraid of!

Carol: Nothing *of which to be afraid*!

Phil: I just said that...

Carol: You can't end sentences with prepositions! "Nothing of which to be afraid" is the proper grammar!

As the conversation goes on, he startles her further, and she draws a gun.

Phil: What do you need that gun out for?

Carol: You mean "out for what do you need that gun?"

Phil: OK, that *can't* be right.

Carol: It *is*!

People who grew up in the hoariest of language-tamer traditions will recognise Carol's response. Regardless of time and place, they have been drilled by a parent or teacher to believe that there is never a time or place to end a sentence in a preposition.

As with the *whom* episode of *Sherlock* that opened this book, the writers of *Last Man on Earth* are selective as to which old stickler shibboleths they care to have their character endorse: Carol lets a "that was me!" slip in the same scene, where old-fashioned grammarians would (wrongly) insist that the only correct way to say this is "that was I!"

But never mind that; as with *Sherlock*'s writers, the writers of *Last Man on Earth* are building a character by showcasing her refusal to let her uncompromising grammar standards slide, even when she may have just met the only other living human being. Her meeting Phil would normally call for tears of relief. She is clearly a bit of a crackpot.

Isn't she right about the grammar, though? Many people think that though the grammar crackpots like Carol out there are unpleasant, you have to give them a grudging respect: they know their grammar, keeping the rest of us a little closer to the light of truth than we would be without them.

The only problem is that Carol's belief is a complete myth. "Don't end a sentence with a preposition" has never, ever been a rule of English grammar. It was first popularised as a preference, not a rule, by John Dryden, the 17th-century poet and essayist. Dryden knew that predecessors like Shakespeare had put prepositions at the end of clauses (he singled out Ben Jonson specifically in his essay), and Dryden admitted to doing so himself. But he thought it more elegant not to, and went back to correct his earlier writings to remove what he called a "fault". As with so many other bogus rules in English, Dryden's rule comes from Latin, where it is indeed impossible to put a preposition at the end of a sentence. But Latin isn't English.

Nonetheless, Dryden's preference made it into a hugely influential English grammar by Bishop Robert Lowth at the end of the 18th century. Here again, Lowth listed it as a preference, not a rule, conceding that sentence-ending prepositions were "an idiom, which our language is strongly inclined to". (It doesn't seem he was trying to be funny, in ending a sentence in a preposition here.) Through a series of repetitions by other grammar-book writers, especially Lowth's successor Lindley Murray, the preference hardened into what many people came to believe as a rule. It's a zombie, one of the most unkillable myths about the English language, passed on through the generations to the teeth-gnashing chagrin of actual experts in English grammar and its history. From conservative to liberal, no serious grammar expert has any time for this fake rule.

So is Carol's "nothing of which to be frightened" wrong? Not quite: there's nothing wrong with her grammar there; English has both possibilities:

Nothing to be frightened of

Nothing of which to be frightened

Where she's wrong is insisting that only one of those is correct. And she's also wrong in another couple of interesting ways. She makes a choice, not technically incorrect but totally unorthodox, in preferring "nothing of which to be frightened" in speech, when this is a form that is common only in formal writing. And she's wrong in upbraiding someone who's also using the language correctly (in fact, more appropriately than she is) in a situation that calls for solidarity. They may be the only two people alive; this is no time for one-upmanship, especially one-upmanship based on a myth.

Many language tamers share Carol's base belief: that there's only one way to do things in English, and any deviation from that is not "proper grammar". Arnold Zwicky, a linguist at Stanford University, has called this belief the One Right Way principle. It has two parts:

1. There is One Right Way to use an expression; a form should have only one meaning.

2. There is One Right Way to express a meaning; a meaning should be expressed by only one form. No true synonyms.

The first clause covers many of the usages that sticklers hate: If *aggravate* means "to worsen", it can't also mean "to irritate". If *enormity* means "monstrosity", it can't mean "hugeness", too. Nearly all semantic changes in individual words, like the cases of *buxom*, *nice* and *silly* discussed earlier, would violate the principle, as long as the word still retains any link to the older meaning. In other words, (1) more or less forbids semantic change. This is more or less like trying to forbid oxidation, or the tides.

But it is the second clause that most often applies to grammar rather than to words, and is of interest here. Many people seem to think – without actually articulating the One Right Way principle – that if something can be done in grammatical form X, it cannot be done in any other way. If prepositions *may* come before the nouns or pronouns they govern, as in "nothing *of which* to be frightened", they may not go anywhere else, as in "nothing to be frightened of".

This rule has so straitjacketed poor Carol that when Phil goes a step further and ends a sentence with not one but two prepositions – "What do you need that gun out for?" – she tortures herself into the construction that Phil simply can't believe: "Out for what do you need that gun?" This time, Phil is justified: "That can't be right." In the expression "What did you do that for?", the "What for" is simply an idiom, synonymous with "why". Analysing it as a preposition (*for*) governing a pronoun (*what*) would mean that it could be reordered as "For what did you do that?" This simply isn't English; a normal native English speaker would just stare at you blankly if you said it in a normal conversation. In the Corpus of Contemporary American English, a collection of 520 million words of speech and writing kept by Brigham Young University, "what did you do that for?" appears 32 times, and the phrase "for what did you..." appears not once. So when Carol tries turning "what for" into "for what", then goes further by pulling the *out* from the end of the sentence and putting it in front of *for what*, the "out for what" result understandably bewilders Phil.

English, like every other language, gives its speakers options – and that's a good thing. Take these uncontroversial stylistic variants:

Possession: *the king's son = the son of the king*

Contraction: *I cannot do that = I can't do that*

Word choice: *Why did you do that? = What did you do that for?*

Word order: *He quickly shut the door = Quickly, he shut the door = he shut the door quickly*

Nobody would say that any of these variants is wrong. But now take these variants. In each pair, the second is considered wrong by people like Carol:

Preposition-stranding: *the man to whom I was talking = the man I was talking to*

Nominative or accusative after "to be": *It was he = It was him*

Split infinitive: *To go boldly = to boldly go*

Which in restrictive relative clauses: *a day that will live in infamy = a day which will live in infamy*

We've already dealt with preposition-stranding (pp. 156–8), the split infinitive (pp. 37–8), and the accusative pronoun after forms of the verb *to be* (pp. 61–2). To this inglorious list belongs the third item in the list above: the idea that you can't use *which* in a "restrictive" relative clause, one that crucially defines the word it refers back to. (A "non-restrictive" relative clause simply adds an extra bit of information.) Many people think that *which* can't be used in sentences like the first one below; they think *which* can only be used in sentences of the second type.

Restrictive: The car **that** I sold cost me $8,000.

Non-restrictive: The car, **which** I sold, cost me $8,000.

But Franklin Roosevelt knew what he was doing with his native language when he called December 7th 1941 "a day which will live in infamy". *Which* has never been confined to non-restrictive clauses; the idea that it should be is a product of H. W. Fowler's desire to neaten up the language. Fowler, whom we met in Chapter 2, noted a century ago that *that* is only used in restrictive clauses, and so thought that *which* should be kept for non-restrictive clauses. No such rule obtained at his time, as he admitted.

But he thought that this preference *should* be a rule – a typical move of the One Right Way school, trying to neaten things up, to reduce the messy variability that is inherent to language. And since Fowler's suggestion, many other usage books – notably Strunk and White's *The Elements of Style* – have repeated it as though it really were a rule rather than a preference. Mixing up preferences and rules is the heart of the One Right Way fallacy: if I *prefer* one thing, some *rule* must exclude the other. Dryden's preference on prepositions became Carol's rule. Fowler's preference on *which* became E. B. White's rule.[1] And so on.

And the bad grammar-book writers and the Carols of the world have slipped another confusion into the One Right Way doctrine: the failure to understand the basic linguistic concept of register. In short, a register is a variety of a language that is usually associated with a particular kind of use. Informal speech among friends is one register; formal public speech is another. Informal e-mail, business letters and academic work all call for different registers in writing.

Mastery of register – including the ability to switch between registers – is a key component of linguistic competence. To be a Carol – to insist on an absurdly formal form of English when you've just met the last man on earth – is to be, at a deep level, not a guardian of high standards but a linguistic klutz, missing one of the main skills that make people sound like people and not automatons.

Geoffrey Pullum, a syntactician at the University of Edinburgh, illustrates the idea by boiling registers radically – and usefully – down to two: Normal and Formal. Many of the options English gives its users come in exactly two varieties: one for use in most speech and relaxed or personal writing, the other for elevated formal speech and most writing of the kind published in print.

Compare Pullum's examples:

Normal	Formal
(1) don't	do not
(2) which he sneered at	at which he sneered
(3) who we're so proud of	of whom we are so proud

Normal	Formal
(4) people who you don't meet much	people whom one does not often meet
(5) he's better than me	he is more accomplished than I
(6) because it wasn't him	for it was not he
(7) a bag you can throw up into	a bag into which one may vomit

The list could go on for quite a while:

Normal	Formal
(8) if you could	should you be able to
(9) if he did that	Were he to do that
(10) anyway	be that as it may (subjunctive)
(11) We ask students to study alone	we ask that students study alone (subjunctive)
(12) Can I ask a question?	May I ask a question?

Note that a few of these comparisons have not one but two grammatical contrasts: sentence (3) has *who* versus *whom*, and moves the preposition to a different place. Sentence (4) contrasts *who* and *whom*, *you* and *one*, and *much* and *often* while (5) handles what case of pronoun should come after *than*: as Pullum and other grammarians have written endlessly, the accusative (*better than me*) has a long and perfectly distinguished history in English, including among great writers, but is more Normal than Formal.

The language tamer wants there to be just a strictly limited set of ways to string words together to get a message across. Just as computer languages are strictly defined, with overlap and duplication to be avoided in principle so as to avoid confusion and waste, natural languages shouldn't tolerate any waste either, goes the theory. And it goes without saying that people like Simon Heffer and Nevile Gwynne from Chapter 2, who write their grammar books from their instincts rather than from an examination of quality English, think that in most of these cases, only the Formal forms are proper English. The Normal forms are deviations, born of personal laziness abetted by cultural decline.

But if the Normal forms are indeed normal, what are they doing there, in apparent excess next to the Formal ones? Why does the language have so much more variability than it needs? One answer is chance; elements of language (both words and bits of grammar) are constantly entering (and sometimes leaving) the language. Inevitably, there will be more than one way to say many things for this reason alone.

But there's another, more profound reason the language gives its users multiple options. Remember, after all, that the users of the language create the forms of the language themselves. Besides random change, there are often good reasons they do so. And in register, we see a good example of the hidden genius of language: the choice of Normal or Formal allows a speaker or writer a valuable second channel of communication, alongside the literal meaning of the words and grammar that (hopefully) add up to a clear proposition, command, question or request. That second channel – the one residing in the register – says something about the occasion, the speaker, the person spoken to, and the perceived relationship, whether of solidary, superiority, politeness, or distance. It's not wasteful, but efficient, to have the choice of register to communicate a lot of what needs saying in an inaudible channel alongside the actual words chosen. In speech, it joins other paralinguistic channels like body language and tone of voice, both of which often say as much – or more – than the propositional content of the words chosen ever could. Imagine the difference between a menacing "would you like to come with me, Mr Smith" and a friendly "hey, Bill, why don't you join me!" delivered with good cheer. The strict content of the words may seem to be the same, but tone of voice and the register of the language do far more; the first will be perceived as commanding and threatening; the second as inviting. In other words, register is doing most of the work here. To restrict yourself only to Formal – to buy into the One Right Way fallacy – is to leave a valuable and versatile tool lying on the ground. Truly gifted speakers know the secret of register.

*

The 44th president of the United States was often said to be such a gifted speaker. But what did this actually mean, when said of Barack Obama? He certainly gave some grand and successful speeches on high-profile occasions: his 2004 keynote speech to the Democratic National Convention, his 2008 campaign speech on the subject of race, his victory speech later that same year.

But Obama was also comfortable switching modes. As a mixed-race boy raised by a white family who later made black South Side Chicago his home and political base, he had to be adept at speaking in different ways so that different audiences could relate to him. A video of him ordering a chilli-dog in Chicago shows the cashier asking him – just elected president – if he needs change, and Obama saying "naw, we straight," with the dropping of the *to be* verb (*are*, in this case) typical of black American English. The presidency increasingly calls on its holders to be able to move back and forth between these modes successfully.

But one mode is particularly difficult, even for gifted speakers. That's speaking extemporaneous Formal, with the full weight of the power of the presidency sitting on your shoulders. In serious sit-down interviews with journalists, Obama was so slow and deliberate that these sessions were often hard to watch, with long pauses, stretched-out phrases, and Obama's famous tic: "ahhh" or "uhhh" to buy himself some time. Formal on the fly – while also knowing your every word will be scrutinised by the world – can be very hard indeed, even for a gifted speaker.

To make the point a little more bluntly, take Obama's predecessor. George W. Bush was considered a linguistic stumblebum, his gaffes the stuff of legend. But those who knew the off-camera, relaxed and personal Bush found him not only warm and fluent but charismatic and charming. Meanwhile, standing behind a podium and delivering a prepared speech, he was not half as bad as his reputation would have you remember; though not as eloquent as some, he certainly was at least competent.

It was, again, those middle situations that tripped Bush up: those that called for an *extemporised* Formal for a man whose default mode was a very relaxed form of Normal. Decrying the obstetricians driven out of practice by the high cost of insurance, he once said "too many good OB/GYNs aren't able to practice their..." – here he paused, wondering whether to re-start his sentence; what is it that doctors practise? Well, good doctors love helping people, right? He continued

"…love with women all across the country." In 2000, he sympathised with a working-class single parent "working hard to put food on your family". Describing the threat of terrorism, he said "Our enemies are innovative and resourceful, and so are we. They never stop thinking about new ways to harm our country and our people, and neither do we."

Extemporaneous Formal takes practice, and Bush had not had a lot of that in the more relaxed register of politics in Texas, where politicians are usually expected to talk like ordinary voters – that is, in Normal. Bush's stump speeches always tilted heavily towards Normal anyway, which is an increasing trend in modern politics generally. It was when he reached for a stylish and serious rhetorical flourish (as in the repeated structure in "Our enemies are innovative and resourceful, and so are we…" above) that he lost track of where he was, and came out with something that set the comedy-show writing teams to high-fiving, their night's work done for them.

No discussion of register and American presidents would be complete without a look at Obama's successor. For many journalists and pundits it was obvious that there was no way Donald Trump would become president. No candidate in the history of the republic, surely, had used the word "rapists" in announcing his bid for the presidency. But Trump, in talking of illegal immigrants from Mexico, threw caution to the wind. Instead of the usual high-flying clichés about America's greatness, the entire speech was a bizarre series of extemporised, often repetitive riffs.

> I've been on the circuit making speeches, and I hear my fellow Republicans. And they're wonderful people. I like them. They all want me to support them. They don't know how to bring it about. They come up to my office. I'm meeting with three of them in the next week. And they don't know – "Are you running? Are you not running? Could we have your support? What do we do? How do we do it?"

> I like them. And I hear their speeches. And they don't talk jobs and they don't talk China. When was the last time you heard China is killing us? They're devaluing their currency to a level that you

wouldn't believe. It makes it impossible for our companies to compete, impossible. They're killing us.

But you don't hear that from anybody else. You don't hear it from anybody else. And I watch the speeches.

I watch the speeches of these people, and they say the sun will rise, the moon will set, all sorts of wonderful things will happen. And people are saying, "What's going on? I just want a job. Just get me a job. I don't need the rhetoric. I want a job."

Surely, such a linguistic incompetent was doomed.

As the campaign wore on, Trump's poll numbers confounded all those who had never heard a candidate talk this way. He was relentlessly Normal; he almost never spoke from a teleprompter or gave a formal speech at all, and he freely digressed from whatever his chosen topic was again and again. On the page, transcripts of his speeches seemed disconnected, even deranged, and highly educated journalists reckoned that it was only a matter of time before the voters saw what they saw: an ignoramus, possibly a mentally ill one.

But the mistake of those journalists was another register mistake. Trump was talking to the audience in front of him, not giving an oration meant to be read later like Lincoln's Second Inaugural. As he said, they "don't need the rhetoric". Reading Trump's quotes out of context is to misunderstand what he was doing. Trump connected with the crowd like a talented comedian, speaking like the members of the crowd did themselves, in a campaign that was targeted endlessly against the coastal elites – free-traders, globalists, multiculturalists, journalists – who had been hoodwinking the common people. Trump almost never went into Formal mode, even when the situation called for it. In other words, he didn't give speeches, or orate; he talked. And it worked.

In many ways, the countless experts and journalists who (to borrow a word from Bush) misunderestimated Trump made the same mistake as the grammar-sticklers: they didn't get the power of switching *down* a register when the time is right. Many voters felt condescended to. They felt that elites, whether academics, Hollywood stars, rich financiers or the Washington establishment, had taken them for granted, only paying attention when it came time to patronise with platitudes about working families and the middle class. Someone who talked like the angry guy at the end of the bar, someone they felt they knew (even if he was a billionaire), was just what they were looking for.

*

If pundits failed to spot Trump's adroit use of Normal, that's not because they don't have at least a tacit understanding of register. Most people do, switching modes from intimate conversation to boardroom presentation without thinking about it. And lessons about register start young, when children first get explicit correction from their parents.

I dislike the "Berenstain Bears" children's books, appearing in a long series since the 1960s, for many reasons. They're too long, they're boring, and they always have a pat moral lesson. Stan and Jan Berenstain's Papa Bear is a predictable doofus. Sensible Mama Bear always sorts things out. One thing that encapsulated what I don't like about them crops up in *The Berenstain Bears and the Bad Dream*. Brother Bear, dying to see a new movie, is begging his mother: "May I see it when it comes, Mama? May I? May I?"

Now, no child reader of the Berenstain Bears has ever said "May I? May I?" spontaneously. But this is presented as just how the Bear Family kids talk, as if it were normal. It may be so in their fictional world, but that could only be if Mama Bear (it would never be Papa) had drilled the children constantly in the unpublished *The Berenstain Bears and the Grammar Scold*: "Can I go to the bathroom, Mama?" "I don't know, *can* you?" "*May* I, Mama?"

The *can/may* distinction perfectly summarises the Normal/Formal distinction, and the way in which far too many parents, teachers and editors insist that only the Formal can ever be right. *Can*, like virtually every other old word in English, has changed over the centuries. Originally it meant to be acquainted with something – as the two consonants hint, it is a distant cousin to *know*. (Ben Jonson wrote in 1637 "She could the Bible in the holy tongue.") Through the typical semantic shifts, it then meant "to know from experience", and then "to have learned to do something, to be intellectually able to", and from there, "to...have the power, ability or capacity to," according to the *OED*. This is *can*'s most common modern meaning.

But the Mama Bears of the world don't want to let the word continue to evolve to the next obvious related meaning given in the *OED*: "Expressing objective possibility, opportunity, or absence of prohibitive conditions: be permitted or enabled by the conditions of the case." Was this meaning already established by the time of *The Berenstain Bears and the Bad Dream*, published in 1988? Yes – for about a thousand years. *Can* meaning "to be permitted" turns up in an Old English text called the *Seven Sleepers*, so old that the *OED* doesn't attempt to date it.

The slightly related definition – "expressing permission or sanction; to be allowed to" is dated back to 1489: "Þe [*the*] lawe saithe suche a man can not make noo testament nor mary himself nor entre in to religyon." It has been in continuous use since. Oscar Wilde puts permissive *can* in the mouth of Lord Augustus in 1893's *Lady Windermere's Fan*:

Cecil Graham: You'll play, of course, Tuppy?

Lord Augustus: Can't, dear boy. Promised Mrs Erlynne never to play or drink again.

Clearly Augustus is talking about permission, not ability, here, and he is an aristocrat, created by one of the greatest wordsmiths in the history of the English language, not a working-class or ill-educated speaker, nor the product of an illiterate writer. *Can* can't mean *may*? Of course it can.

May of course means *may*, too. And so, in the One Right Way tradition, some language tamers want to clean up the language and make *only may* mean *may*. But this is – as every child knows on some level – not Normal. To ask "can I have a drink of water?" and be reprimanded by a teacher or a parent – "I don't know, *can you*?" – has irritated countless children. They know perfectly well what they mean, and they know perfectly well that their parents know what they mean. In other words, they know that *can* for permission is Normal, and they haven't yet had it drummed into their heads that *may* is Formal – and that some people consider only Formal to be correct.

This has lifelong consequences. Parents are constantly correcting small children's English: the child makes one of those cute mistakes like "maked", and the parent corrects to *made*. But most of a child's learning comes not from explicit instruction, but from passive soaking up of the language used around her. Children will grow out of *maked* even without parental corrections, because *maked* is not any kind of Normal.

But children do not, until they are drilled, grow out of *can I?* when asking permission. That's because, by all the evidence the child has available, this is how everybody talks nearly all of the time, with *may* confined to some kind of fringe situations that the child can safely ignore during the monumental task of acquiring the language. In fact, though *can* has meant *may* for a thousand years, the sticklers are on to something: *may* is in fairly sharp decline in English, both in Britain and in America (as are *must* and *shall*), while *can* is holding strong, as the figure below shows. This is not because people don't learn properly anymore; it is because Normal is edging out Formal.

Change in pmw frequency from 1961 to 1991 for the core modals in UK and UK corpora, expressed as a percentage of 1961 data ("pmw" is "per million words")

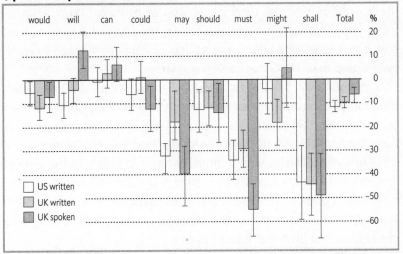

Source: Bas Aarts, Sean Wallis and Jill Bowie, "Profiling the English verb phrase over time: modal patterns", in I. Taavitsainen, M. Kytö, C. Claridge and J. Smith (eds), *Developments in English: Expanding Electronic Evidence.* Cambridge University Press (2015)

When children are suddenly told that what they know their parents and virtually everyone else says, and what they have been saying all their lives thus far, is "wrong", there's an early disconnect between the child's native competence and the new idea of an invisible but Platonically correct language out there, one that nobody seems to be using.

The lessons will go on from there: "Don't say 'it was her', say 'it was she'." "Don't say 'me and Billy went', say 'Billy and I went'." "Don't say 'ain't'. 'Ain't' ain't in the dictionary." This advice varies a bit in quality. *Billy and I went* is perfectly normal, and *Billy and me went* is highly informal or dialect. *Ain't* is, in fact, in any good dictionary today, but it too is either dialectal or informal.

But so much of this kind of advice goes against a child's linguistic instincts – learned from parents as well as other respected adults – that it comes as a repeated minor humiliation. Nobody likes to be told they're wrong when they're quite sure they're right, and when their parents have been heard saying some of the very same things the child has just said.

As school begins, some formal terminology is introduced, and the lessons come from teachers as well as parents: "Don't split an infinitive." "You can't put a preposition at the end of a sentence." And now a new label gets put on the advice: grammar. You need to learn proper grammar. That's not good grammar.

The child now has not just a humiliation, but a humiliator: this thing called grammar. Linguists, who truly love grammar, describe it as the set of rules that generate well-formed sentences in a language. But the schoolchild learns, through this kind of teaching, that grammar is a set of rules for torturing your natural sentences into an unnatural form that will satisfy a teacher. This engenders in many children a lifelong hatred of "grammar". This can become an alienation from English class generally, and so from the kind of skilled formal writing that they will need to succeed in so many avenues of life.

What's the alternative? No one has ever seriously proposed letting all schoolchildren merely write what feels comfortable to them, without ever guiding them towards mastery of the grammar (and mechanics and spelling) of written English. But it is in fact the case that many school systems, starting in the 1960s, in both Britain and America, started de-emphasising grammar. To that point, for several centuries, "grammar" had been dominated by prescriptivist, Latin-based thinking that made teachers tell their students that their written and spoken English was riddled with mistakes, and that they had to learn rules like "don't end a sentence with a preposition" before they could have "good grammar".

By the 1960s, generations of learners and many teachers had become fed up. Educational reformers overreacted, though: they dropped much of the formal teaching of grammar entirely, rather than improving it. David Crystal, a linguist and critic of hoary prescriptivism, describes his shock at facing a lecture-hall full of undergraduates in the 1970s, discussing the "don't end a sentence with a preposition" rule, when a student asked "Please, what's a preposition?" He asked the class how many others didn't know; most of the hands went up. One student hazarded that it had something to do with riding a horse: "I was always told that a pre-position was what one had to adopt when preparing to mount."[2]

And so things went for years after that, until many of those students became teachers themselves – and lacked the grammatical wherewithal to teach students how to break down a sentence into its parts for analysis. Those that did do any "grammar" were left to focus on basic writing faults like *its/it's*, *to/too/two*, *their/they're/there* and the like, plus the old prescriptivist standbys: don't split an infinitive, nor end a sentence with a preposition. It was the worst of all worlds: children learning to hate grammar without ever actually learning the intricate wonders of actual grammar.

Some school systems have tried to bring grammar back. But when pendulums swing, they swing hard. In Britain, Michael Gove, the education secretary for the Conservative-led government from 2010 to 2014, himself a writer (as a journalist), pushed for the re-introduction of explicit learning of the parts of a sentence and how they go together. In some ways this was progressive. It introduced terms like "determiner", a part of speech recognised by linguists but not formerly by many English teachers and which includes words like *a*, *an*, *the*, *my*, *your*, *this*, *that*, *each* and *some*. (These form a part of speech because they all perform the same syntactic function, specifying a noun more closely. They have traditionally been thrown into other bins, being called adjectives for example, though they fail many tests for adjective-hood.)

But Gove's reforms introduced this kind of thing for a high-stakes exam that children were to take at age 11. It included challenges like "tick one box to show which part of the sentence is a relative clause," "circle all the determiners in the sentence below," and "tick one box in each row to show how the modal verb affects the meaning of the sentence." It asks students "which of the following is a command?", listing four sentences, only one of which is a grammatical imperative, but all of which have the force of a command (like "could you please shut the door?") Note that the tests do not, at least at this stage, confirm whether students can actually use any of these devices, but merely whether they can spot them on the page and regurgitate their names.

Some might say "but this is necessary for them to become good writers later." It's a tempting conclusion – especially for a grammar nut like me. But it turns out to have no research whatsoever behind it. Though it seems like common sense, one study has even found that this was the worst of several approaches that were carefully compared to see which got students writing the best prose. In 2007 Steve Graham and Dolores Perin, two academics, compared dozens of teaching strategies in a meta-analysis, a study of studies considered a kind of gold standard in academia. (Any one study may have flaws, but looking at a large batch of them and combining their findings means that those flaws should wash out.) Graham and Perin found 11 strategies that were proven to work – things like practising summarisation, pre-writing and collaborative writing assignments. But in a curious side-note, they noted that explicit grammatical instruction not only did not have any benefit, but had a slightly negative effect. This puzzled Perin and Graham themselves; they conclude that it is probably because grammar is taught too abstractly, in isolation from actual writing and its goals. As such, it was worse than a distraction; it was teaching time wasted, time that could have been applied to better strategies.[3]

An important side-note at this point: the tests sat by English 11-year-olds test spelling, punctuation *and* grammar, not just grammar. Many readers of this book will associate "grammar" with such things as capitalisation or the use of semicolons. But linguists (and I join them) use "grammar" to mean the rules used to assemble meaningful words from smaller units, and how to put words together to make meaningful sentences. Grammar covers things like subjects, verbs, phrases, clauses, tenses, cases, moods, parts of speech, and so on. Things like capitalisation and full stops are conventional ways of *signalling* various grammatical functions, and children do need to begin learning them, along with spelling, almost as soon as they begin to learn to write. But strictly speaking, commas and quotation marks are orthography, not grammar.

Oddly enough, the forbidding-sounding stuff of grammar, unlike punctuation, is exactly what children learn naturally in the act of being small children and using the language. Students don't need to be able to name a relative clause to be able to use one; children as young as 2 years 5 months produce sentences like "Look at dat train *Ursula bought*," and by 3 years 1 month they are marking them with *that*, as in "Here's a tiger *that's gonna scare him*."[4] The same is true of most of the grammar of English. There are really only a few tricky cases like *whom*, and they are tricky precisely because they are relatively rare and so often avoided in speech. Grammar is learned – at least in one's native language – by using the language, not by being taught formal terminology.

So why teach it? One reason is mastering those remaining tricky cases. Another is that grammar is intellectually mesmerising in and of itself, for the right kind of student. But a third reason, and perhaps the most important one for pedagogical purposes, is that talking *about* language and how it works is a useful skill for all kinds of students, no matter what their interests and abilities. And this brings us back to register, and to Normal and Formal.

The tricky cases that need to be taught explicitly to children in school belong almost exclusively to Formal. Normal is, by definition, what comes naturally to a native speaker. But Formal English includes all of the grammatical bits and pieces like *whom*, word order like *the man about whom I was talking*, and nominative case after the copula like *it was she*. These form part of the literary language that is a critical part of English-speakers' cultural heritage. Students need to learn Formal. But they should learn it for what it is: a specific kind of language for certain important purposes, and not the One Right Way.

This is all the truer for the many students who come to English with a home dialect that is further from standard Normal English. Black Americans, white southern Americans, working-class Londoners and speakers of many other dialects, for example, have *you was*, *he was* and *they was* as part of their home dialect, along with many other features that the average teacher will tell them are "wrong" when they get to school. Their predictable disconnect with "grammar" – this invisible rulebook out there that dictates they're almost always wrong – will be even stronger than the one that many speakers of standard English have. That's because standard Normal is closer to standard Formal. For the non-standard-dialect speaker, many more bits of their pronunciation, word choice and grammar will differ from Formal. Students who are continually told that they simply can't speak correctly are far more likely to decide that the world of school simply isn't for them. Evidence shows that students corrected for natural parts of their home dialect withdraw from participation,[5] and are more likely to perform poorly and misbehave.

Far more sensible is to use the differences between registers as a pedagogical tool, to teach kids about Formal and Normal. This is a way to show them that what they learned at home is one way to use the language, and that school will teach them another. Children need to know that mastery of Formal is still a key qualification for entry into the best-paid and most prestigious jobs, and that is not going to change in the foreseeable future.

So students should be told that while at home their mothers and fathers might say "we was", in class they are expected to say and write "we were". They should be told that it's important to "button up" one's English for certain occasions, in the same way that it's important to dress the right way for some occasions. A truly full-spectrum linguistic competence means mastering both Normal and Formal, or, for many students, Formal, standard Normal *and* a non-standard dialect like black American or southern white or Scots dialectal English. This goes for students just as it does for the most powerful people in the world. If fluent register-switching is good enough for Barack Obama, it's good enough for the classroom and its students. In top-flight careers like business and politics, as in life, people are expected to be both warm and authoritative, engaging and informative, fun and serious. Language is part of that.

Most 11-year-olds, like those learning about relative clauses, modal verbs and determiners in England, are not quite ready for this kind of material. Even if they can learn what a relative clause is, it is very hard to imagine such a young child using this knowledge to write better.

At this point, children are still learning the contours of their native language by hearing it and reading it, not by explicit description of it. But it's not too early to teach a bit of basic register, the difference between different kinds of language use in different scenarios. The goal, for young minds like this, should be exposure to varieties of the language from the highest and most traditional Formal to the most eloquent dialectal Normal. There should be a place both for the posh and ambitious voices in Jane Austen and for the country and black voices of Mark Twain in any literary education worth the name.

A child who slips up and uses a bit of non-standard grammar – something especially likely to happen with poorer children not exposed to standard Normal at home – shouldn't be told that what they grew up with is ignorant. People have a natural tendency to be attached to their homes, their families and their communities. Children like this should be told that there's an important kind of standard English that they need to be able to turn on at school, even if they choose to turn it back off when they're at home with family and friends.

The comedians Keegan-Michael Key and Jordan Peele made one of the most brilliant comedy sketch shows of all time largely around examining exactly these issues. Both are the sons of white and black parents, and so are usually coded as "black" in American thinking. Both were raised by white mothers in middle-class homes, and both are university educated. While the world may see them as black, they see themselves as people who constantly have to tweak up or down various mental knobs like "Black" and "Formal" in their own minds when they speak. In a sketch in the first-ever episode of their five seasons of *Key & Peele*, Key is standing at a street crossing talking on the phone to his wife about a date at the theatre that night in impeccable standard – that is, white-sounding – English when suddenly another black man (Peele) walks into view. Key's English changes suddenly.

> Because you're my wife and you love the theatre and it's your birthday. Great. Unfortunately the orchestra's already filled up but they do still have seats that are still left in the dress circle so [at this point, Peele walks up to the same pedestrian crossing light where Key can see him] if you want me to get them theatre tickets I'm'a do that right now... Naw, they got that one dude in it that you

love, man, he gonna be in it. Right, naw, I'm'a pick yo ass up at six thirty-then...

As the light changes, Peele walks away and says to his friend on his own phone, "Oh my god, Christian, I almost just got mugged right now."

In a subsequent stand-up sketch, though, the duo explains that no black man in a group of black men wants to sound the whitest, even if, by default, each of them sounds "whiter than Mitt Romney in a snowstorm". The theme would come up again and again over the course of *Key & Peele*'s run: a black man in America can't afford to sound black all the time, nor white all the time. Linguists call this "code-switching", and for many people it's a fact of daily life, a social survival skill.

It's also a fascinating topic for study; *Key & Peele* should be required viewing in every sociolinguistics class in the land. But register is not just for college: young children are ready to learn that there are different ways of talking for different situations. After all, some children learn to use "sir" and "ma'am" with all grownups (especially in the American South) or "sir" and "miss" with teachers (in Britain). They know they can swear around their friends but not in class. Children are nothing if not situationally aware.

This doesn't mean that teaching register and situational appropriateness should be a substitute for grammar. It should be a complement, and an introduction: "some people speak like this sometimes and like that at other times. You may speak one way at home, but you'll need to master some new skills for writing." The idea that kids are too stupid to handle variation – that they must be taught the One Right Way, lest their "bad habits" (ie, Normal, or their home dialects) slip into their writing – is nonsense. Far more children grow up like Key and Peele, exposed to multiple kinds of English and learning to switch between and control them, than grow up surrounded by nothing but impeccable Formal.

Older children, exposed to years of good reading and of early practice in writing, are more ready for the fairly abstract terminology of grammar, relative clauses and all. Waiting until they have a good feel for their language is not "dumbing down". It's a matter of preparing students with the right sequence of lessons. Explicit grammar teaching does not prepare children to read, write and speak; it's the other way round. Years of reading, writing and speaking prepare them to learn to analyse the language through explicitly talking about its grammar.

*

What about a more radical approach? It is a commonplace among linguists to argue that languages and dialects are all more or less infinitely expressive. Since nothing is bigger than infinity, this entails the notion that no language or dialect is really structurally superior to any other. One language may have a word that another lacks, but usually that means that the second language just needs a couple of words to say what the first language says in just one word.

To give an example, many languages lack a distinction between blue and green. One word covers them both. But this doesn't mean they can't perceive the difference, and if they need to express it, they have the option of saying "X like a tree" versus "X like the sky". This is not really inferior, but just slightly more cumbersome than English's one-word *blue* and *green* solutions. Russian has two words for light blue (*goluboi*) and dark blue (*sinii*) but this does not make Russian superior to English, either.

Educated people have a general sense that this is true of big prestigious languages like Russian, French, German and English – that it is basically preposterous to talk about any one of them being superior to another. But the same people have a strong sense that non-standard, stigmatised dialects are broken-down versions of the standard, and that speakers of those dialects need to have their language "fixed" by eliminating the dialect's "mistakes". When Henry Higgins takes on Eliza in George Bernard Shaw's *Pygmalion*, to teach her proper educated English, he doesn't do so out of the goodness of his heart. He does it because he can't stand not to:

> A woman who utters such depressing and disgusting sounds has
> no right to be anywhere – no right to live. Remember that you are
> a human being with a soul and the divine gift of articulate speech:
> that your native language is the language of Shakespeare and
> Milton and The Bible; and don't sit there crooning like a bilious
> pigeon.

In real life, these prejudices can be even uglier. In the murder trial of George Zimmerman, a white man who killed an unarmed black teenager, Trayvon Martin, in 2012, Rachel Jeantel, who had been on the phone with Martin, was one of the star witnesses for the prosecution. But John Rickford, a Guyanese expert in black American English at Stanford, argues that her testimony was heavily discounted because of her use of the dialect. He cites on-line responses to her: "an animal"; "the missing link between monkeys and humans"; "you could swap her out for a three-toed sloth and get the same witness value and response." Zimmerman was found not guilty of murder.

But in truth, dialects don't stand in a relationship to each other like an original and a poorly learned version, akin to a bad copy. They're more like two related species, with a common ancestor and most features in common, as well as systematic differences. Not only is neither superior in any linguistic sense but the non-standard dialect, the "bad copy", may in ways be more sophisticated than the prestige standard. Black American English famously omits the copula verb (*to be*) in many sentences (*she at my house*), while including it as *be* in other sentences (*she be coming over to my house*). But this isn't random or broken-down. The *be* in the second example means that someone does something often or habitually: she comes over to my house a lot.

Even if a non-standard dialect and the prestige standard may be linguistic equals, they aren't social equals. The very definition of a standard is that it's held up as the only, or the only acceptable, version of the language in schools, universities, businesses and so many other places. So some linguists – aware that there is nothing linguistically "broken" about dialects like black American dialect – want to break down the status distinction. And specifically, they have repeatedly proposed different versions of the idea that children might be taught in schools in their home dialect, rather than in standard English.

One attempt to do this came in the 1970s with a series of "dialect readers". They were based on the insight that a child who speaks only a minority dialect is doing two different things when learning to read, and both of them are hard: one is decoding the letters on the page, and the other is making sense of a version of the language that isn't their own. In the 1960s, a Scottish-American linguist named William Stewart reported that a 12-year-old girl named Lenora, a speaker of black American English who had been classified as a problem reader, saw, in his typewriter, a version of "A Night Before Christmas" that he had been writing in black vernacular for a Christmas Card:

> It's the night before Christmas, and here in our house,
> It ain't nothing moving, not even no mouse.
> There go we-all stockings, hanging high up off the floor,
> So Santa Claus can full them up, if he walk in through our door.

Lenora immediately began reading the lines fluently. But when Stewart showed her the original poem in standard English, all her "problem reader" behaviours returned. Stewart then repeated the experiment with other speakers like Lenora, with the same result.

This prepared the ground for more formal pedagogical experiments in using dialect for teaching reading. In the 1970s, this took the form of a reading program of short pamphlet-length books – called *Bridge*. One story began

> You ever hear of the *Titanic*? Yeah, that's right. It was one of them
> big ships. The kind they call an ocean liner. Now this here ship
> was one of the biggest and baddest ship ever to sail the sea. You
> understand? It was suppose to be unsinkable. Wind, storm,
> iceberg – nothing could get next to it. It was a superbad ship, the
> meanest thing on the water. It could move like four Bloods in
> tennis shoes. It was out of sight!

Despite Stewart's anecdotal results, there is no large-scale peer-reviewed evidence that users of the *Bridge* readers became better readers than those who learned with traditional reading materials. (One study that did show improvement was unpublished, and its methods and data have been called too opaque to count as strong support.)

Still, related approaches have returned to intellectual vogue several times since. In the most famous case, in the mid-1990s, the school board in Oakland, California proposed a program of teaching black students using a knowledge of their home dialect, which the proponents called "Ebonics". The name, and an overblown theory that black English was heavily shaped by West African languages, helped make the effort a national laughing-stock. Comedians and editorial-writers assumed

– wrongly – that the idea was to teach every subject to children entirely *in* dialect. The school board's original draft resolution did seem confusingly to suggest this, but as the superintendent repeatedly made clear, the approach was always to "use the vernacular to teach the standard", as Rickford puts it.

One problem with this approach is that black American English, like every other kind of language, varies from place to place, time to time and speaker to speaker. Rural southern black people don't speak just like urban northern ones. And some speakers will speak heavier versions of the dialect than others. Many dialect-speakers (like Key and Peele) can move on a continuum between fully standard and the strongest form of the vernacular. Others might just have a hint of the pronunciation and a few grammar features of the dialect. Some will have none at all. This diversity makes it hard to design any teaching materials that would address all black Americans. Just as there is no One Right Way for standard English, it's hard to imagine an official, prescriptivist One Right Way for black American or any other kind of non-standard English.

A second obstacle is probably even more insurmountable; finding enough teachers able and willing to teach in dialect. Patriann Smith, a specialist in literacy at Texas Tech, proposes a "translingual" classroom that integrates dialect difference into all language teaching, with all trainee teachers required to demonstrate a knowledge of at least one non-standard English dialect. This might be intellectually commendable, but politically, it would be poison, the Ebonics controversy on steroids. The half-informed newspaper articles and editorials are sadly predictable: not only would the kids be encouraged to speak their "ghetto" English but the teachers would be made to learn it, too! Imagine poor idealistic trainee Molly White from Kansas being forced by some loony-left inner-city education bureaucrat to sit in Ebonics class and learn to conjugate her verbs: *I be goin' to the sto', you be goin' to the sto', he, she or it be goin' to the sto'...*

But Smith is on to an important problem. Most teachers in American schools subscribe to the One Right Way policy, even if they don't call it that. This is grammatically off-base, according to the Normal-versus-Formal register analysis we've been through here: Normal forms like *that's the man I was talking to* are not in any way inferior to Formal forms like *that's the man with whom I was talking*. And when it goes to full-on dialect, not just register, the One Right Way policy does even more harm, making many kids from minority-dialect backgrounds start feeling defective as soon as they open their mouths.

It's hard to design a perfect system that would help these kids learn standard English while not making them feel stupid. But Smith is on to another big thing: any change has to start with the teachers. Many of the teachers of the subject called English have degrees in "English" from a university. But such a degree will have focused on the close reading of literature, not on the systematic exploration of English grammar and usage itself. In America at least, few "English" degree programs, even elite ones, require such a class. Much less are most of today's English teachers versed in the study of *variation* in (non-literary) English, the crucial topic here. How language changes according to register, dialect and so on are core topics at university – but in the Linguistics department, not in English, with which the Linguistics people have almost no interaction.

Big and diverse countries like America and Britain need updated thinking in language education. Too many students leave school either with the idea that grammar is their enemy, or with no grammar teaching at all. If all teachers of English were, at the very least, required to have one class (or better, a full year) in the linguistics of English, the One Right Way mindset would start to crack under the weight of its inaccuracies and inconsistencies. A new generation of teachers could approach kids' developing English with a full suite of skills, from teaching the difference between formal written and everyday spoken English, to coaching kids from non-standard dialect backgrounds to recognise the differences between the dialects. The goal, always, is to get them to master the standard, but not necessarily by eradicating their home dialect. It means getting them, in effect, to be bidialectal.

Grammar does have rules. But teachers should think not just of rules, but tools. Learning about the variation between different kinds of language is not just fascinating in its own right. It just might work, too. Three different studies have found the "contrastive analysis" approach successful. This is the pedagogical technique in which (say) black-English speakers are explicitly told that *we was* in their dialect translates into *we were* in the standard, and so forth. One study in

Chicago found that students taught contrastive analysis reduced the occurrence of ten salient black-English features (like *we was*) in their writing by 59%. Students in a control group, taught the old-fashioned way, saw no significant change.[6]

Using language well doesn't mean observing every strait-laced prescriptivist rule in the book at all times – this makes for a very poor, awkward communicator like poor Carol and her "out for what do you need that gun?" Good prescriptivists realise this. Mark Halpern, a rock-ribbed prescriptivist with whom I've engaged in some long and often mutually frustrating debates, has made one good point about situational appropriateness:

> Observance of what prescriptivists consider the best usages may backfire on the user if trotted out in inappropriate circumstances, as when addressing members of a milieu in which verbal precision and grace are positively disfavored, as being elitist or snobbish, for instance; you don't say "whom" in a biker bar.

Halpern is making a (witting or unwitting) category error when he confuses "verbal precision and grace" with Formal grammar. Plenty of people are ploddingly awful in perfectly grammatical standard English. And plenty of people are precise and graceful speaking some other variety. In cultures the world over, including illiterate ones, leaders tend to be gifted, charismatic speakers. In other words, bikers value fluency too.

But you don't say "whom" in a biker bar, nor do you write "we was" in a high-school essay. This is, in the end, not all that hard to wrap the mind around. The language tamers who want everyone to use *whom* at every available opportunity seem to think that diversity is a problem to be eliminated, fearing that people simply can't use one set of rules here, and another set there. But people do it all the time. Being able to vary between Normal and Formal as needed is not some exotic skill. Given how many people are bidialectal, it is, in itself, happily, unremarkably normal.

7

Apologies to Orwell

IN 2001, AMERICA'S economic conservatives saw a dream come true. They had spent years loathing the estate tax, levied on inheritances. The tax hit only estates of over $650,000 for an individual or $1.3m for a married couple, affecting just 2% of the adult deaths in 1999.[1] But conservatives hated it in principle (and richer conservatives in practice, too), and in the 1990s, they hit on a particular strategy to undermine public support for it, a strategy that now has the force of legend. While Newt Gingrich, a Republican, was Speaker of the House, and with the guidance of Frank Luntz, a Republican messaging guru, the party's leaders adopted en masse a new phrase for the tax: the "death tax". After several years of campaigning against the death tax, George W. Bush was elected president in 2000, and in 2001 he signed a bill that eliminated it. Conservatives were thrilled.

Liberals, meanwhile, were apoplectic. It seemed to reward exactly those Americans who didn't need any rewarding. But more galling still, the repeal was signed by a president who was the son of a president, born in wealthy Greenwich, Connecticut, educated at Yale and Harvard, with family connections that jump-started his business career. If any family is the kind that comes to mind with the word "estate", it might be the Bushes. The father, President George H. W. Bush, really was a bit of a patrician. But the son had picked up a twang from growing up in Texas, and liked to pose as a country boy. So liberals were doubly outraged: the fake-ordinary scion of a rich family eliminates a tax that once helped real ordinary people, all by using a clever linguistic trick, diverting attention from the "estate" to a purported tax on death itself.

Following that success, Luntz took on the aura of a kind of messaging mastermind, an evil genius. It seemed he had discovered a deep insight

184 TALK ON THE WILD SIDE

into the frailty of the human mind. In turn he inspired a new wave of political thinking informed by linguists, psychologists and cognitive scientists whom we will meet shortly. In the post-"death tax" world, liberals would fight back and try to win political debates by winning the battle of labelling. If you can get someone to use your language, you're halfway to convincing them, goes the theory.

These political language tamers don't see themselves as manipulators. They believe that the enemy has deceitfully chosen wrong, misleading language, and that voters will see the light when the wording is altered to show things as they truly are. It assumes implicitly that this approach works. And this approach has not only the support of those academic cheerleaders but a grounding in the tradition of great writing on politics and language.

But is it actually true? Can tweaks of language win otherwise unwinnable political battles? Language matters, including in politics. (You'd hardly expect a language columnist with an education in political science to conclude otherwise.) But its power is easily exaggerated. Rewording, reframing, and rethinking the whole enterprise of how to communicate with voters can be helpful, but it does not get you off the hook of actually winning political arguments.

The death-tax story is widely told, but not always understood. In one version of it, Luntz poll-tested three versions, asking three groups of voters if they would approve a repeal of the "estate tax", the "inheritance tax" and the "death tax". Luntz said that while a bare majority wanted repeal of the "estate tax", and somewhat more would repeal the "inheritance tax", a full three-quarters favoured killing the "death tax". He was off to tell Newt Gingrich, and the tax was soon dead, goes the story.

But there are plenty of wrinkles to this. Luntz's story of going from a bare majority to three-quarters support for repeal is not the only poll out there (and remember that Luntz is in the business of selling his ability to move polls). Another poll, by the Kaiser Family Foundation, Harvard University and National Public Radio, found that shifting from "estate tax" to "death tax" moved support for repeal from 54% to only 60%.[2]

Now, a lobbyist or activist in an evenly divided political battle will take six percentage points wherever they can get it; every bit helps.

But what helps even more than that? For the forces pushing for repeal, millions of dollars from rich families and anti-tax groups to fund the case for repeal didn't hurt: The Gallo wine-making family, the Mars candy-making family behind M&Ms, the heirs to Campbell's soup and others bankrolled an effort to make it seem as though the tax would hit many small businesses and farmers.[3]

Was there no white magic that could stand against these black arts? As it turns out, another useful trick is available: explaining the policy, even briefly. When the Kaiser/Harvard/NPR pollsters asked those who favoured repeal whether they would still do so if the threshold for the tax were simply raised, the results were surprising:

Keep estate tax as is:	17%
Keep tax but only on estates of $1m or more:	26%
Keep tax but only on estates of $5m or more:	11%
Keep tax but only on estates of $25m or more:	7%
Eliminate tax even on estates of $25m or more:	26%
Don't know/refused:	15%

Now it seems that a majority (54%) supports a tax on estates of $5m or more. Opposition to the tax as unfair in principle, even on the biggest of estates, was limited to a hardcore of just 26% of the population.

The key to the "death-tax" repeal was not, in other words, only the magic of the phrasing. It was public ignorance of the threshold of the tax itself, and how likely a family was to pay it. Though only 2% of families were likely to pay the tax, 49% of those polled by Kaiser/Harvard/NPR said that "most" families have to pay it. No wonder they favoured repeal; it was repeal of a grossly unfair – but wholly mythical – tax on the average family. Frank Luntz may well point to the poll-boost of his "death-tax" phrasing, whether six percentage points or 25, but that's nothing next to the power of briefly examining the policy. Talk of raising the threshold flips the numbers from 17% support for the tax to as high as 61%. Merely mentioning a threshold of $1m gets the numbers up to 43% support for keeping the tax, and remember, before the 2001 repeal, the threshold was already higher than that: most families would only have paid tax on an estate worth $1.3m. Facts can be powerful things.

It's well known that wording in poll questions can affect the outcomes hugely. Whether intentionally or unintentionally, Luntz's poll seems to have been worded in a way to maximise the effect of the "death tax" phrasing, and the Kaiser/Harvard/NPR poll may have somehow subtly minimised that effect. Plus, many distracted poll respondents, being asked successively whether they'd support a tax at the $1m threshold, the $5m threshold and the $25m threshold, might have felt gradually pressured by the poll-taker, feeling that their positions were increasingly being shown as unreasonable. It's easy to imagine a respondent "caving" and saying they'd support a tax on estates of $5m or $25m after feeling slightly browbeaten, even if they didn't believe in it.

Reams of social science show that many tiny factors can affect how people answer questions, from the wording of the question to the colour of the paint on the wall to the attractiveness of the questioner. Our thoughts are constantly shifting, and so we are easily swayed; new information, distracting factors and plenty of other irrelevant things can press someone, whether a voter answering a telephone poll or a subject taking part in a psychological study, into answering this way or that. Because this kind of research is difficult to do, it is hard to prove how many voters were actually persuaded by the "death-tax" phrasing.

But the story has taken on legendary status, cited in virtually any discussion on this topic, by conservatives eager to repeat their success and by those on the left hoping to fight back. Therefore it's worth looking in some depth into the pros and cons of political strategies that aim to achieve big political gains by small changes in terminology.

One objection leaps out. There is no way to make anyone accept your preferred terminology or use it. The "death tax" framing of the estate tax was eagerly taken up by opponents of the tax, but by hardly anyone else – certainly not the tax's supporters. To this day, "estate tax" is still far more common in Google searches: more than six times as common as "death tax" for the five years from 2012 to 2017. The phrasing of "death tax" may have motivated die-hard opponents of the tax to fight all the harder for its repeal, but contrary to what the myth suggests, "death tax" never caught on as the preferred term of most Americans.

This should be predictable: on issue after issue, the two sides in America's bitterly divided politics use different words for nearly everything. The most venerable is, of course, the division between opponents of legal abortion, who call themselves "pro-life" and their opponents "pro-abortion", and those who favour legal abortion, calling themselves "pro-choice" and their opponents "anti-choice". Every other linguistic label of this debate is polarised. Late-term abortions are called "partial-birth" abortions by pro-lifers and "dilation and extraction" by those who support the right to have them. Pro-lifers like to talk about "abortion clinics" if not ginning up the outrage by talking of outright "abortion mills". Pro-choicers talk about "family planning" or "women's health" clinics, and the chief provider of these services to many Americans, especially poorer ones, is called Planned Parenthood – itself a term of choice.

It's unlikely that either side has persuaded many solid supporters of the other side merely by their choice of terminology. A staunch pro-lifer is unlikely to hear the word "women's health" and suddenly decide she is for access to abortion after all. Of course, it's possible that both sides have to fight hard for their terminology even to preserve a rough draw in the debate; it would hardly make sense for pro-choicers to start calling themselves "pro-abortion". Terminology matters just for keeping your own side together. But to convince the other side takes more than that.

*

There is another reason that re-jiggering political phrasing is unlikely to yield automatic political wins for any side of any long-running political conflict. Words are, as we have seen so many times in this book, inherently unstable; they change literal meaning over time – especially over longer stretches. Remember how *buxom* went from meaning "pliable" to meaning "big-breasted".

Words with strictly literal meanings and no secondary connotations don't change quite so quickly. For example, "iron" has secondary meanings and metaphorical extensions ("iron will", "an iron constitution", "to iron a shirt", "a 9-iron"), because of iron's frequent use in our daily life. But invisible "nitrogen" doesn't, so that it means exactly what it did when it was (as far as the *OED* knows) first written down in 1789.

"Buxom" meant literally bendable in the physical sense, which is how it naturally went on to mean "obedient". "Obedient" naturally moves on from there to other meanings: happy and gay, then physically healthy, then plump, then curvy for a woman. Each leap is a short one.

Political words – because they deal with sensitive and contentious things in the political realm – are chock-full of those secondary associations. Not all people could give a technical definition of *socialism, feminism, communism, fascism, terrorism* and *neoconservatism* that would please an expert in those topics. But asking an ordinary person what other concepts he associates with those words will quickly tell you a lot about his politics.

So simply repackaging something with a new word, one with more positive associations, doesn't work because as soon as the new word becomes associated with the old thing, the old thing's associations start attaching to the new word. This is famously the case with what Steven Pinker calls the "euphemism treadmill": the people we once respectably called *cripples* became the *handicapped*, and from there, the *disabled*, and so on. I was mildly shocked in Brazil at seeing disabilities referred to in Portuguese as *deficiências* – deficiencies. The word is perfectly polite and official in Portuguese, but it has picked up a different set of associations in English. These things are fairly random and situational, not inherent to a word.

Another famous case in which conservative Republicans in America flipped the script on their liberal Democratic opponents involved not rebranding with a new word but trashing the old one. *Welfare* is a grand old English word first attested in the 14th century as a state of well-being. It went on to mean things like "abundance" and even "extravagant living" (an obsolete meaning that died out in the 16th century). Note how naturally "extravagant living" flows from "well-being".

The political sense of *welfare* is older than many people think; originally American, it was first attested in 1886, still with a positive sense: the *OED* defined it as "organized provision for the basic physical and material well-being of people in need". But by 1933, we have the phrase "on welfare" ("you see, there are a lot of people on welfare down there," from an article in the New Orleans *Times-Picayune*). The *OED*'s first clearly negative citation comes from 1955: "Signe ... said that she was criticized for being on the welfare."

Political junkies know the rest. By the 1970s, Ronald Reagan was campaigning to reinvent the Republican Party as an anti-government party. Among the staples of his campaign was the so-called "welfare queen", a character that made it into speech after speech of Reagan's. According to a report of a 1976 campaign stop,

> "There's a woman in Chicago," the Republican candidate said recently to an audience in Gilford, N.H., during his freeswinging attack on welfare abuses. "She has 80 names, 30 addresses, 12 Social Security cards and is collecting veterans' benefits on four nonexisting deceased husbands." He added:

> "And she's collecting Social Security on her cards. She's got Medicaid, getting food stamps and she is collecting welfare under each of her names. Her tax-free cash income alone is over $150,000."

Reagan was accused of wildly exaggerating the woman's story. She did indeed face criminal charges, but according to the same report, "Miss Taylor is now charged with using not 80 aliases but four. The amount the state is charging that she received from her alleged fraud is not $150,000 but $3,000."[4]

But what's $147,000 against an unforgettable story? The seed of the "welfare queen" story fell on fertile ground. Americans prize self-reliance: remember that criticism of being "on welfare" went back to 1955. "Welfare" quickly became racially charged, too: liberals accused Reagan of stoking white voters' latent racism against a stereotype of a black woman having endless kids and cheating the system. (Reagan, however, had made no mention of race.)

But the battle lines were drawn: "welfare" was no longer "well-being", or even "assistance for the needy". It was a hand-out to the undeserving, even to fraudsters and cheats. Or it was a term of abuse cynically manipulated by racist conservatives. Whatever it was, it was politically radioactive. By 1992, Bill Clinton, a Democrat, was campaigning to "end welfare as we know it". He would win that year's election, and ultimately sign a bill that proponents called welfare "reform", but which Ted Kennedy, a left-wing icon and senator, called "legislative child abuse". "Welfare" benefits were cut back and time-limited. Today, in another round of the never-ending rebranding, welfare payments are known in America as "Temporary Assistance to Needy Families", commonly called TANF, so that one needn't even say the word "needy". "Food stamps", similarly, are now called SNAP – "Supplemental Nutrition Assistance Program". Opponents of a generous social safety net can either continue talking about "welfare" and "food stamps", or tarnish "TANF" and "SNAP", eventually requiring them to be rebranded again.

Much the same has happened in Britain to the word "benefits". What could, in its original sense, be more positive? But now it is nearly as associated with lazy scroungers as "welfare" once was in America. A Channel 4 television show, *Benefits Street*, which ran in 2014, was touted by the producers as showing "the reality of life on benefits, as the residents of streets in areas hit hard by recession invite cameras into their tight-knit communities". But critics on the left deplored it as demeaning the poor with sensationalism shorn of context. Even for those who never saw the show, the name said it all.

As "death tax", "welfare" and "benefits" show, linguistic jiu-jitsu can work two ways: you can rebrand something cleverly, or you can work to create new associations with an old brand. It is worth paying attention when your political antagonists are trying to pull this off. And it is worth trying a version of either of these tricks yourself. But neither process proves that language somehow precedes thinking, or in other words that if you can change the language you can necessarily change minds.

*

Mere labels are one thing. It may seem easy to rebut the notion that you can't "polish a turd", "put lipstick on a pig" or otherwise put a new shine on an unpleasant old thing and expect it to sell. But there is serious thinking – and science – behind the idea that language does go deeper than mere labels. This is the idea that people think not in words, exactly, but in deep-seated mental metaphors. This entails the conclusion that if you can get people not merely to swap labels but to swap metaphors, you can bring them to a new way of thinking.

Many readers will associate "metaphor" with English class: as the teacher explains, when the poet says "It is the east, and Juliet is the sun," he does not mean that Juliet is a mass of incandescent gas, or a gigantic nuclear furnace. It means that the sun brings hope and warmth, as does the sight of one's beloved.

But for linguists and cognitive scientists, metaphor is all the more interesting for being all the more workaday and common than "Juliet is the sun." Far from being a device that wordsmiths and poets use to arrest our imagination in new ways, most metaphor is the opposite: it is an unremarkable constant in our mental life, it is mostly unconscious, and it causes our thoughts not to run off in new directions but to stay stuck in a habitual groove, like the melody of a pleasing but unoriginal pop song on an old record.

Now, I came up with that "record" metaphor quickly after a few moments' pondering. But that was only after writing, then erasing, another metaphor: "stuck in a rut". I erased "stuck in a rut" because it's a cliché, but it perfectly illustrates a nearly unconscious metaphor. I realised that while I've read "stuck in a rut" hundreds of times in my life, I was hazy on exactly what the non-metaphorical meaning of "rut" was. According to the *OED*, confirming a notion I half-knew, it's originally "A (deep) furrow or track made in the ground, especially in a soft road, by the passage of a wheeled vehicle or vehicles." That explains a lot; most of us don't have physical, non-metaphorical ruts in our lives because there are no more soft roads in most of our lives, and even where there are, they are driven on by tyres with wide and soft rubber footprints, not sharp narrow cart-wheels that cut ruts. "Rut" is, for most English-speakers, not something they've ever seen in the world, but pure metaphor.[5]

According to one of the keenest students of metaphor in the modern era, George Lakoff, a linguist and cognitive scientist, most metaphors are of the "stuck in a rut" variety – unconscious, hardly considered – and not the "Juliet is the sun" variety – poetic and arresting. Lakoff and Mark Johnson published, in 1980, a little book called *Metaphors We Live By*, which examined the ubiquity of metaphor in common, everyday language, and, they argued, in everyday thinking.[6]

Lakoff and Johnson proposed a few overarching metaphors that explain a lot of the surface-level metaphors that depend on them. For example, the metaphor "time is money" explains the prevalence of lots of other expressions, like *spending, wasting, budgeting, giving, donating* and *saving* time, or describing someone as living on *borrowed* time.

Lakoff and Johnson went further, though, showing that metaphors are not skin-deep but computational. Time is not only money, they argued, but a "limited resource" and "a valuable commodity", which is why we can *use up, have enough of* or *run out of* time, as we can with a limited resource, and we can *have, give, lose* and *thank someone for* time, as with a valuable commodity. These linguistic expressions are all harmonious, since the meta-metaphors are harmonious too: time is money, which is both a valuable commodity and a limited resource. If "time is money" logically entails that "time is a limited resource" and that "time is a valuable commodity", and we speak with time metaphors that "compute" in a system of sub-categorisation in the same way that the overarching metaphors do, Lakoff and Johnson felt they had evidence that mental metaphors were systematic, suggesting that much of our thinking itself is metaphorical.

But that did not mean that it was eternal, universal or unchangeable. In Western cultures, for example, the future is "ahead" of us, in a mental metaphor of time as a road along which you travel forward. But in some others, the future is "behind": after all, the past, which is ahead of you, is visible, since you know its contents, but the future, unknown, is behind your back. So metaphors go deep, but they are cultural and contingent. And they can, Lakoff thinks, be changed.

Lakoff is a Democrat, a liberal in the American political sense, and since the rise of his theory that metaphors are deeply seated in human cognition, he has made a name for himself as an advisor to political activists, encouraging them to reframe political issues in new metaphors that he feels are more consonant with reality. Lakoff doesn't believe that there is no such thing as objective reality and that all is metaphor. But he believes that some metaphors more accurately describe reality than others – and that conservatives have misled Americans with deceptive metaphors.

Lakoff is perhaps best known for the notion that most Americans may see their country as a kind of big family, and that their politics are based on a notion of what kind of metaphorical parent (government) the family needs. Republicans believe that that family needs a strict father, and Democrats think that it needs a nurturing parent. (He avoids "mother" here; Democrats have long suffered from being labelled the "mommy party".) The strict-father metaphor, according to Lakoff, ties together what otherwise might seem like three irreconcilable strands of traditional Reagan-era Republicanism: hawkish foreign policy, social conservatism and free-market economics. In Lakoff's metaphor, the strict father protects the family (defence), punishes moral and sexual transgressions (social conservatism) and believes that sink-or-swim is the best way to teach wayward children to work hard (laissez-faire economics). Democrats, by contrast, believe that children need a parent who will support, teach, give resources, offer room to experiment and learn, and so on.

But more broadly, Lakoff has argued that Democrats are consistently "out-framed" by Republicans. In his 2004 book *Don't Think of an Elephant*, he argued that once Republican frames are out there, they are irresistible, in the same way that telling someone not to think of an elephant makes them think of an elephant. It's strategically critical, he argues, not to be suckered into using the opposing side's frames. Republicans portray taxes as an affliction, and so promise "tax relief". Democrats are too quick to follow, promising their own version of the same. So he thinks they should reframe taxes, emphasising the good things they pay for, calling them not a burden, but "membership fees".

There is some good evidence for the power of framing effects in politics – and not only from the polls of Frank Luntz. Lera Boroditsky, a psychologist who specialises in language and thought at the University of California San Diego, has researched how simple differences in metaphor make a big difference in the kind of policy solutions people support.

For example, she and Paul Thibodeau gave one group of experimental subjects a news paragraph about a fictional town, Addison, beginning "Crime is a *beast* ravaging the city of Addison" (emphasis mine), and went on to describe the crime problem in detailed statistics. When questioned afterwards, 71% of the subjects recommended some form of tougher law-and-order policies for Addison. But when Boroditsky gave a different group the exact same paragraph, with one word swapped, "Crime is a *virus* ravaging the city of Addison," the results were very different. Now only 54% recommended tougher law-and-order policies. They were more likely to suggest policies that resembled a public health approach, rather than a punitive one, things like education and after-school programmes.

Interestingly, amping the metaphor up made little difference; in a different test condition, the metaphor was made more salient: "crime is a *wild beast preying* on" Addison, versus "crime is a *virus infecting*" Addison. Doubling up on the metaphorical language yielded results indistinguishable from those achieved by the mere swap of "beast" for "virus".[7] So it took just a nudge – that one word, rather than laying it on thick – to get all of the effect required. What's more, the trick works subtly. When asked after their responses what made the subjects reply as they did, most cited the statistics. Virtually no one noticed – or at least admitted to noticing – the lure of the metaphor.

This seems to be strong evidence of Lakoff's strongest claim. When he was asked which of his decades of research findings could be labelled "Lakoff's law", he chose a simple one: "frames trump facts." Elaborating further, he said that "Conventional frames are pretty much fixed in the neural structures of our brains. In order for a fact to be comprehended, it must fit the relevant frames. If the facts contradict the frames, the frames, being fixed in the brain, will be kept and the facts ignored."[8]

In the decade-plus since Lakoff wrote that, with the rise of social media as a "digital newsstand", the fear that people ignore news that doesn't fit their pre-existing views has only grown. Voters self-segregate, "liking" and sharing news stories in their social media feeds that comport with what they always believed. Psychologists have long recognised the larger phenomenon of "confirmation bias": it pleases people to read what they already know (or at least believe) to be true, a fact that can even be shown in scans of the brain, where pleasure centres are activated by confirmation of previous beliefs.

So people are hard to get to change their mind, even with the cleverest phrasing. Yes, Boroditsky got an impressive 17-percentage-point change by swapping *beast* for *virus*. But note that in either condition, a clear majority of people preferred law-and-order solutions. A new framing (the virus) helped push them from their previous position somewhat – but most people stayed where they were. Something besides linguistic framing is at work.

Another objection to Lakoff's law – "frames trump facts" – comes from Lakoff's own logic. If a pre-existing frame makes a voter reject facts that are dissonant with the frame, what on earth will make them accept an entirely new frame? Everyone knows a college Marxist who is now a die-hard anarcho-capitalist, or a former evangelical Christian who's now an out-and-proud atheist. But such conversions are relatively rare – and we're all the more likely to notice them because of the famous zeal of the convert. But if Lakoff is right that most people don't really want to change their minds – and he very much seems to be right about that – then trying to get them to accept a rival frame is like trying to find converts to Islam in the pews of a Southern Baptist church. American conservatives are not unaware of the frame of the government as the provider of useful benefits, a good value for money, like joining a worthy club. They just reject it. American liberals are not unaware of the frame of taxes as a burden. They just reject it. Of course, in a polarised media environment, each side will hear messages with supportive frames more than messages with opposing ones. But if the idea of almighty frames really is right, Lakoff is going to have a lot of work getting conservatives to even briefly listen to his "taxes-as-membership-fees" frame once, much less enough times to change minds.

In any case, there are good reasons to doubt that frames are almighty. Boroditsky's experiment seemed to show that most people already seemed to have a "beast"-like view of crime, and the "virus" framing only pushed a few of them in a new direction. And remember, this is an experiment in a psychology lab, where the stakes are close to zero. Participants are being asked to respond to strange questions without really knowing why. That the manipulation of a single variable in test conditions like this causes a strong effect is interesting, but it hardly proves that this effect will be anywhere near as big in the real world. Voters – as Lakoff knows – go to the polls with a whole set of values, frames, identities, histories and irrational prejudices as well as, in most cases, a few policy positions that are reasonably well-informed and thoroughly thought through. They might be affected by what news story they last read, their morning breakfast conversation, or even variables that shouldn't matter like whether their football team won the night before, whether it's raining on polling day or whether they are hungry when they go into the booth.

Relentlessly disciplined messaging with new and powerful frames by one side or the other of a political debate might be enough to sway a small few voters in a tight contest in which voters are constantly being bombarded with messages from both sides. But to truly win debates requires this kind of messaging over long periods of time, getting rising new generations to accept your frames and not the other side's, as well as gradually winning a tiny few converts from the other side and picking up as many of the (increasingly rare) non-partisan undecided as possible. This is the work of decades.

Frames can help, but they are not magic. And whatever Lakoff may think, facts do matter. People may ignore facts if they can, choosing instead to stick with their pre-existing frame. And many people simply don't have much time to absorb the facts: political activists and journalists don't know what it's like to have a job where your 9-to-5 duties actually forbid you from reading political news, rather than requiring it. So many people might well go with the frame when they simply don't have time for the facts. But when they can be convinced to listen for a few moments, as when the pollsters on the estate tax gave respondents different thresholds at which the tax might kick in, the facts are powerful – far more so than the linguistic transmogrification of "estate" to "death" tax.

How do you get people to listen to new facts and arguments, then? In today's political environment, everyone is an expert in the facts – or claims to be. People get all they think they need from their social-media feeds, and sympathetic news channels and websites. The old arbiters of accepted facts – in America, the quality newspapers, and in Britain, the BBC – are increasingly written off as partisan hackery.

People have no problem discounting those arbiters now that they have so many choices. Framing, a narrow linguistic idea born in cognitive science, seems less powerful than confirmation bias, a larger idea born of reams of psychology research. Language experts can be forgiven for focusing on language, which can have some effect. But it is not the miracle cure it is sold as. People are stubborn, and there's no easy way to change that, linguistic or otherwise.

But even if it's hard to get all people to listen to all the facts all of the time, it's still possible to get some people to hear some of the facts some of the time. And that requires patience, patience of the kind the pitch-men for "framing" don't want to admit is needed. Suddenly bombarding a cousin you haven't seen in years with criticism for her politics on social media may make you feel righteous, but it isn't going to do anything to change her mind. Whether it's framing or plain-vanilla confirmation bias, most people don't take well to it. But carefully taking care of the relationship – asking about her kids, commenting on her cat pictures or whatever – prepares the ground for you to gradually introduce a contentious conversation.

When that point comes, it's probably not a good idea to say "Taxes are not an affliction! You're the victim of a frame! Taxes are really membership fees that buy you privileges in a democracy!" Most people really don't like paying taxes, and it has little to do with metaphor. Money's tight; like time, it's a scarce resource, exactly one of those deep-seated concepts Lakoff identified in *Metaphors We Live By*. Nobody likes parting with a scarce resource, no matter what the framing.

So even though Lakoff encourages his side never to adopt the other's framing, another good bit of psychology is simply to establish, in a conversation, the notion that you know where the other side might be coming from. "Look, I don't like paying taxes, either. Who does? But if you think about it another way, I do like having a school for my kids, and a road to that school, and a policeman protecting the road. So it's almost like I pay to join a nice community... you might think of it even as a membership fee."

My Danish wife reports that her parents, like many (though not all) Danes, are proud to pay their taxes, under precisely this logic. This isn't because they have been hoodwinked by language. In America, the tax office is called the Internal Revenue Service. In Britain, it's Her Majesty's Revenue and Customs. Both bureaucracies seem to want to avoid mentioning what the body in question actually does. In Denmark, the tax authority is called Skat, which means... Tax.[9] But this "framing" doesn't stop Danes from paying their taxes, sometimes with grudging respect, sometimes even with pride. No need for metaphorical "membership fees" here: Danes simply think taxes are the price to be paid for the services they want.

This is partly because the Danish state works well; people there expect it to. They don't think they will see as much of their tax wasted as it might be in Britain or America. And this is partly because Denmark's centre-left parties spent decades building the idea of a welfare state as a good thing: "welfare" (*velfærd*) has none of the taint in Danish that it has in English.

Not that Danish policy preferences are fixed forever; Denmark has seen its welfare state expand past the point of affordability, and has gradually rolled it back, in a mostly consensual process. This hardly seems a possibility in countries with overheated two-party politics like Britain, and especially America. In Scandinavia, many parties compete for power. But where only two parties alternate in power, what damages one party is almost always to the benefit of the other. This has made for a politics of calling one's opponents fools and liars, rather than trying to gently convince their voters to give a new approach a try. Fixing politics in bitterly divided countries – America, and increasingly Britain – seems harder than ever.

This is all the more reason to prepare for a long period of first extending empathy to the people you're trying to convince, then patiently introducing new facts and arguments as well as new metaphors and frames. What works with an individual – slowly developing fellow-feeling and understanding before trying to convince them – is what is also needed in trying to win a majority of voters to one's own political side.

Lakoff and a collaborator, Elisabeth Wehling, who studied in his linguistics department at Berkeley, write in *The Little Blue Book*, a guide for America's Democrats, that "most Americans care about their fellow citizens. This is the moral basis of Democratic thought, and we think the public will respond to it." That most Americans are in effect moral Democrats and don't yet know it – but can be brought there with a frame shift – sounds a lot like wishful thinking.

Van Jones, a Democratic activist, calls Lakoff "a Jedi master" of language in a blurb for *The Little Blue Book*. The Jedi mind-trick of the *Star Wars* films can, of course, be accomplished with a wave of the hand and a firm-sounding "these are not the droids you're looking for." Real life is much harder than that. Anyone selling a short-cut around the long and hard work of persuasion is selling a fantasy – and also selling it to themselves.

*

There's another fantasy out there about political language. It has to do not so much with content, but with style. For decades, wise political commentators and journalists have – rightly – attacked the language that governments sometimes use. The Internal Revenue Service really is a tax service; Departments and Ministries of Defence spend a lot of time on the attack.

The culprit is always the same, according to the pundits: the use of overblown, confusing or misdirecting language instead of plain English. This stacks the deck against ordinary citizens who just want to know what their government is up to. And the Ur-Text of this complaint against obfuscating officials is George Orwell's celebrated 1946 essay "Politics and the English Language".

In it, Orwell complained of political language that

> A mass of Latin words falls upon the facts like soft snow, blurring the outline and covering up all the details. The great enemy of clear language is insincerity. When there is a gap between one's real and one's declared aims, one turns as it were instinctively to long words and exhausted idioms, like a cuttlefish spurting out ink.

Not for Orwell the clapped-out, dying metaphor. In the same essay, he describes a writer whose "stale phrases choke him like tea leaves blocking a sink." My own personal favourite Orwell metaphor comes in his description of those "who come flocking towards the smell of 'progress' like bluebottles to a dead cat".

It's certainly true that reading Orwell's essay, and especially the six rules of writing that close his essay, will improve most people's writing. They are

1. Never use a metaphor, simile, or other figure of speech which you are used to seeing in print.
2. Never use a long word where a short one will do.
3. If it is possible to cut a word out, always cut it out.
4. Never use the passive where you can use the active.
5. Never use a foreign phrase, a scientific word, or a jargon word if you can think of an everyday English equivalent.

6. Break any of these rules sooner than say anything outright barbarous.

But Orwell, in the service of his own crisp style, made these rules rather too absolute. Critics have had plenty of fun with them: The "out" in rule 3 can be cut, twice. And the very first sentence of "Politics and the English Language" contains an unnecessary passive:

> Most people who bother with the matter at all would admit that the English language is in a bad way, but it is generally assumed that we cannot by conscious action do anything about it.

Geoffrey Pullum, who coined the terms "Normal" and "Formal" discussed in Chapter 6, has found that Orwell's essay has slightly more clauses in the passive voice than the typical passage of English prose.

Orwell's rules really are decent ones for inexperienced writers (so long as they're considered guidelines, not rules). But he was far too confident that there was something deeper that would result from following his rules: namely, that they would make it near impossible to say stupid and dishonest things, or to fall into lock-step dogma, without realising that one is doing so: "If you simplify your English, you are freed from the worst follies of orthodoxy. You cannot speak any of the necessary dialects, and when you make a stupid remark its stupidity will be obvious, even to yourself."

Orwell had witnessed the rise of the two great murderous -isms in Europe, fascism and communism. Both turned their violence on their own people, with a ferocity that could not be put in plain language. As Orwell put it, a defender of Stalin's purges can't just come out and say "I believe in killing off your opponents when you can get good results by doing so." The same might be said for Hitler's *verschärfte Vernehmung* and *Endlösung*, "sharpened interrogation" and "final solution", which in plain language are torture and mass murder.

Orwell's notion that plain language will make awful politics unbearable is simple, appealing – and largely wrong. Remember that for people to recognise a falsehood, they need to know the truth. Orwell, like Lakoff, assumes that once deception is stripped away (Lakoff's misleading frames, Orwell's bewildering, overlong, cliché-filled humbug), the truth will be plain. But there's a plausible – even tested – way to show that Orwell is wrong. It's called populism.

The year 2016 rocked Western politics. First, in June, Britain voted for Brexit: to leave the European Union, against the advice of the overwhelming majority of politicians, economists, academics, business leaders and elite journalists. Then, in November, America rejected a former secretary of state and senator, Hillary Clinton, for a political novice and a billionaire with a habit of saying appalling things, Donald Trump. In both cases, the experts misread the sentiment of a part of their country far away from the big cities where journalists tend to live and work.

And in both cases, those angry voters, ready to vote for change of almost any kind, were seduced not by "cuttlefish squirting out ink", but by politicians making it perfectly clear what they wanted and how they planned to get it. When they lied, the lies were often perfectly clear to anyone who cared to learn the least bit about the facts. But either the lies were not recognised as such, or voters didn't care.

First take Brexit. Its master slogan was simple: "Let's take back control." Brussels, the metonym for the European Union, was an undemocratic weight on Britain's ancient freedoms, its democracy and the "Mother of All Parliaments", the legislature at Westminster. Brexit's proponents toured the country in a bus that featured the slogan "We send the EU £350m a week. Let's fund the NHS [UK National Health Service] instead. Vote Leave." The £350m figure was fake; it was a net number that didn't take into account the money Britain got back from the EU. And no one on the Leave side had any serious interest in putting any big extra sums – much less £350m a week – into the health service. But when supporters of staying in the EU pointed this out, they were dismissed as "elites" with no standing to talk about what the real British people – sick of elites – wanted. There was absolutely nothing wrong with the language on the side of the bus, which obeys all of Orwell's rules. The problem was voters' grasp of the facts.

The polite faces of the Leave campaign were Boris Johnson, who had just been the Conservative mayor of London, and Michael Gove, the former justice and education secretary. But its real powerhouse was Nigel Farage, the leader of the United Kingdom Independence Party. Mainstream politicians dismissed Farage as a buffoon – it is hard to find a politician more often photographed with a pint of beer and a cigarette in his hands. But that was part of his appeal. And so was his language – as different from that of a polished politician as they come. In a typical speech, he said

> So who are we? Who is the typical UKIP voter? I'll tell you something about the typical UKIP voter – the typical UKIP voter doesn't exist. When I look at the audiences in those theatres there is a range of British society from all parts of the spectrum. Workers, employers, self-employed. Big businessmen, corner shop owners. Well off, comfortably off, struggling. Young as well as old. Not ideologues. Some left, some right, mostly in the middle. Some activists, some haven't voted for twenty years. One thing many have in common: they are fed up to the back teeth with the cardboard cut-out careerists in Westminster. The spot-the-difference politicians. Desperate to fight the middle ground, but can't even find it. Focus groupies. The triangulators. The dog whistlers. The politicians who daren't say what they really mean. And that's why UKIP attracts this eclectic support. Because when we believe something – we don't go "are you thinking what we're thinking?" We say it out loud.[10]

There are a few clichés in there ("fed up to the back teeth", "cardboard cut-out"). But by and large, this too is a text that follows Orwell's rules. It even reads a bit like Orwell: Its sentences are short, as are all of the words; about the fanciest words are "spectrum", "eclectic" and "ideologue". And he ends with a macho declaration about political language itself, in the plainest possible English: "we say it out loud." What he wanted was perfectly clear, too. In the Brexit of his dreams,

> We get our money back.

> We get our borders back.

> We get our Parliament back.

> We get our fisheries back.

> We get our own seat on the bodies that actually run the world.

> We get back the ability to strike free-trade deals.

"Elites" could cavil at the facts implied here. But the pounding, repetitive phrasing was perfectly clear and punishingly effective. Whatever the causes of the narrow victory for Brexit, obfuscating language was not it.

That same summer, Donald Trump was shifting into general-election mode in America, having wrapped up the Republican nomination for president. He had swept away more than a dozen Republican rivals who had tried to belittle him as a newcomer out of his depth. Something about his campaign generated an energy among his voters that none of his rivals could match. And much of it had to do with his speech. He loved to rib Jeb Bush, a former governor of Florida who had raised huge sums for his campaign, as "low energy". And he was; Bush seemed an owlish, slightly tired professor next to the shouting, staccato Trump.

As argued in Chapter 6, Trump's style was successful precisely for being anything but that of a seasoned politician giving an elegant speech. He spoke almost entirely off the cuff:

> Look, having nuclear – my uncle was a great professor and scientist and engineer, Dr John Trump at MIT; good genes, very good genes, OK, very smart, the Wharton School of Finance, very good, very smart. You know, if you're a conservative Republican, if I were a liberal, if, like, OK, if I ran as a liberal Democrat, they would say I'm one of the smartest people anywhere in the world. It's true! But when you're a conservative Republican they try – oh, do they do a number – that's why I always start off: Went to Wharton, was a good student, went there, went there, did this, built a fortune. You know I have to give my like credentials all the time, because we're a little disadvantaged. But you look at the nuclear deal, the thing that really bothers me – it would have been so easy, and it's not as important as these lives are. Nuclear is powerful; my uncle explained that to me many, many years ago, the power, and that was 35 years ago. He would explain the power of what's going to happen and he was right – who would have thought? But when you look at what's going on with the four prisoners – now it used to be three, now it's four – but when it was three and even now, I would have said it's all in the messenger, fellas. And it is fellas because, you know, they don't, they haven't figured that the women are smarter right now than the men, so,

you know, it's gonna take them about another 150 years. But the Persians are great negotiators. The Iranians are great negotiators. So, and they, they just killed, they just killed us.

Unedited transcripts like this rocketed around the internet, forwarded by voters alarmed that anyone could consider voting for a man who produced such a stream of non-sequiturs, the rhetorical equivalent of a bunch of beer cans, crisp bags and the odd shiny pool of oil floating down a filthy river. But the effect of passing these excerpts around was not what the people sharing them hoped. The chief result was to blind Trump's opponents to how effective he was.

Real speech is full of starts and stops, non-sequiturs, ellipses, and so on. For example, examine this linguistic 12-car pile-up.

> We need to have a much more intentional explicit plan for NATO to engage with African countries and regional organizations, uh, not because the United States is not prepared to invest in security efforts in Africa, but rather to ensure that, uh, we are not perceived as trying to uh, dominate the continent. Rather we wanna make sure that we're prep-, uh, seen as, uh, a reliable partner, and there are some advantages to some European countries with historical ties, uh, being engaged, uh, in uh, and uh, in ha-, in, taking advantage of relationships. The francophile countries obviously is gonna to be able to do certain things better than we can, uh, and, uh, you know, one of, one of the, uh, things we, we wanna make sure of, though is that, uh, when, when the average African thinks about US, uh, engagement in Africa, I don't want them to think our only interest is avoiding terrorists from spilling out into, uh, the world stage.

It's an embarrassing mess: "francophile" substituted for "francophone", subjects and verbs not matching up, sentences not ending properly, and one "uh" after the other. The speaker is Barack Obama. He was talking to the editor and the foreign editor of *The Economist* on Air Force One, with a tape recorder in front of him. Obama is a good speaker, but this kind of thing – a bad passage in an otherwise lucid interview – is typical of all speakers, even good ones.

For those passing around similar, unedited transcripts of Trump, the joke was on them. While he could maunder on and get off topic quite frequently, the unscripted and personal way he said nearly everything he said was mesmerising to many voters who had never heard a politician talk like this.

And these populists were not only successful with their style; they were clear about content, in blunt language meant to shock the audiences into thinking "I've never heard anyone say these things." Farage was explicit, saying that UKIP would not be cowed by taboo: "we say it out loud." Trump did the same, hardly hiding his plans. "We are going to build a wall and Mexico is going to pay for it." "I would immediately start renegotiating our trade deals with Mexico, China, Japan and all of these countries that are just absolutely destroying us." "I will get rid of gun-free zones on schools and ... on military bases." "We're going to get Apple to start building their damn computers and things in this country instead of in other countries." Say what you like, but Orwell's heavy snowfall of obscuring language is nowhere to be seen.

Since Orwell's death, the nature of political speech has changed. In the 1940s, politicians still strove for an elevated register when they spoke in public. Beginning in the 1960s, they began aiming to look more authentic, of the people. They didn't go all the way – whether Obama or Bush, most aimed to keep some kind of dignity in their words. But demotic was in, and Demosthenes was out. By Trump, this trend had reached a peak: it was all emotion and plain words, with no hint of aiming for dignity or what used to be called "rhetoric" in the good sense. Normal, at least in the mouth of the 45th president, had utterly crushed the need for Formal.

Yet despite what Orwell might have hoped, this plain speech did nothing to stop Trump. It may indeed have been his biggest weapon. If he lied, voters either didn't know, or they gave him a pass. And if he promised something unconscionable, like torturing terrorism suspects – "I'd bring back a hell of a lot worse than waterboarding" – many people either gave him a pass on that too, or they actively thought it was a great idea. When people want bad things, the man who promises them those things in the plainest possible language is going to win.

*

The political language tamers are not good guys or bad guys as a batch. It's a matter of your starting point: the good guys are always on your side, and the bad guys are on the other. The good guys want to clear away misleading language to reveal the truth; the bad guys want to hoodwink honest folk with tricky language. The good guys want to find the real labels for things; the bad guys want to pass off poison as a healing tonic.

But what all political language tamers share is a view that these language games work. At a first approximation, they seem to be right, if polls are to be believed. But whether political consultants trying to sell a quick rebranding, or more sophisticated metaphor-mongers selling a reframing, they may be giving themselves too much credit, and the voters too little.

Many voters really are ill-informed. So it goes in a big and diverse society in which most people's job is not politics. But most people try to learn what they can about their country's policies, and they try to vote according to their interests and their values. It is too cynical to suggest that the great majority are under a kind of spell that can be undone with a counter-spell.

Plain language is no reliable white magic either. Speaking in short words and simple syntax doesn't always mean, as Orwell thought, that "when you make a stupid remark its stupidity will be obvious." It can have the effect of making a purveyor of lies and atrocious morals sound like a lonely voice of honesty in a world of politicians taking too much care. Authenticity really does sell – even authentic awfulness: "we say it out loud."

In fact, even Orwell seemed not to know quite where he stood on language taming. In *Nineteen Eighty-Four*, he gave us the ultimate example of a language so heavily engineered by the totalitarian state that the removal of the word *freedom* had made such a thought unthinkable in the minds of the people. But in real life, this is, fortunately, too pessimistic by half. People can think of all kinds of things they don't have a word for, and where needed, they can easily invent one.

Orwell is known to have taken an interest in invented languages, perhaps hoping that the right one might make meanings more concrete and, presumably, make dishonesty more difficult. He studied C. K.

Ogden's stripped-down "Basic English" and another invented language, Interglossa. But these, too, he rejected.

He also rejected nannying prescriptivism, as well as Anglo-Saxon purism:

> The defence of the English language ... has nothing to do with correct grammar and syntax, which are of no importance so long as one makes one's meaning clear, or with the avoidance of Americanisms, or with having what is called a "good prose style". On the other hand, it is not concerned with fake simplicity and the attempt to make written English colloquial. Nor does it even imply in every case preferring the Saxon word to the Latin one, though it does imply using the fewest and shortest words that will cover one's meaning.

In other words, in an enduring irony, Orwell's great essay on clarity failed to make any clear proposals for fixing English, beyond a simple principle that is easier to declare than it is to follow: think about what you want to say, then say it clearly. Orwell's failure to come up with a fix shows that the weight of fixing a broken politics can't fall on language alone. People need facts and arguments to make their case, not just labels, frames nor even just plain talk. A democracy can't be better than its voters. So there is no easy way – linguistic or otherwise – around the hard slog of educating them to make good decisions.

Conclusion: Weirder and more wonderful

LIKE MANY LANGUAGE LOVERS, I grew up as a bookish kid. Like many kids who spent their childhoods stuck in books, I was a bit of a know-it-all, and not always a gracious one. I would cut people off when they were saying something I thought was wrong, or finish their story when I knew the ending. As an adult, I was lucky to find a job where being a smart-aleck is basically in the job description. My motto is "fun facts are only fun if they're true."

That said, a book full of myth-bustings, even if successfully executed, would be hollow; the reader could well walk away thinking "great: now I 'know' a lot less than I did when I started." Even if pulled off, even if a public service, such a book would be a bit of a downer, a kind of negative success.

But I have tried here not just to puncture myths, but to sketch a set of beliefs about language that add up to not just a coherent whole, but a positive, optimistic one. First, I hope I've left the impression that language is worth a systematic, detailed study. The field of linguistics doesn't have half the sex-appeal of some of its related disciplines, like psychology, and that's a shame. Too much public commentary on language comes from self-appointed authorities who have never learned to check what they say before they say it. I'm "self-appointed", too. But I've tried hard to stick to facts that I can document. And documenting the facts about language – as well as seeing what those facts add up to, as generalisations – is what linguistics is all about. I hope readers who have enjoyed this book will go on to get their language facts from people who have spent their life assiduously garnering them, not from soap-box prophets.

But second, I have tried to sketch a theory of language itself in this book. That theory is meant to be not only compelling intellectually. It's also meant to give the reader a reason to approach language with a sense of wonder, and even optimism – too often in short supply.

In Chapter 1, we looked at the most radical language tamers possible. Ludwig Zamenhof hoped to bring the world to peace with a universal language, easy to learn and culturally neutral: Esperanto. He seems to have been wrong on two counts. One is that knowing a common language does not necessarily promote world peace, as the world's many civil wars have offered too much proof of. But second, people don't simply learn a language because it's useful; they are compelled to learn a language with a vibrant culture and literature that lots of people they want to talk to already speak. With all respect to the idealists, that has never really quite happened with Esperanto; it seems fated to remain a scattered dream. English, for all its flaws, has become the world's auxiliary language. But around the world, the good news is that huge amounts of money and classroom-hours are still spent in the teaching and learning of foreign languages. People want to understand each other. Esperanto may not have triumphed, but the dream of understanding has never died.

Lojban is a far more radical experiment, testing the engineering limits of language. Can a language be invented that dispenses with the messy ambiguity of natural language? Yes. Can it be learned? It seems so. Can it be spoken fluently? Some Lojbanists claim to, but most of them struggle. Does it lead, according to the Sapir–Whorf hypothesis, to more logical thinking? There is no proof of this, and even Lojban's fans don't care much about that element anymore.

So what's the good news? The creation of a logical language by a person (James Cooke Brown) who spoke an illogical natural language – English – is in itself a refutation of the strongest formulation of the Whorfian hypothesis. If "the limits of my language are the limits of my world," as Wittgenstein claimed, and "my language" is illogical, I shouldn't be able to think up a logical one. Yet Brown did exactly that when he sat down, with his flawed human brain, conditioned by a flawed language, and invented Loglan. People can take a step back and question their own grammar and vocabulary, no matter how deeply conditioned by their native language they are. In other words language – thank goodness – is not a mental prison, the limits of your world.

Nor is it pure logic. But plenty of real-world language sticklers think it is. Nevile Gwynne thinks that proper grammar is a logical prerequisite for the good life. But his claims, too, are self-refuting: he doesn't actually know that much about grammar, and yet he's made a tidy fortune and reputation flogging his little grammar book. English grammar is most certainly not logical; singular *they* is proof enough by itself that English-speakers will press whatever tools they need into service to make sure the language can do what they want it to. They've been doing this with singular *they* since the 14th century. Anyone who tells you that this is a modern "abomination", as Simon Heffer, the British journalist and Gwynne-style grammar-book writer does, should be handed a library card, a reference book written by a true expert and two weeks' vacation.

The good news is that people who want a good reference book are spoiled for choice. There are great grammar writers who make no absurd claims about the logic of thought. Whether such readers want a relatively tradition-based guide, like Bryan Garner, or a more modern, evidence-driven one, like Steven Pinker, what they will have is exactly that: a guide, not a scold. English is messy; controversies abound; sometimes these books will disagree. But a small investment in a good couple of books can ensure that any guidance you accept is built on facts and history, not superstition. Buy a few of these books, read their different suggestions – and decide for yourself. There is no Académie Anglaise, only the collected decisions of millions of English-speakers who care about their language. You are one, too. You get a vote.

Yet more proof that language is weirder, and more wonderful, than a grammar of pure logic comes from decades of efforts to get computers to learn language. The early approaches to getting computers to understand, use and translate language were a bit like the Lojban approach: strip language to its abstract rules, and teach a machine those rules. What are machines good for if not rule-governed processing?

But it turned out that this would never work; the rules are too many, the exceptions too manifold, to ever hand-code them all into software, even over the course of decades. The geeks in the artificial-intelligence labs were forced to start over with "dumb", brute-force approaches, throwing large amounts of real language data – recordings, translations, etc – at machine-learning algorithms. This worked better for simulating "intelligence" than all the clever coding of rules ever could. And the advent of digital neural networks, based on a metaphor of the brain itself – have made machine learning more powerful still.

In other words, after the blind alley of the "rules-based" approach, computers were set loose to learn, roughly, like a human child: from the facts of the world, lots of them, inductively, from the ground up. A few rules can be grafted on top, to steer the machine right in ambiguous or confusing cases. (Think *whom*.) But the power is in learning from facts, not rules.

Machines still struggle to integrate real-world facts ("A sparrow is a kind of bird"), practical knowledge (in "the box is in the pen," the "pen" must be an enclosure, not a writing instrument), pragmatic linguistic competence ("Can you pass the salt?" is not a request for information), ambiguity resolution (how to know which recently mentioned item an "it" refers back to), and so forth. An average five-year-old human will clean the best computer system's clock on these tasks. And that child can bring such linguistic and paralinguistic abilities together to have a passable conversation. The world's most amazing linguistic computer is still the human mind, a marvel that still hides many secrets for linguists, psychologists and computer scientists to discover.

Language changes, and it often seems to be doing so in a bad way. Pronunciation changes, making it look like people no longer take care to learn how to speak properly. Words take on new meanings, confusing older speakers. Words switch grammatical categories, nouns becoming verbs and so on. Vogue new words come into existence, crowding out perfectly good words that were already there. And at its deepest level, the grammar of a language changes: once upon a time, speakers of English could not only use *whom*, but (a thousand years ago) could put a case ending on every noun in the language. When the grammar changes, people understandably feel like something is lost.

Yet the good news can be stated clearly: no language has ever fallen apart. As annoying as any single change may seem, this stunning fact stands in perfect refutation of pedants and "kids-today" grousers, from ancient times through to the present. This is surprising, though: everything else falls apart. Even stone buildings crumble, and of course organic matter rots. If language is, as I've contended throughout this book, best thought of as an organic thing, how does it not rot, too?

Metaphors can be confusing as well as enlightening, and it is important to take care here. In looking at long-term change, language should be seen not as an organism, but as an ecosystem with the power to heal and regenerate itself. Perhaps a single word will suffer a grim fate, like a prey animal does at the claws of a ruthless predator. But the elements of the system work together as a system, to make sure that neither predators nor prey over-proliferate, a remarkable instance of "spontaneous order" that, having arisen, tends to take care of itself.

If the "spontaneous order" of language is a testament to the good things millions of humans can do when they put their minds together, language nationalism – like nationalism in general – can show up the bad things millions of humans can do when they put their minds together. In the modern age of nationalism, many nations are defined by language itself: "we are the people who speak this language here." But languages have messy, contested borderlands, all around the world. And speakers of a single language have a habit of wanting a single country.

No two people can be standing on the same patch of ground at any given time. And in our world of sovereign states, no bit of the earth can belong to two countries at the same time. But the good news, here, is that these rules do not apply to the real-estate of the human mind. A person can speak a regional language, the main national language, and a foreign language – and in fact, exactly this status is common in places from Africa to India and China. Startling as it seems to native English-speakers in Western countries, most of the world is multilingual, and multilingualism is especially common in the world's poorest places, where small-language groups rub shoulders.

Some states are dominated by a single language. But many aren't: decent multilingual and multicultural societies like Canada and Switzerland show that having multiple languages does not inevitably lead to confusion and dissolution. These places have made multiple identities a very part of the overarching identity. It's not a magic formula. It's not even that hard. New countries struggling to deal with multilingualism, like Ukraine, could learn a lot from the places that have dealt with it for centuries. National languages are no bad thing, but boosting national language X doesn't have to mean banishing minority language Y.

And people can handle multiple dialects and registers. Contrary to those who think there is an eternal and single right way of speaking or writing, most of us naturally modulate our language from situation to situation, from conversation partner to conversation partner. Comedy is made of the depiction of a nerdy kid unable to adopt the lingo when he tries to join the cool kids, or the streetwise character unable to switch off the sass-mouth when meeting a bunch of stuffy rich folks. But it's a fictional set-up. Most of us effortlessly possess this kind of competence: even if some people master the switching better than others, nobody needs to be told not to say "whom" in a biker bar. It's yet another obvious refutation of a traditional language-tamer creed, the One Right Way principle. One Right Way actually means linguistic incompetence. Happily, most people are smarter than that.

In the last chapter, we looked at the fact that even a brilliant linguist, George Lakoff, and the rightly celebrated George Orwell didn't know how to fix political language. On the face of it, this looks like bad news. Is there nothing to be done? After all, many people of all political persuasions can agree that the last few years have shown politics in the democratic world to be in pretty bad shape.

But then again, whether you're reading this in 2018 or 2028 or 2038, that will probably be the case, just as you could have easily found people saying it in 2008, 1998, and so on. Politics is messy, and democratic politics is messiness squared. Since human beings are imperfect, getting them together to make complicated decisions is necessarily so.

So the fact that there are no quick solutions in "reframing", or in preferring Orwell's plain language, or anything else, the messiness of politics is not really a function of language, but of the people who speak it. Kant was on to something when he said that "Out of the crooked timber of humanity, no straight thing was ever made." That includes politics – and language, too.

As a final consolation, we return, strangely enough, to *Nineteen Eighty-Four*. Benign language tamers fail – but so do the malign ones. People rightly worry about manipulative language coming to dominate our life, about politicians mastering double-talk to hide what they're up to. That much is plain from the frequency of the words "Orwellian" and "Newspeak" in English books:

Rise in the frequency of "Orwellian" and "Newspeak", according to Google Books

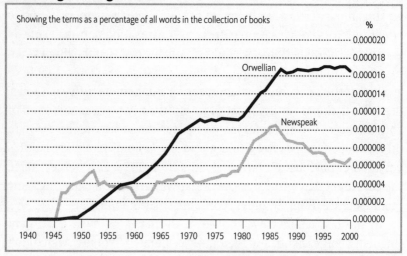

Source: Google Books ("Orwellian Newspeak")

But if our enduring interest in spotting Orwellian language seems like bad news – there seems to be a lot of it about – it's also good news. The bastards have never won. We don't speak in – much less do we think in – Newspeak. Even as politicians and their consultants have become ever more professional in their crafting of lies, evasion and bullshit, people have never stopped recognising it, and calling it what it is.

*

Language resists taming and ordering for the same reason it resists malign manipulation. It is distributed among billions of users, human beings, each of whom uses it in a different way for different purposes. In this, it recalls politics itself. Political conservatism teaches that human nature is hard to change, even with clever engineering by clever planners, so it's best not to try. And in a related but different vein, classical liberalism teaches that humans are basically decent, and flourish best when left to their business.

These two streams have shaped how we think about the ideal society: pluralist and free, because the alternatives are worse. In our politics, the most successful places in the world have chosen democracy, with all its chaos, all its flaws, over one-man rule. In economics, the richest places in the world have chosen markets, with all their irrationality, with all their booms and busts, over central planning.

In language, there is no less reason to trust the masses over the masters.

Notes

Introduction: The case of the missing whom

1.　Figures are for 2011. UNESCO Institute for Statistics Fact Sheet, September 2013, No. 26.
2.　See McWhorter's 2013 TED talk. https://www.ted.com/talks/ john_mcwhorter_txtng_is_killing_language_jk

1.　Bringing the universe to order

1.　Jorge Luis Borges, *The Analytical Language of John Wilkins*, in *Otras Inquisiciones, 1937–1952*.
2.　Arika Okrent, *In the Land of Invented Languages*, Spiegel & Grau (2009), pp. 212–13.
3.　Esperantists cite a figure of 2 million speakers of Esperanto, based on a study by the late Sydney Culbert of the University of Washington. But John Wells, an Esperantist and emeritus professor of linguistics at University College London, has estimated the number of true fluent speakers to be more likely in the hundreds of thousands, making it a thousandth the size of Spanish.
4.　https://mw.lojban.org/papri/User:Bob_LeChevalier
5.　Geoffrey Sampson on *The Complete Lojban Language* in the *Journal of Linguistics*, Vol. 35, no. 2 (Jul 1999), pp. 447–8.
6.　Opponents of Chomsky's "universal grammar" and Pinker's "language instinct" say that there are no significant features shared among all the world's languages – not even nouns and verbs. Resolving that debate is beyond my remit here, but no one in the debate would argue – even given the world's hugely diverse languages – that there is a natural language that functions like Lojban.
7.　Yes, Latinists, *lingua francas*. If this English-style plural is good enough for Nick Ostler, who wrote a wonderful history of *lingua francas*, *The Last Lingua Franca*, it's good enough for me.

2. Is language logic?

1. N. M. Gwynne, *Gwynne's Grammar: The Ultimate Introduction to Grammar and the Writing of Good English*. Incorporating also *Strunk's Guide to Style* (p. 5), Ebury Publishing, Kindle Edition. Biographical details come from the *Daily Telegraph*'s Elizabeth Grice, "The Glamour of Grammar", April 13th 2013, at http://www.telegraph.co.uk/education/9987974/The-glamour-ofgrammar-an-object-lesson.html

2. For the Hellenophiles and Bible experts: the phrase "his trespasses" does not appear in the original Greek. The King James translators were winging it a bit, since "if you forgive not each one his brother" would look a bit odd with no object like "his trespasses".

3. Merriam-Webster online, at https://www.merriam-webster.com/words-at-play/to-boldly-split-infinitives.

4. Examples go on for page after page in George O. Curme, *A Grammar of the English Language. Volume III: Syntax*, DC Heath and Company (1931), pp. 460–65.

5. *Merriam Webster's Concise Dictionary of English Usage* (2002), p. 598. Merriam-Webster.

6. Gwynne, op. cit., p. 27.

7. Ibid., p. 69.

8. Berit Brogaard, "The Feral Child Nicknamed Genie", *Psychology Today*, July 10th 2017.

9. Steven Pinker, *The Language Instinct: How the Mind Creates Language*. First published 1994. Harper Perennial edition published 2000, p. 62.

10. At the time of this writing, April 2018, the papers were available online at http://originsofman.angelfire.com/pdf/galileo.pdf; http://originsofman.angelfire.com/pdf/newton.pdf; and http://originsofman.angelfire.com/pdf/einstein.pdf

11. See the discussion at Merriam-Webster's webpage: https://www.merriam-webster.com/words-at-play/is-it-wrong-to-say-between-you-and-i

12. *Merriam-Webster's Dictionary of English Usage*, pp. 262–3.

13. Bryan Garner, "Shall We Abandon 'Shall'?", *ABA Journal*, August 1st 2012, at http://www.abajournal.com/magazine/article/shall_we_abandon_shall/

14. Steven Pinker, *The Sense of Style*, Viking Penguin (2014), pp. 112–13.

3. Machines for talking

1. Jack Copeland, *Artificial Intelligence: A Philosophical Introduction*, Wiley (1993), Chapter 9.

2. Kevin Warwick and Huma Shah, "Can Machines Think? A Report on Turing Test Experiments at the Royal Society", *Journal of Experimental & Theoretical Artificial Intelligence*, June 29th 2015, at http://www.tandfonline.com/doi/full/10.1080/0952813X.2015.1055826

3. This account is from the University of Pennsylvania's Mark Liberman, in his presentation to the Centre Cournot, a Paris-based part of the Fondation de France that supports scientific research. Shared with the author by Liberman.

4. Marcel Druon, a former permanent secretary of the French Academy, once suggested making French the sole legal language of the European Union, on account of its allegedly unmatched logic. Again, we see that for an expert native speaker, the rules just make sense. It can sometimes take an outsider to point at the system – like the positioning of French adjectives – and say "this makes no sense."

5. February 2nd 2012. I wrote about this under "Headline Headaches" at the old Johnson blog on Economist.com: http://www.economist.com/blogs/johnson/2012/02/journalese

6. From the University of California, Berkeley pages of assistant researcher John Brandon Lowe, at http://www.linguistics.berkeley.edu/~jblowe/Lx158/schedule/shrdlu.html

7. "Candide: A Statistical Machine Translation System", by Stephen DellaPietra and Vincent DellaPietra, IBM's principal investigators, at https://aclweb.org/anthology/H/H94/H94-1100.pdf

8. http://blogs.warwick.ac.uk/steverumsby/entry/a_new_google

9. The eagle-eyed or linguistically trained will see that a second step is required. If the stem of a verb ends in an "unvoiced" consonant – one of the ones like p, t and k where the vocal cords don't vibrate – then the -d ending becomes unvoiced, too. In other words, it becomes a -t sound, as in *walked*, which sounds like *walkt*. And if there's already a d- or t-sound at the end of the stem, it would be hard to hear the past-tense ending, so a dummy vowel is put in to separate the stem from the ending, which is why we say *skidded* and *flirted*. Pinker and Prince posit that speakers first apply the grammatical rule ("add d") and then apply the phonological rule ("devoice, or add an 'e', as needed").

4. Buxom, but never nice

1. Languages do *die*, of course – when young people stop learning a language, and old people pass away, until the last speaker dies. But this is a different phenomenon. The proposition here is that no living language has ever become unusable because of lack of attention to grammar or other rules.

2. See, for example, April McMahon's chapter "Restructuring Renaissance English" in Lynda Mugglestone, ed., *The Oxford History of the English Language*, Oxford University Press (2006). She discusses competing views of how coherent the shift was, as well as differing views of how it began, and whether it did so as a "drag chain" or a "push chain"; in a drag chain,

one element moves into an empty space, and the next element in the chain moves to occupy the slot left empty by the first move. The way I have described it in the text, following many scholarly accounts, is as a push chain.

3. Johnson's preface as found on Jack Lynch's website: https://andromeda. rutgers.edu/~jlynch/Texts/preface.html

4. That is, "Ich am vn-wys & wonderliche nyce", from *The Romance of William of Palerne*.

5. March was once the beginning of the Roman year, hence *Sept*ember (seventh), *Oct*ober (eighth) and *Nov*ember (ninth).

6. *Johnson's Dictionary: An Anthology*, edited by David Crystal, Penguin (2005), p. xiii.

7. For this discussion, I'm talking about hashtags as used to find tweets and to label one's own so that others can find them. This doesn't apply to the popular use of hashtags as a kind of ironic side-comment, like "Just spilled coffee on my new suit. #awesome".

8. Bernard Comrie, *Language Universals and Linguistic Typology*. Second edition. Chicago: University of Chicago Press (1989), as cited by the Summer Institute of Linguistics at http://www-01.sil.org/linguistics/ glossaryoflinguisticterms/whatisanisolatinglanguage.html

9. At Pereltsvaig's blog, http://www.languagesoftheworld.info/historical-linguistics/more-on-word-order-morphological-types-and-historical-change.html. Pereltsvaig leans heavily on R.M.W. Dixon, *Ergativity*, Cambridge University Press (1994), pp. 182–5.

10. Gary Lupyan and Rick Dale, "Language Structure is Partly Determined by Social Structure". (2010), PLoS ONE 5(1): e8559. (doi:10.1371/journal. pone.0008559)

11. These two hypotheses are given in more detail in Daniel Nettle, "Social Scale and Structural Complexity in Human Languages", *Philosophical Transactions of the Royal Society B* (2012) 367, 1829–36, at https://www. danielnettle.org.uk/download/093.pdf

5. Language tamers with armies and navies

1. For a fuller treatment of Yugoslavia, see Robert Lane Greene, *You Are What You Speak*, Delacorte (2011), chapter 5.

2. Radio Free Europe/Radio Liberty, "Southern Slavic? Balkan Nationalists Balk at Common Language Initiative", March 30th 2017, at https://www. rferl.org/a/balkans-without-borders-sarajevo-declaration-common-language/28400837.html

3. Bernard Spolsky, *Language Policy*, Cambridge University Press (2004), p. 12.

4. That is, in the first official language, "Ós í an Ghaeilge an teanga náisiúnta is í an phríomhtheanga oifigiúil í. Glactar leis an Sacs-Bhéarla mar theanga oifigiúil eile."

5. See *Nationalia* online, "Government propaganda makes Chinese people think that Uyghurs deserve to be suppressed and killed", April 6th 2017, at http://www.nationalia.info/interview/10957/government-propaganda-makes-chinese-people-think-that-uyghurs-deserve-to-be-suppressed-and

6. Formerly known internationally by its Russian name, Lvov. Names are highly political in this part of the world.

7. "Bill 101" on Historica Canada, at http://www.thecanadianencyclopedia.ca/en/article/bill-101

8. "Once they start laughing at you, you're through", *The Economist* online, March 11th 2013, at http://www.economist.com/blogs/johnson/2013/03/language-policy

9. The original provision in Law 101 required students who wanted to study in English to have had one parent educated in English in Quebec. It was later changed, so that students with a parent educated mostly in English anywhere in Canada could themselves study in English.

10. Office québécois de la langue française, "Langue et éducation au Quebec 2017: Éducation préscolaire et enseignement primaire et secondaire," at http://www.oqlf.gouv.qc.ca/ressources/sociolinguistique/2017/20170331_etude1.pdf

6. Whom in a biker bar

1. We know the rule is White's because Strunk had not included the rule in the book that White later amended and turned into a bestseller.

2. David Crystal, *Making Sense: The Glamorous Story of English Grammar*, Profile (2017), pp. xiii–xiv.

3. Steve Graham and Dolores Perin, "Writing Next: A Report to the Carnegie Corporation of New York", 2007, at https://www.carnegie.org/publications/writing-next-effective-strategies-to-improve-writing-of-adolescents-in-middle-and-high-schools

4. Holger Diessel and Michael Tomasello, "The Development of Relative Clauses in Spontaneous Child Speech", *Cognitive Linguistics*, 11(1/2) (2000), 131–51, at http://www.personal.uni-jena.de/~x4diho/The%20development%20of%20relative%20clauses%20in%20spontaneous%20child%20speech.pdf

5. A. Piestrup, "Black Dialect Interference and Accommodation of Reading Instruction in the First Grade" (Monographs of the Language Behavior Research Laboratory, No. 4). Berkeley: University of California, 1973. Cited in John Rickford, "Linguistics, Education and the Ebonics Firestorm", in

Shondel Nero, *Dialects, Englishes, Creoles and Education*, Lawrence Erlbaum Associates (2006).

6. Rickford, ibid., cites the Aurora University study in Hanni Taylor, *Standard English, Black English and Bidialectalism*, Peter Lang (1989).

7. Apologies to Orwell

1. Jonathan Weisman, "Linking Tax to Death May Have Brought its Doom", *USA Today*, May 20th 2001.

2. National Public Radio/Kaiser Family Foundation/Kennedy School of Government, "National Survey of Americans' Views on Taxes" (2003). Full results available at http://www.npr.org/news/specials/polls/taxes2003/20030415_taxes_survey.pdf

3. Weisman, op. cit.

4. *New York Times*, citing the *Washington Star*, February 15th 1976, at http://www.nytimes.com/1976/02/15/archives/welfare-queen-becomes-issue-in-reagan-campaign-hitting-a-nerve-now.html?_r=0

5. For those stuck in a different mental "rut", the cart-track meaning has nothing, etymologically, to do with the meaning referring to a period in which male deer compete for the right to mate with the local females. The first, "cart-track" word is cognate to the word "route". The second is from Latin for *rugitus*, the action of roaring, as deer do when they fight, and is cognate to the modern Spanish word *ruido* and French *bruit*, "noise".

6. Lakoff was already a distinguished linguist by 1980. Unbelievably, the original copy-editor at the University of Chicago Press suggested to him and Johnson that the title be changed to "Metaphors By Which We Live", because of course the copy-editor bought the old, bogus rule that you can't end a sentence in a preposition. Lakoff apparently didn't like the suggestion, or many of the copy-editor's other changes, and responded with a 23-page, single-spaced letter. The copy-editor resigned from the project.

7. Paul H. Thibodeau and Lera Boroditsky, "Metaphors We Think With: The Role of Metaphor in Reasoning", *PLoS One*, February 23rd 2011, at https://doi.org/10.1371/journal.pone.0016782

8. Edge.org, "2004: What's Your Law", at https://www.edge.org/response-detail/10696

9. *Skat* also means "Treasury", but the taxation idea is clear: people say *jeg betaler skat*, "I pay taxes".

10. Farage's speech to the 2013 UKIP conference, at https://blogs.spectator.co.uk/2013/09/nigel-farages-speech-full-text-and-audio

Acknowledgements

THIS BOOK IS IN YOUR HANDS thanks to Peter McGuigan and Caspian Dennis for representing it, Andrew Franklin and Clive Priddle for publishing it, and Ed Lake for expertly editing it. A second thanks goes to Caspian for naming it. Zanny Minton-Beddoes and Fiammetta Rocco brought the "Johnson" column on language into *The Economist*; I double-dipped into their generosity, by using materials from my column for the book, and by taking time off from my daily duties to write the rest of it. My wife, Eva Høier Greene, provided more than just the personal support for which most authors can thank their spouses. She also brought a brilliantly critical eye on the manuscript that only an intimate companion of the author can bring: "I know what you think you're saying, but..."

Others who helped with the text, either reading chunks, helping me find sources or answering my questions – in some cases originally for work published in *The Economist* – include Emilie Champliaud, John Cowan, Olga Fischer, Bryan Garner, Macduff Hughes, Oliver Kamm, Mark Liberman, Laurie Mackenzie, Victor Mair, John McWhorter, Steve Pinker, Geoff Pullum, Gwenno Saunders, Rhisiart Tal-e-Bot and Terry Winograd.

Index

Lane Greene is an American journalist, best known for his work for *The Economist* and his book about the politics of language, *You Are What You Speak: Grammar Grouches, Language Laws, and the Politics of Identity.*

PublicAffairs is a publishing house founded in 1997. It is a tribute to the standards, values, and flair of three persons who have served as mentors to countless reporters, writers, editors, and book people of all kinds, including me.

I. F. STONE, proprietor of *I. F. Stone's Weekly*, combined a commitment to the First Amendment with entrepreneurial zeal and reporting skill and became one of the great independent journalists in American history. At the age of eighty, Izzy published *The Trial of Socrates*, which was a national bestseller. He wrote the book after he taught himself ancient Greek.

BENJAMIN C. BRADLEE was for nearly thirty years the charismatic editorial leader of *The Washington Post*. It was Ben who gave the *Post* the range and courage to pursue such historic issues as Watergate. He supported his reporters with a tenacity that made them fearless and it is no accident that so many became authors of influential, best-selling books.

ROBERT L. BERNSTEIN, the chief executive of Random House for more than a quarter century, guided one of the nation's premier publishing houses. Bob was personally responsible for many books of political dissent and argument that challenged tyranny around the globe. He is also the founder and longtime chair of Human Rights Watch, one of the most respected human rights organizations in the world.

•   •   •

For fifty years, the banner of Public Affairs Press was carried by its owner Morris B. Schnapper, who published Gandhi, Nasser, Toynbee, Truman, and about 1,500 other authors. In 1983, Schnapper was described by *The Washington Post* as "a redoubtable gadfly." His legacy will endure in the books to come.

Peter Osnos, *Founder*

31901064364443